BILL BRYSON

THE PENGUIN DICTIONARY OF
TROUBLESOME WORDS

GUILD PUBLISHING
LONDON

This edition published 1984 by
Book Club Associates
by arrangement with
PENGUIN BOOKS

First published 1984
Published simultaneously by Penguin Books

Filmset in Monophoto Times by
Northumberland Press Ltd, Gateshead
Printed in Great Britain by
Richard Clay (The Chaucer Press) Ltd,
Bungay, Suffolk

CONTENTS

INTRODUCTION

This book might more accurately, if less convincingly, have been called *A Guide to Everything in English Usage That the Author Wasn't Entirely Clear About Until Quite Recently*. Much of what follows is the product of questions encountered during the course of daily newspaper work: should it be 'fewer than 10 per cent of voters' or 'less than 10 per cent'? Does someone have 'more money than her' or 'than she'?

The answers to such questions are not always easily found. Seeking the guidance of colleagues is, I discovered, dangerous: raise almost any point of usage with two journalists and you will almost certainly get two confident, but entirely contradictory, answers. Traditional reference works are often little more helpful because they so frequently assume from the reader a familiarity with the intricacies of grammar that is – in my case, at any rate – generous. Once you have said that in correlative conjunctions in the subjunctive mood there should be parity between the protasis and apodosis, you have said about all there is to say on the matter. But you have also, I think, left most of us as confused as before. I have therefore tried in this book to use technical terms as sparingly as possible (but have included a glossary at the end for those that do appear).

For most of us the rules of English grammar are at best a dimly remembered thing. But even for those who make the rules, grammatical correctitude sometimes proves easier to urge than to achieve. Among the errors cited in this book are a number committed by some of the leading authorities of this century. If men such as Fowler and Bernstein and Quirk and Howard cannot always get their English right, is it reasonable to expect the rest of us to?

The point is one that has not escaped the notice of many structural linguists, some of whom regard the conventions of English usage as intrusive and anachronistic and elitist, the domain of pedants and old men. In *American Tongue and Cheek*, Jim Quinn, a sympathizer, savages those who publish 'private lists of language peeves. Professional busybodies and righters of imaginary wrongs, they are the Sunday visitors of language, dropping in weekly on the local poor to make sure that everything is up to their own idea of standard ...' (cited by William Safire in *What's The Good Word?*).

There is no doubt something in what these critics say. Usage authorities can be maddeningly resistant to change, if not actively obstructive. Many of our most seemingly unobjectionable words – precarious, intensify, freakish, mob, banter, brash – had to fight long battles, often lasting a century or more, to gain acceptance. Throughout the nineteenth century reliable was opposed on the dubious grounds that any adjective springing from rely ought to be relionable. Laughable, it was insisted, should be laugh-at-able.

Even now, many good writers scrupulously avoid hopefully and instead write the more cumbersome 'it is hoped' to satisfy an obscure point of grammar, which, I suspect, many of them could not elucidate. Prestigious is still widely avoided in Britain in deference to its nineteenth-century definition, and there remains a large body of users who would, to employ Fowler's words, sooner eat peas with a knife than split an infinitive. Those who sniff decay in every shift of sense or alteration of usage do the language no service. Too often for such people the notion of good English has less to do with expressing ideas clearly than with making words conform to some arbitrary pattern.

But at the same time, anything that helps to bring order to a language as unruly and idiosyncratic as English is almost by definition a good thing. Even the most ardent structuralist would concede that there must be at least some conventions of usage. Otherwise we might as well spell fish (as George Bernard Shaw once wryly suggested) as ghoti: 'gh' as in tough, 'o' as in women, and 'ti' as in motion. By the most modest extension it should be evident that clarity is better served if we agree to preserve a distinction between its and it's, between 'I lay down the law' and 'I lie down to sleep', between imply and infer, forego and forgo, flout and flaunt, anticipate and expect and countless others.

No one, least of all me, has the right to tell you how to organize your words, and there is scarcely an entry in the pages that follow that you may not wish to disregard sometimes and no doubt a few that you may decide to scorn for ever. The purpose of this book is to try to provide a simple guide to the more perplexing or contentious issues of standard written English – or what the American authority John Simon, in an unguarded moment, called the normative grapholect. If you wish to say 'between you and I' or use fulsome in the sense of lavish, you are entirely within your rights and can certainly find ample supporting precedents among many distinguished writers. But you may also find it useful to know that such usages are at variance with that eccentric, ever-shifting corpus known as Good English.

Most of the entries that follow are illustrated with questionable usages from leading British and American newspapers and magazines. I should perhaps hasten to point out that the frequency with which some publications are cited has less to do with the quality of their production than with my own reading habits. *The Times* of London easily appears more often than any other publication, but then it is my job to read *The Times*.

I have also not hesitated to cite errors committed by the authorities themselves. It is, of course, manifestly ungrateful of me to draw attention to the occasional lapses of those on whom I have so unashamedly relied for almost all that I know. My intention in so doing was not to embarrass or challenge them, but simply to show how easily such errors are made, and I hope they will be taken in that light.

It is to those authorities – most especially to Theodore Bernstein, Philip Howard, Sir Ernest Gowers and the incomparable H. W. Fowler – that I am most indebted. I am also deeply grateful to my wife, Cynthia, for her infinite patience; to Donald McFarlan and my father, W. E. Bryson, for their advice and encouragement; to Alan Howe of *The Times* and, not least, to Keith Taylor, who was given the thankless task of editing the manuscript. To all of them, thank you.

A Note on Presentation

To impose a consistent system of presentation in a work of this sort
can result in the pages of the book being littered with italics,
quotation marks or other typographical devices. Bearing this in mind,
I have employed a system that I hope will be easy on the reader's
eye as well as easy to follow.

Within each entry, the entry word and any other similarly derived
or closely connected words are italicized only when the sense would
seem to require it. Other words and phrases – synonyms, antonyms,
correct/incorrect alternatives, etc. – are set within quotation marks,
but again only when the sense requires it. In both cases, where there
is no ambiguity, no typographical device is used to distinguish the
word.

◙ A ◙

a, an. Do you say a hotel or an hotel? A historian or an historian? The convention is to use *a* before an aspirated 'h' (a house, a hotel, a historian) and *an* before a silent 'h'. In this second category there are only four words: hour, heir, honour (US honor) and honest, and their derivatives. Some British authorities allow *an* before hotel and historian, but almost all prefer *a*.

Errors involving *a* and *an* are no doubt more often a consequence of carelessness than of ignorance. They are particularly common when they precede a number, as here: 'Cox will contribute 10 percent of the equity needed to build a $80 million cable system' (*Washington Post*). Make it *an*. Similarly, *a* is unnecessary in the following sentence and should be deleted: 'With a 140 second-hand wide-bodied jets on the market, the enthusiasm to buy anything soon evaporated' (*Sunday Times*).

abdicate, abrogate, abjure, adjure, arrogate, derogate. All six of these words have been confused in a startling variety of ways. Abdicate, the least troublesome of the six, means to renounce or relinquish. Abrogate means to abolish or annul. Abjure means to abstain from, or to reject or retract. Adjure means to command, direct or appeal to earnestly. Arrogate (a close relation of *arrogance*) means to appropriate presumptuously or to assume without right. And derogate (think of *derogatory*) means to belittle.

Those, very baldly, are the meanings. It may help you a little if you remember that the prefix *ab-* indicates 'away from' and *ad-* 'towards'. It might help the rest of us even more, however, if you were to remember that all of these words (with the possible exception of abdicate) have a number of shorter, more readily understood and generally less pretentious synonyms.

abjure. See ABDICATE, ABROGATE, ABJURE, ADJURE, ARROGATE, DEROGATE.

abrogate. See ABDICATE, ABROGATE, ABJURE, ADJURE, ARROGATE, DEROGATE.

accrue does not mean simply to increase in size, but rather to be added to bit by bit. A balloon, for instance, cannot accrue. Except in its legal and financial senses, the word is better avoided.

acoustics. As a science, the word is singular ('Acoustics was his line of work'). As a collection of properties, it is plural ('The acoustics in the auditorium were not good').

acute, chronic. These two are sometimes confused, which is a little puzzling since their meanings are sharply opposed. *Chronic* pertains to lingering conditions, ones that are not easily overcome. *Acute* refers to those that come to a sudden crisis and require immediate attention. People in the Third World may suffer from a chronic shortage of food. In a bad year, their plight may become acute.

adage frequently, and unnecessarily, appears with 'old' in tow. An adage is by definition old.

adjure. See ABDICATE, ABROGATE, ABJURE, ADJURE, ARROGATE, DEROGATE.

admit to is always wrong, as here: 'Pretoria admits to raid against Angola' (*Guardian* headline). Delete *to*. You admit a misdeed, you do not admit to it.

adverse, averse. 'He is not adverse to an occasional brandy' (*Observer*). The word wanted here was *averse*, which means reluctant or disinclined (think of *aversion*). *Adverse* means hostile and antagonistic (think of *adversary*).

aerate. Two syllables. Not *aereate*.

affect, effect. As a verb, *affect* means to influence ('Smoking may affect your health') or to adopt a pose or manner ('He affected ignorance'). *Effect* as a verb means to accomplish ('The prisoners effected an escape'). As a noun, the word needed is almost always *effect* (as in 'personal effects' or 'the damaging effects of war'). *Affect* as a noun has a narrow psychological meaning to do with emotional states (by way of which it is related to *affection*).

It is worth noting that *affect* as a verb is usually bland and often almost meaningless. In 'The winter weather affected profits in the building division' (*The Times*) and 'The noise of the crowds affected his play' (*Daily Telegraph*), it is by no means clear whether the noise and weather helped or hindered or delayed or aggravated the profits and play. A more precise word can almost always be found.

affinity denotes a mutual relationship. Therefore, strictly speaking, one should not speak of someone or something having an affinity for another, but rather should speak of an affinity with or between. When mutuality is not intended, sympathy would be a better word. But it should also be noted that a number of authorities and many dictionaries no longer insist on this distinction.

agenda. Although a plural in Latin, *agenda* in English is singular. Its English plural is *agendas* (but see DATA).

aggravate in the sense of 'exasperate' has been with us at least since the early seventeenth century and has been opposed by grammarians for about as long. Strictly, *aggravate* means to make a bad situation worse. If you walk on a broken leg, you may aggravate the injury. People can never be aggravated, only circumstances. Fowler, who calls objections to the looser usage a fetish, is no doubt right when he says the purists are fighting a battle that was long ago lost. But equally there is no real reason to use *aggravate* when 'annoy' will do.

aggression, aggressiveness. 'Aggression in US pays off for Tilling Group' (*Times* headline). Aggression always denotes hostility, which was not intended here. The writer of the headline meant to suggest only that the company had taken a determined and enterprising approach to the American market. The word he wanted was aggressiveness, which can denote either hostility or merely boldness and assertiveness.

aggressiveness. See AGGRESSION, AGGRESSIVENESS.

aid and abet. A tautological gift from the legal profession. The two words together tell us nothing that either doesn't already say on its own. The only distinction is that *abet* is normally reserved for contexts involving criminal intent. Thus it would be unwise to speak of,

15

say, a benefactor abetting the construction of a church or youth club. Other redundant expressions dear to lawyers are 'null and void', 'ways and means' and 'without let or hindrance'.

alias, alibi. Both words derive from the Latin root *alius* (meaning 'other'). *Alias* refers to an assumed name and pertains only to names. It would be incorrect to speak of an impostor passing himself off under the alias of being a doctor.

Alibi is a much more contentious word. In legal parlance it refers to a plea by an accused person that he was elsewhere at the time he was alleged to have committed a crime. More commonly it is used to mean any excuse. Fowler calls this latter usage mischievous and pretentious, and most authorities agree with him. But Bernstein, while conceding that the usage is a casualism, contends that there is no other word that can quite convey the meaning of an excuse intended to transfer responsibility. Time will no doubt vindicate him – many distinguished writers have already used *alibi* in its more general, less fastidious sense – but for the moment all that can be said is that in the sense of a general excuse, many authorities consider *alibi* unacceptable.

alibi. See ALIAS, ALIBI.

allay, alleviate, assuage, relieve. *Alleviate* should suggest giving temporary relief without removing the underlying cause of a problem. It is close in meaning to 'ease', a fact obviously unknown to the writer of this sentence: 'It will ease the transit squeeze, but will not alleviate it' (*Chicago Tribune*). *Allay* and *assuage* both mean to put to rest or to pacify and are most often applied to fears. *Relieve* is the more general term and covers all these meanings.

allegory. See FABLE, PARABLE, ALLEGORY, MYTH.

alleviate. See ALLAY, ALLEVIATE, ASSUAGE, RELIEVE.

all right. A good case could be made for shortening *all right* to *alright*. Not only do most of us pronounce it as one word, but also there are very good precedents in *already*, *almost* and *altogether*, which were formed by contracting *all ready*, *all most* and *all together*, and even in *alone*, which was originally *all one*. In fact, many writers

– all too many, as it happens – appear to think that *alright* has gained acceptance already, as these two examples show: 'You came away thinking: "The guy's alright"' (*Observer*); 'The engine cuts out and someone says: "Poor chap, I hope he will be alright"' (*The Times*). English, however, is a fickle tongue, and *alright* continues to be looked on as illiterate and unacceptable and consequently it ought never to appear in serious writing.

allusion. 'When the speaker happened to name Mr Gladstone, the allusion was received with loud cheers' (cited by Fowler). The word is not, as many suppose, a more impressive synonym for reference. When you allude to something, you do not specifically mention it. Thus it would be correct to write: 'In an allusion to the President, he said: "Some people make better actors than politicians"'. But you leave it to the reader or listener to make his own deduction about what it is specifically you are implying. The word therefore is closer in meaning to implication or suggestion.

along with. See TOGETHER WITH, ALONG WITH.

altercation. 'Three youths were slightly injured in the altercation' (*Chicago Tribune*). No one ever gets physically hurt in an altercation. It is a heated exchange of words and nothing more.

alternative. Although the word derives from the Latin *alter*, meaning 'either of two', almost all the authorities agree that a strict interpretation of its meaning is needlessly pedantic and impractical. Only Partridge insists that three alternatives would be wrong.

Alternative and *alternate* are frequently confused, particularly in their adverbial forms. *Alternate* means by turns: first one, then the other. Day alternates with night. *Alternative* means offering a choice. The most common misuse is seen here: 'The journey may be made by road or alternately by rail' (cited by Fowler). The writer meant *alternatively* – though in fact the sentence would say no less without it. *Alternative* is in any case better avoided when there is no suggestion of a compulsion to choose. An army under attack has the alternative of fighting or retreating, but it is loose to say that someone has the alternative of making a journey by road or by rail when he might well choose not to go at all.

although. See THOUGH, ALTHOUGH.

ambiguous, equivocal. Both mean vague and open to more than one interpretation. But whereas an ambiguous statement may be vague by accident or by design, an equivocal one is calculatedly unclear.

ambivalent. 'It makes an ideal compromise for those who have always been ambivalent about Spain in high season' (*Guardian*). *Ambivalent* is better avoided when all you mean is of two minds or indecisive or ambiguous. Strictly speaking, it refers to a psychological state in which a person suffers from two irreconcilable desires. By extension, according to most authorities, it may be used to denote a situation involving strongly contradictory or conflicting views. But its use in any other sense is, as Partridge would say, catachrestic.

amid, among. 'Throughout the afternoon and evening the rescuers searched among the rubble for survivors' (*Guardian*). *Among* (or *amongst*) applies to things that can be separated and counted, *amid* (or *amidst*) to things that cannot. Since the rescuers were not searching one rubble and then another rubble, the word here should have been *amid*.

among. See AMID, AMONG; BETWEEN, AMONG.

amoral, immoral. Occasionally confused. Something that is immoral is evil or dissolute and contrary to the prevailing creed. The word amoral pertains to matters in which the question of morality is disregarded or does not arise. Thus an amoral person (one who does not distinguish between right and wrong) may commit an immoral act.

The use of the Greek prefix *a-* with the Latin-derived word *moral* pained Fowler, who suggested that *nonmoral* would be an improvement. But even he conceded that such a view was largely wistful. Today *nonmoral* is entirely acceptable, but only a pedagogue would insist on it.

an. See A, AN.

ancient. '[She] drew up in a car that can best be described as ancient' (*Observer*). Something that is ancient is not merely old, it is very old – at least several hundred years. A better word here would be *antiquated*, which refers to things that are out of fashion or no longer produced.

and. The belief that *and* should not be used to begin a sentence is without foundation. And that's all there is to it.

A thornier problem is seen here: 'The group has interests in Germany, Australia, Japan and intends to expand into North America next year' (*The Times*). This is what Fowler calls bastard enumeration and Bernstein, with more delicacy, calls a series out of control. The problem is that the closing clause ('intends to expand into North America next year') does not belong to the series that precedes it. It is a separate thought. The sentence should say: 'The group has interests in Germany, Australia *and* Japan, and intends to expand into North America next year'. (Note that the inclusion of a comma after 'Japan' helps to signal that the series has ended and a new clause is beginning.)

The same problem is seen here: 'Department of Trade officials, tax and accountancy experts were to be involved at an early stage in the investigation' (*Guardian*). *And* here is being asked to do two jobs at once: to mark the end of a series and to join 'tax' and 'accountancy' to 'experts'. It isn't up to it. The sentence needs to say: 'Department of Trade officials *and* tax and accountancy experts'. This reluctance by writers to supply a second *and* is common, but always misguided.

and/or. Bernstein calls this construction 'both a visual and a mental abomination' and he is right. If you mean *and* say 'and', if you mean *or* say 'or'. In the rare instance when you really do mean both, as in 'a $100 fine and/or 30 days in jail', say 'a $100 fine or 30 days in jail or both'.

and which. 'The rights issue, the largest so far this year and which was not unexpected, will be used to fund expansion plans' (*The Times*). *And which* should almost always be preceded by a parallel *which*. The sentence above would be unexceptionable, and would read more smoothly, if it were changed to: 'The rights issue, which was the largest so far this year and which was not unexpected . . .'. Occasionally the need for euphony may excuse the absence of the first *which*, but such instances are rare and usually the omission is no more than a sign of slipshod writing. The rule applies equally to such constructions as *and that, and who, but which* and *but who*. (See also THAT, WHICH).

another. 'Some 400 workers were laid off at the Liverpool factory and another 150 in Bristol' (*Daily Telegraph*). Strictly speaking, *another* should be used to equate two things of equal size and type. In this instance it would be correct only if 400 workers were being laid off in Bristol also. It would be better to write 'and 150 more [or others] in Bristol'.

anticipate. 'First-year losses in the video division were greater than anticipated' (*The Times*). To anticipate something is to look ahead to it and prepare for it, not to make a reasonable estimate, as was apparently intended here. A tennis player who anticipates his opponent's next shot doesn't just guess where it is going to go, he is there waiting for it. The word is only vaguely a synonym for expect. Grammarians, in a mercifully rare stab at humour, sometimes quote the old joke about an engaged couple who anticipated marriage – the point being that anticipating a marriage is quite a different matter from expecting one. In the example above, the use of the word is contradictory. If the company had anticipated the losses, it wouldn't have found them larger than expected.

anxious. Since *anxious* comes from *anxiety*, it should contain some connotation of being worried or fearful and not merely eager or expectant. You may be anxious to put some unpleasant task behind you, but, unless you have invested money in it, you are unlikely to be anxious to see a new play.

anybody, anyone, anything, any time, anyway, anywhere. *Any time* is always two words, *anything* and *anywhere* always one. The others are normally one word, except when the emphasis is on the second element (e.g., 'He received three job offers, but any one would have suited him').

A common fault occurs here: 'Anyone can relax, so long as they don't care whether they or anyone else ever actually gets anything done' (*Observer*). *Anyone* and *anybody* are singular and should be followed by singular pronouns and verbs. The sentence would be more grammatical as 'so long as he doesn't care whether he or anyone else ever actually gets anything done'. For a discussion, see NUMBER (4).

anyone. See ANYBODY, ANYONE, ANYTHING, ANY TIME, ANYWAY, ANYWHERE.

anything. See ANYBODY, ANYONE, ANYTHING, ANY TIME, ANY-
WAY, ANYWHERE.

any time. See ANYBODY, ANYONE, ANYTHING, ANY TIME, ANY-
WAY, ANYWHERE.

anyway. See ANYBODY, ANYONE, ANYTHING, ANY TIME, ANY-
WAY, ANYWHERE.

anywhere. See ANYBODY, ANYONE, ANYTHING, ANY TIME, ANY-
WAY, ANYWHERE.

appendices, appendixes. Either is correct. *The Concise Oxford* prefers
the first, *The American Heritage* prefers the second.

appendixes. See APPENDICES, APPENDIXES.

appraise, apprise. 'No decision was likely, he said, until they had been
appraised of the damage' (*Sunday Times*). The word wanted here was
apprise, which means to inform. *Appraise* means to assess or evaluate.
An insurance assessor appraises damage and apprises owners.

appreciate has a slightly more specific meaning than many writers give
it. If you appreciate something, you value it ('I appreciate your help')
or you understand it sympathetically ('I appreciate your plight'). But
when there is no sense of sympathy or gratitude or esteem (as in 'I
appreciate what you're saying, but I think it's nonsense'), 'understand'
or 'recognize' would be better.

apprise. See APPRAISE, APPRISE.

approximate means 'near to', so *very approximate* ought to mean 'very
near to'. The difficulty is that when most people speak of a very
approximate estimate, they mean a very tentative one, not a very close
one. Gowers, in *The Complete Plain Words*, roundly criticizes the
usage as loose and misleading. But Fowler classes it among his
'sturdy indefensibles' – words and phrases that are clearly illogical,
and perhaps even lamentable, but which have become so firmly
entrenched that the purists may as well throw in their towels. In this
Fowler is no doubt right.

Where the authorities do find common ground is in the belief that *approximate* and *approximately* are cumbersome words and are usually better replaced by 'about' or 'almost' or 'nearly'.

a priori, prima facie. Occasionally confused. *Prima facie*, meaning 'at first sight' or 'on the surface of it', refers to matters in which not all of the evidence has been collected, but in which such evidence as there is points to certain conclusions. *A priori* refers to conclusions drawn from assumptions rather than experience.

apt. See LIABLE, LIKELY, APT, PRONE.

arbitrate, mediate. The functions of these two words are quite separate. Arbitrators are like judges in that they are appointed to hear evidence and then to make a decision. They remain aloof from the disputing parties. Mediators, on the other hand, are more like negotiators in that they shuttle between opposing sides trying to work out a compromise or settlement. They do not make judgements.

Difficulties sometimes also arise in distinguishing between an arbitrator and an arbiter. Whereas an arbitrator is appointed, an arbiter is someone whose opinions are valued but in whom there is no vested authority. Fowler sums up the distinction neatly: 'An arbiter acts arbitrarily; an arbitrator must not'.

argot. See JARGON, ARGOT, LINGUA FRANCA.

aroma does not refer to any smell, but only to pleasant ones. Thus 'the pungent aroma of a cattleyard' (*Washington Post*) is wrong.

arrogate. See ABDICATE, ABROGATE, ABJURE, ADJURE, ARRO-GATE, DEROGATE.

artefact, artifact. The first spelling is preferred in Britain, the second in America, but either is correct. In either case it is something shaped by human hand and not merely any very old object, as was apparently thought here: 'The team found bones and other artefacts at the site' (*Guardian*). Bones are not artefacts. The word is related to *artifice*, *artificial* and *artisan*, all of which imply the work of man.

articles, omitted. Some writers, in an apparent effort to make their writing punchier, adopt a habit of dropping the word *the* at the start of sentences, as in the three following examples, all from *The Times*: 'Monthly premium is £1.75'; 'Main feature of the property is an Olympic-sized swimming pool'; 'Dividend is again being passed'. Inevitable result is stilted sentences. Reader is apt to find it annoying. Writer who does it persistently should have his typewriter taken away.

artifact. See ARTEFACT, ARTIFACT.

as. See LIKE, AS.

as ... as. 'Housing conditions in Toxteth may be as bad, if not worse than, any in Britain' (*Observer*). The problem here is what grammarians call an incomplete alternative comparison. If we remove the 'if not worse' phrase from the sentence, the problem becomes clearer: 'Housing conditions in Toxteth may be as bad ... than any in Britain'. The writer has left the 'as bad' phrase dangling incompleted. The sentence should say 'as bad *as*, if not worse than, any in Britain'.

assassin. Until fairly recently the word applied not just to murderers, but also to those who attempted to murder, so to talk of a "would-be assassin' or 'a failed assassin' would be tautological. But, because of the proliferation of such crimes in the last twenty years, an assassin today is taken to mean someone who succeeds in his attempt. Thus there can no longer be any objection to appending a qualifying adjective to the word.

assuage. See ALLAY, ALLEVIATE, ASSUAGE, RELIEVE.

attain. 'The uncomfortable debt level attained at the end of the financial year has now been eased' (*The Times*). *Attain*, like 'achieve' and 'accomplish', suggests the reaching of a desired goal. Since an uncomfortable debt level is hardly desirable, it would have been better to change the word (to 'prevailing', for example) or, in this instance, to delete it.

auspicious. Beloved by public speakers ('On this auspicious occasion'), the word does not simply mean special or memorable. It means propitious, promising, of good omen.

avenge, revenge. Generally, *avenge* indicates the settling of a score or the redressing of an injustice. It is more dispassionate than *revenge*, which indicates retaliation taken largely for the sake of personal satisfaction. The corresponding nouns are *vengeance* and *revenge*.

average. 'The average wage in Australia is now about £150 a week, though many people earn much more' (*The Times*). And many earn much less. That is what makes £150 the average. When expressing an average figure, it is generally unnecessary, and frequently fatuous, to elaborate on it. (See also MEAN, MEDIAN, AVERAGE.)

averse. See ADVERSE, AVERSE.

awake. For a word that represents one of life's simplest and most predictable acts, *awake* has an abundance of forms: *awake, awoke, awaked, awaken, awakened*. Specifying the distinctions is, as Fowler notes, a difficult business, but in any case they present fewer problems than their diversity might lead us to expect. There are, however, two problems worth noting:

1. *Awoken*, though much used, is not standard. Thus this sentence from an Agatha Christie novel (cited by Partridge) is wrong: 'I was awoken by that rather flashy young woman.' Make it *awakened*.

2. As a past participle, *awaked* is preferable to *awoke*. Thus, 'He had awaked at midnight' and not 'He had awoke at midnight'. But if ever in doubt about the past tense, you will never be wrong if you use *awakened*.

awfully. See TERRIBLY, AWFULLY, HORRIBLY, ETC.

awhile. 'I will stay here for awhile' is incorrect because the notion of 'for' is implicit in *awhile*. Make it either 'I will stay here awhile' or 'I will stay here for a while'.

▣ B ▣

bait, bate. 'Robin's exploits were listened to with baited breath' (*Mail on Sunday*). Unless Robin's listeners were hoping to catch fish, their breath was *bated*. The word is a cousin of *abated*.

barbaric, barbarous. *Barbaric* emphasizes crudity and a lack of civilizing influence. A loincloth might be described as a barbaric costume. *Barbarous* stresses cruelty and harshness and usually contains at least a hint of moral condemnation, as in 'barbarous ignorance' or 'barbarous treatment'.

barbarous. see BARBARIC, BARBAROUS.

basically. The trouble with this word, basically, is that it is greatly overused and generally unnecessary, as here.

bate. See BAIT, BATE.

bathos. From the Greek *bathus*, meaning 'deep', *bathos* can be used to indicate the lowest point or nadir, or triteness and insincerity. But its usual use is in describing an abrupt descent from an elevated position to the commonplace. It is not, as is sometimes supposed, the opposite of pathos, which is to do with feelings of pity or sympathy.

be (with a participle). Often a wordy way of getting your point across, as here: 'He will be joining the board of directors in March' (*The Times*). Why not just say: 'He will join the board of directors in March'?

before, prior to. There is no difference between these two except that *prior to* is longer, clumsier and awash with pretension. If, to paraphrase Bernstein, you would use 'posterior to' instead of 'after', then by all means use *prior to* instead of *before*.

behalf. There is a useful distinction between *on behalf of* and *in behalf of*. The first means acting as a representative, as when a lawyer enters a plea on behalf of a client. It often denotes a formal relationship. *In behalf of* indicates a closer or more sympathetic relationship and means acting as a friend or defender.

'I spoke on your behalf' means that I represented you when you were absent. 'I spoke in your behalf' means that I supported you or defended you.

behove (US **behoove**). An archaic word, but still sometimes a useful one. Two points need to be made:

1. The word means necessary or contingent, but is sometimes wrongly used for 'becomes', particularly with the adverb 'ill', as in, 'It ill behoves any man responsible for policy to think of how best to make political propaganda' (cited by Gowers).

2. It should be used only impassively and with the subject 'it'. 'The circumstances behove us to take action' is wrong. Make it, 'It behoves us in the circumstances to take action'.

bereft. 'Many children leave school altogether bereft of mathematical skills' (*The Times*, cited by Kingsley Amis in *The State of the Language*). To be bereft of something is not to lack it but to be dispossessed of it. A spinster is not bereft of a husband, but a widow is (the word is the past participle of *bereave*).

besides means 'also' or 'in addition to' and not 'alternatively'. Partridge cites this incorrect use: '... the wound must have been on the right side of his face -- unless it was made by something besides the handle of the gear-lever'. Make it 'other than'.

between, among. There is a long-standing misconception, still tenaciously clung to by some, that *between* applies only to two and *among* to more than two, so that we should speak of dividing some money between the two of us, but among the four of us. That is correct as far as it goes, but it doesn't always go very far. It would be absurd, for instance, to say: 'We sat down among the three lakes' or 'We decided to build our house among the forest and the town and the mountain'.

More logically, *between* should be used to indicate reciprocal relationships and *among* collective ones. If, for example, we referred to trade talks among the Common Market countries, it would suggest collective discussions, whereas trade talks between them could indicate any two of them meeting separately. *Between* emphasizes the individual, *among* the group.

A second problem with *between* is seen here: 'The layoffs will affect between 200 to 400 workers' (*The Times*). Used in this sense, *between* denotes the extremes of a range, not the range itself. Thus you should say either 'between 200 and 400' or 'from 200 to 400'.

between you and I. John Simon calls this 'a grammatical error of unsurpassable grossness'. It is perhaps enough to say that it is very common and that it is always wrong. The rule is that the object of a preposition should always be in the accusative. More simply, we don't say 'between you and I' for the same reason that we don't say 'give that book to I' or 'as I was saying to she only yesterday'. A similar gaffe is seen here: 'He leaves behind 79 astronauts, many young enough to be the children of he and the others . . .' (*Daily Mail*). Make it 'of him'.

biannual, biennial, bimonthly, biweekly. Biannual means twice a year and biennial means every two years (or lasting for two years). About that there is no trouble. Bimonthly (or bi-monthly) should mean every two months, but is often taken to mean twice a month. Similarly, biweekly (or bi-weekly) should mean every two weeks, but is often misconstrued as meaning twice a week. Clarity probably would be better served, at least with these last two, if you were to write 'twice a week', 'every two months' and so on.

biennial. See BIANNUAL, BIENNIAL, BIMONTHLY, BIWEEKLY.

bilateral. See UNILATERAL, BILATERAL, MULTILATERAL.

bimonthly. See BIANNUAL, BIENNIAL, BIMONTHLY, BIWEEKLY.

biweekly. See BIANNUAL, BIENNIAL, BIMONTHLY, BIWEEKLY.

blatant, flagrant. The words are not quite synonymous. Something that is blatant is glaringly obvious and contrived ('a blatant lie') or noisily obnoxious ('blatant electioneering') or both. Something that is flagrant is shocking and reprehensible ('a flagrant miscarriage of justice'). If I tell you that I regularly travel to the moon, that is a blatant lie, not a flagrant one. If you set fire to my house, that is a flagrant act, not a blatant one.

blazon. '[She] blazoned a trail in the fashion world which others were quick to follow' (*Sunday Times*). Trails are blazed. To blazon means to display or proclaim in an ostentatious manner.

blueprint as a metaphor for a design or plan is much overworked. If the temptation to use it is irresistible, at least remember that a blueprint is a completed plan, not a preliminary one.

born, borne. Both are past participles of the verb *bear*. *Born* is limited to the idea of giving birth ('He was born in December'). *Borne* should be used for the sense of supporting or putting up with ('He has borne the burden with dignity'), but is also used in the sense of giving birth in active constructions ('She has borne three children') and in passive constructions followed by 'by' ('The three children borne by her . . .').

borne. See BORN, BORNE.

both. Three small problems to note:
1. *Both* should not be used to describe more than two things. Partridge cites a passage in which a woman is said to have 'a shrewd common sense . . . both in speech, deed and dress'. Delete *both*.
2. Sometimes it appears superfluously: '. . . and they both went to the same school, Charterhouse' (*Observer*). Either delete *both* or make it '. . . they both went to Charterhouse'.
3. Sometimes it is misused for 'each'. To say that there is a supermarket on both sides of the street suggests that it is somehow straddling the roadway. Say either that there is a supermarket on each side of the street or that there are supermarkets on both sides. See also EACH.

both . . . and. 'He was both deaf to argument and entreaty' (cited by Gowers). The rule involved here is that of correlative conjunctions, which states that *both* and *and* should link grammatically similar things. If *both* is followed immediately by a verb, *and* should also be followed immediately by a verb. If *both* immediately precedes a noun, then so should *and*. In the example above, however, *both* is followed by an adjective (deaf) and *and* by a noun (entreaty).

The sentence needs to be recast, either as 'He was deaf to both argument [noun] and entreaty [noun]' or as 'He was deaf both to argument [preposition and noun] and to entreaty [preposition and noun]'.

The rule holds true equally for other such pairs: 'not only ... but also', 'either ... or' and 'neither ... nor'.

bottleneck, as Gowers notes, is a useful, if sometimes overworked, metaphor to indicate a point of constriction. But it should not be forgotten that it is a metaphor and therefore capable of cracking when put under too much pressure. To speak, for instance, of 'a worldwide bottleneck' or 'a growing bottleneck' sounds a note of absurdity. Bottlenecks, even figurative ones, don't grow and they don't encompass the earth.

bravado should not be confused with bravery. It is a swaggering or boastful display of boldness, often adopted to disguise an underlying timidity. It is, in short, a false bravery and there is nothing courageous about it.

breach, breech. Frequently confused. *Breach* describes an infraction or a gap. It should always suggest *break*, a word to which it is related. Thus a breach of international law is a violation. *Breech* applies to the rear or lower portion of things. A breech delivery is one in which the baby is born feet first. A less common error is seen here: 'Washington remained hopeful that Secretary of State Cyrus Vance might breech the gap on his trip to the Middle East' (*Time*, cited by Simon). Here the writer was doubly wrong. He was apparently thinking of *breach* but meant bridge.

breech. See BREACH, BREECH.

bulk. A few authorities insist that bulk should be reserved for contexts involving volume and mass and not employed as a general synonym for 'the majority' or 'the greater part'. Thus they would object to 'the bulk of the book' or 'the bulk of the American people'. But two considerations militate against this view. First, as Fowler points out, *bulk* in its looser sense has been with us for at least 200 years and is unlikely now to slink off under the icy gaze of a handful of purists. And second, as Bernstein maintains, there is no other word that conveys quite the same idea of a generalized, unquantified assessment. So use it as you will.

burgeon does not mean merely to expand or thrive. It means to bud or sprout and therefore indicates an incipient action. It would be correct to talk about the burgeoning talent of a precocious youth, but to write of 'the ever-burgeoning population of Cairo', as one writer on the *Daily Telegraph* did, is wrong. Cairo's population has been growing for centuries, and nothing, in any case, is ever-burgeoning.

but used negatively after a pronoun presents a problem that has confounded careful users for generations. Do you say, 'Everyone but him had arrived' or 'Everyone but he had arrived'? The authorities have never been able to agree.

Some regard *but* as a preposition and put the pronoun in the accusative – i.e., me, her, him or them. So just as we say, 'Between you and me' or 'Give it to her', we should say, 'Everyone but him had arrived'.

Others argue that *but* is a conjunction and that the pronoun should be nominative (I, she, he or they), rather as if the sentence were saying, 'Everyone had arrived, but he had not'.

The answer perhaps is to regard *but* sometimes as a conjunction and sometimes as a preposition. Two rough rules should help you:

1. If the pronoun appears at the end of the sentence, you can always use the accusative and be on firm ground. Thus, 'Everyone was there but him'; 'Nobody knew but her'.

2. When the pronoun appears earlier in the sentence, it is almost always better to put it in the nominative, as in 'No one but he knew'. The one exception is when the pronoun is influenced by a preceding preposition, but such constructions are relatively rare, often clumsy and usually better reworded. Two examples might be: 'To everyone but him life was a mystery' and 'Between no one but them was there any bitterness'. (see also THAN (3).)

But ... however. Since both words indicate a shift in direction, they should not appear together in a sentence. 'But that, however, is another story' should be 'But that is another story' or 'That, however, is another story'.

Caesarean. 'The baby, weighing more than 8 lb, was delivered by caesarian section' (*The Times*). The preferred spelling is *Caesarean* (upper-case 'C') in both Britain and the United States.

calligraphy. 'Both ransom notes have been forwarded to calligraphy experts in Rome' (*Daily Mail*). The writer meant 'graphology experts'. Calligraphy is an art. It means beautiful handwriting – so, incidentally, to talk of beautiful calligraphy would be redundant.

can, may. You have probably heard it a thousand times before, but it bears repeating that *can* applies to what is possible and *may* to what is permissible. You can drive your car the wrong way down a one-way street, but you may not (or must not or should not). In spite of the simplicity of the rule, errors abound. Here is William Safire writing in *The New York Times* on the pronunciation of *junta*: 'The worst mistake is to mix languages: You cannot say "joonta" and you cannot say "hunta".' But you can – and quite easily. What Safire meant was 'should not' or 'may not' or 'ought not'.

caption. Partridge objects to the use of *caption* to describe the words beneath an illustration, 'instead of above, as it should be', apparently on the assumption that the word derives from the Latin *caput* ('head'). In fact, it comes from *capere* ('to take'), and in any case the usage is now firmly established.

careen, career. Occasionally confused when describing runaway vehicles and the like. To careen in that sense should convey the idea of swaying or tilting dangerously. If all you mean is uncontrolled movement, use career.

career. See CAREEN, CAREER.

ceiling, floor. *Ceiling* used figuratively in the sense of an upper limit is a handy word, but, like many other handy words, is apt to be overused. When you do employ it figuratively, you should never forget that its literal meaning is always lurking in the background, ready to spring forward and make an embarrassment of your metaphor. Philip Howard cites the memorable case of the minister in the Attlee Government who excited confusion and exercised purists by announcing plans to put 'a ceiling price on carpets'. Better still perhaps was this two-faced headline in the *Daily Gulf Times*: 'Oil ministers want to stick to ceiling'.

Floor in the sense of a lower limit is, of course, equally likely to result in incongruities. Occasionally the two words get mixed together, as in this perplexing sentence, cited by both Howard and Fowler: 'The effect of this announcement is that the total figure of £410 million can be regarded as a floor as well as a ceiling'. (See also TARGET.)

celebrant, celebrator. 'All this is music to the ears of James Bond fan club members . . . and to other celebrants who descend on New Orleans each Nov. 11 . . .' (*The New York Times*). Celebrants take part in religious ceremonies. Those who gather for purposes of revelry are celebrators.

celebrator. See CELEBRANT, CELEBRATOR.

Celeste, Mary. The *Mary Celeste*, an American brigantine whose ten passengers and crew mysteriously disappeared during a crossing of the Atlantic in 1872, is sometimes used metaphorically – and almost always is misspelled, as here: 'At last, the sound of people in the City's Marie Celèste' (*Daily Mail*). Make it *Mary*.

celibacy. 'He claimed he had remained celibate throughout the four-year marriage' (*Daily Telegraph*). Celibacy does not, as is generally supposed, necessarily indicate abstinence from sexual relations. It means only to be unmarried, particularly if as a result of a religious vow. A married man cannot be celibate, but he may be chaste.

cement, concrete. The two are not synonyms. Cement is merely a constituent of concrete, which also contains sand, gravel, and crushed rock.

centre round or **around** (US **center around**). 'Their argument centres around the Foreign Intelligence Surveillance Act' (*The Times*). *Centre* indicates a point, and a point cannot encircle anything. Make it 'centre on' or 'revolve around'.

chafe, chaff. The one may lead to the other, but their meanings are distinct. To chafe means to make sore or worn by rubbing (or, figuratively, to annoy or irritate). To chaff means to tease good-naturedly. A person who is excessively chaffed is likely to grow chafed.

chaff. See CHAFE, CHAFF.

chair (as a verb). 'The meeting, which is to be chaired by the German Chancellor, will open tomorrow' (*The Times*). A few authorities, among them Bernstein and *The New York Times Manual of Style and Usage*, continue to resist *chair* used in the sense of 'preside over', as it has been above. They would be happier if the quotation said something to the effect of 'The meeting, whose chairman will be the German Chancellor . . .'. Bernstein includes the usage among his 'fad words' – that is, words resorted to for no other purpose than effect. He rightly ridicules those writers who, in the pursuit of novelty, would 'elevator themselves to their penthouses, get dinner-jacketed and go theatering'. When *chair* first appeared as a verb (in the 1920s), it no doubt seemed just as ludicrous and contrived. But time has, I think, removed the sheen of presumptuousness from the usage, and most dictionaries, including the 1982 *Concise Oxford*, now accept it without comment.

choose. See OPT, CHOOSE.

chronic. See ACUTE, CHRONIC.

circumstances, in the and **under the.** Some newspapers, according to Partridge, insist on the first and forbid the second, which is unfortunate because they can be usefully distinguished. *In the circumstances* should indicate merely that a situation exists: 'In the circumstances, I began to feel worried'. *Under the circumstances* should denote a situation in which action is necessitated or, more rarely, inhibited: 'Under the circumstances, I had no choice but to leave'.

claim. Properly, *claim* means to demand recognition of a right. You claim something that you wish to call your own – an inheritance, a lost possession, a piece of land, for instance. But increasingly it is used in the sense of assert or contend, as here: 'There are those who claim that the Atlantic Treaty has an aggressive purpose' (cited by Gowers).

climax

For years authorities have decried this looser usage and for years hardly anyone has heeded them. The battle, I think, is now nearly lost – even 69 per cent of the normally conservative members of *The American Heritage Dictionary* usage panel accept the word as a synonym for assert. But the authorities' case is worth hearing, if only because they remain so resolute in their dislike of the usage.

Their contention rests on the argument that there is no need for the word in its looser sense, and in this they are quite right. 'Assert', 'declare', 'maintain', 'contend', 'allege', 'profess' and even the much neglected 'say', 'says' or 'said' can almost always fit more accurately into the space usurped by *claim*.

But against this must be placed the weight of common usage, which is clearly imposing, and the fact (to quote Fowler, who doesn't like the word) that 'there is no doubt a vigour about *claim* – a pugnacity almost – that makes such words [as assert, etc.] seem tame by comparison'.

Whatever your position, it is worth bearing in mind that there are occasions when the word is clearly out of place. Fowler cites this headline from a newspaper in Hawaii: 'Oahu barmaid claims rape'. The suggestion appears to be that the unfortunate woman either contends she has committed a rape or would like one to call her own. Whichever, it is execrable.

climax. One or two authorities, notably Bernstein, continue to disapprove of *climax* in the sense of a culmination or high point. The word, they point out, comes from the Greek for ladder and properly ought to indicate a sequence in which each element is an advance upon the previous one. Fowler, however, raises no objection to its use as a synonym for culmination, and most dictionaries now give that as its primary meaning.

On two other points the authorities do agree – that the word should not be used as a verb ('The event climaxed a memorable week') and that it should never be used to indicate the lowest point in a series ('Our troubles reached their climax when the engine wouldn't start').

climb up, climb down. *Climb down*, as a few purists continue to point out, is a patent contradiction. But there you are. Idiom has embraced it, as it has many other patent absurdities, and there is no gainsaying it now. *Climb up*, on the other hand, is always redundant when *climb* is used transitively – which is to say most of the time. An exceptional intransitive use of *climb* would be: 'We sat down awhile before climbing up again'. But in a sentence such as 'He climbed up the ladder', the *up* does nothing but take up space. (See also PHRASAL VERBS and UP.)

close proximity is tautological. Make it 'near' or 'close to'.

co-equal. 'In almost every other regard the two are co-equal' (*Guardian*). A fatuous addition to the language. *Co-* adds nothing to *equal* that *equal* doesn't already say alone.

cognomen applies only to a person's surname, not to his full name or given names. Except jocularly, it is a pretentious and unnecessary word.

collectives. Deciding whether to treat nouns of multitude – words like *majority*, *flock*, *army*, *Government*, *group*, *crowd* – as singulars or plurals is entirely a matter of the sense you intend to convey. Although some authorities have tried to fix rules, such undertakings are almost inevitably, as Fowler says, wasted effort. On the whole, Americans lean to the singular and Britons to the plural, often in ways that would strike the other as absurd (compare the American 'The couple was married in 1978' with the British 'England are to play Hungary in their first World Cup match'). A common error is to flounder about between singular and plural, as here: 'The group, which *has* been expanding vigorously abroad, *are* more optimistic about the second half' (*The Times*). Even Samuel Johnson stumbled when he wrote that he knew of no nation 'that *has* preserved *their* words and phrases from mutability'. In both sentences, the italicized pairs of words should be either singular both times or plural both times.

collide, collision. 'The lorry had broken down when another car was in collision with it' (*Standard*). Such sentences, which are common in newspapers, are wrong in two ways. First, a collision can occur only when two or more *moving* objects come together. If a car runs into a wall, a lamp-post, a broken-down lorry or any other stationary object, it is not a collision. The second fault lies in the expression 'in collision with'. Many writers, anxious not to impute blame in articles dealing with accidents, resort to this awkward and inelegant phrase, but generally unnecessarily. From a legal standpoint it could be imprudent to say, 'Mr X's car collided with Mr Y's yesterday'. But rather than shelter under an ugly phrase, it would be just as safe, and much more idiomatic, to say: 'Mr X's car and Mr Y's collided yesterday'.

collision. See COLLIDE, COLLISION.

collusion. 'They have been working in collusion on the experiments for almost four years' (*Guardian*). *Collusion* should always carry a pejorative connotation, suggesting fraud or underhandedness. In the example above, describing the work of two scientists, the word wanted was cooperation or collaboration.

comic, comical. 'There was a comic side to the tragedy' (*The Times*). Something that is comic is intended to be funny. Something that is comical is funny whether or not that is the intention. Since tragedies are never intentionally amusing, the word wanted here was comical.

comical. See COMIC, COMICAL.

commence. 'The Princess' mother, who gave up modeling ... after commencing her not very happy marriage ...' (*Time*). An unnecessary genteelism. What's wrong with 'beginning'?

commiseration. See EMPATHY, SYMPATHY, COMPASSION, PITY, COMMISERATION.

common. See MUTUAL, COMMON.

comparatively. 'Comparatively little progress was made in the talks yesterday' (*Guardian*). Compared with what? *Comparatively*, like 'relatively' (which see), is better used only when a comparison is being expressed or clearly implied. It is better avoided when all you mean is 'fairly' or 'only a little'.

compare to, compare with. These two can be usefully distinguished. *Compare to* should be used to liken things, *compare with* to consider their similarities and differences. 'He compared London to New York' means that he felt London to be similar to New York. 'He compared London with New York' means that he assessed the two cities' relative merits. *Compare to* most often appears in figurative senses, as in 'Shall I compare thee to a summer's day?' So unless you are writing poetry or love letters, *compare with* is usually the expression you want. The distinction, it should perhaps be noted, is heeded more often in theory than in practice – *The American Heritage Dictionary* (Second College Edition), for instance, encourages the observance of the distinction in its entry for *compare* but then allows Henry Kucera to disregard the rule twice in his foreword – but it is a useful one and worth preserving.

A separate problem sometimes arises when writers try to compare incomparables. Fowler cites this example: 'Dryden's prose ... loses nothing of its value by being compared with his contemporaries'. The writer has inadvertently compared prose with people when he meant to compare prose with prose. It should be 'with that of his contemporaries'.

compassion. See EMPATHY, SYMPATHY, COMPASSION, PITY, COMMISERATION.

compel, impel. Both words imply the application of a force leading to some form of action, but they are not quite synonymous. *Compel* is the stronger of the two and, like its cousin *compulsion*, suggests action undertaken as a result of coercion or irresistible pressure: 'The man's bullying tactics compelled me to step forward'. *Impel* is closer in meaning to 'encourage' and means to urge forward: 'The audience's ovation impelled me to speak at greater length than I had intended'. If you are compelled to do something, you have no choice. If you are impelled, there is more likely to be an element of willingness.

compendium. No doubt because of the similarity in sound to 'comprehensive', the word is often taken to mean vast and all-embracing. In fact, a compendium is a succinct summary or abridgment. Size has nothing to do with it – it may be as large as *The Oxford English Dictionary* or as small as a scrap of paper. What is important is that it should provide a complete summary in a brief way. The plural can be either *compendia* or *compendiums*. *The OED* prefers the former, Fowler and most other dictionaries the latter.

complacent, complaisant. The first means self-satisfied, contented to the point of smugness. The second means affable and cheerfully *complaisant*

obliging. If you are complacent, you are pleased with yourself; if you are complaisant, you wish to please others. Both words come from the Latin *complacere* ('to please'), but *complaisant* reached us by way of France, which accounts for the difference in spelling.

complaisant. See COMPLACENT, COMPLAISANT.

complete. Partridge includes *complete* in his list of false comparatives – that is, words that do not admit of comparison, such as 'ultimate' and 'eternal' (one thing cannot be 'more ultimate' or 'more eternal' than another). Technically, he is right, and you should take care not to modify *complete* needlessly. But there are occasions when it would be pedantic to carry the stricture too far. As the Morrises note, there can be no real objection to 'This is the most complete study to date of that period'. Use it, but use it judiciously.

compound. 'News of a crop failure in the northern part of the country will only compound the government's economic and political problems' (*The Times*). Several authorities have deplored the usage of *compound* in the sense of worsen, as it is employed above and increasingly elsewhere. They are right to point out that the usage springs from a misinterpretation of the word's original and more narrow meanings, though that in itself is insufficient cause to shirk it. Many other words have arrived at their present meanings through misinterpretation (see, for instance, INTERNECINE).

A more pertinent consideration is whether we need *compound* in its looser sense. The answer must be no. In the example above, the writer might have used instead 'multiply', 'aggravate', 'heighten', 'worsen', 'exacerbate', 'add to', 'intensify' or any of a dozen other words.

We should also remember that *compound* is already a busy word. Most dictionaries list up to nine quite distinct meanings for it as a verb, seven as a noun and nine as an adjective. In some of these, the word's meanings are narrow. In legal parlance, for instance, *compound* has the very specific meaning of to forgo prosecution in return for payment or some other consideration (it is from this that we get the widely misunderstood phrase 'to compound a felony', which has nothing to do with aggravation). To use *compound* in the sense of worsen in such a context is bound to be misleading.

Most dictionaries now recognize the newer meaning, so it would

38

be imprudent to call the usage incorrect. But it is a usage we don't need and one that is better avoided.

comprise. 'Beneath Sequoia is the Bechtel Group, a holding company comprised of three main operating arms ...' (*The New York Times*). If you remember nothing else from this book, remember at least that 'comprised of' is always wrong. Comprise means to contain. The whole comprises the parts and not vice versa. In this example, the writer should have said 'a holding company comprising three main operating arms' or 'composed of three main operating arms'.

conceived. 'Last week, 25 years after it was first conceived ...' (*Time*). Delete 'first'. Something can be conceived only once. Similarly with 'initially conceived' and 'originally conceived'.

concept. People just cannot leave this word alone. Originally a concept was a general idea or theory derived from specific instances, and in that capacity it served us unassumingly for 400 years. Then, in the late 1960s, sociologists and politicians and advertising people discovered it. Suddenly the word was being equated with gracious living ('a new concept in urban lifestyles') or hard thinking ('conceptual framework') or diligent planning ('a media promotion concept'). Today, having squeezed the life from *concept*, they have gone looking for more pretentious variants and given us *conceptuate* and *conceptuant* and *conceptacle*. Very often the words hold no meaning at all, as in this advertisement from *The Age* cited by Kenneth Hudson: 'The personal characteristics of the appointee will include ... conceptual appreciation'. Such a phrase, as Hudson notes, is beyond comprehension. If all you mean is 'idea', use 'idea'.

concrete. See CEMENT, CONCRETE.

consensus. 'The general consensus in Washington ...' (*Chicago Tribune*). A tautology. Any consensus must be general. Equally to be avoided is 'consensus of opinion'. Finally, note that consensus is spelled with a middle 's', like 'consent'. It has nothing to do with 'census'.

consummate. As an adjective, the word is much too freely used. A consummate actor is not merely someone who is very good at acting, he is someone who is so good as to be unrivalled or nearly un-rivalled. It should be reserved to describe only the very best.

contact as a verb (as in 'I'll contact you next month') is still frowned on by most authorities, including almost two-thirds of the *American Heritage* usage panel. The authorities are right to object when a more specific word would do. But, as Bernstein asserts, there are times when the vagueness of *contact* can be useful. If I say, 'I'll contact you tomorrow', it leaves open the question of whether I will do it by phone or letter or telex, in person or through a third party. If English usage were in the hands of rational people like scientists and mathematicians, this expanded meaning would no doubt be considered a useful way of expressing a complex set of options simply. But English usage is not and the usage must be considered at best colloquial.

contagious, infectious. Diseases spread by contact are contagious. Those spread by air or water are infectious. Used figuratively ('contagious laughter', 'infectious enthusiasm'), either is all right.

contemptible, contemptuous. *Contemptible* means deserving contempt; *contemptuous* means to bestow it. *Contemptuous* gained currency in the sixteenth century – but too late to catch Shakespeare. In *Much Ado About Nothing*, he has Pedro declare that Benedick 'hath a con-temptible spirit'. He meant, at least by modern standards, contemptu-ous.

contemptuous. See CONTEMPTIBLE, CONTEMPTUOUS.

continual, continuous. *Continual* refers to things that happen repeatedly but not constantly. *Continuous* indicates an unbroken sequence. 'It rained continuously for three days' means it never stopped raining. 'It rained continually for three days' means there were some interrup-tions.

continuous. See CONTINUAL, CONTINUOUS.

contrary, converse, opposite, reverse. All four are sometimes confused, which is perhaps understandable since their distinctions tend to blur. Briefly, a *contrary* is a statement that contradicts a proposition. A *converse* reverses the elements of a proposition. An *opposite* is something that is diametrically opposed to a proposition. And the *reverse* can be any of these.

Take the simple statement 'I love you'. Its opposite is 'I hate you'. Its converse is 'You love me'. And its contrary would be anything that contradicted it: 'I do not love you', 'I have no feelings at all for you', 'I like you moderately'. The reverse could embrace all of these meanings.

conurbation. 'It was around dusk when the Union Jack replaced the Argentinian flag above the tiny conurbation of Goose Green' (*The Times*). A conurbation is a megalopolis where two or more sizable communities have sprawled together, such as Pasadena–Los Angeles–Long Beach in California or Bradford–Leeds in England. It can never be tiny.

converse. See CONTRARY, CONVERSE, OPPOSITE, REVERSE.

convince, persuade. There is a distinction worth preserving between these two words. Briefly, you convince someone that he should believe, but persuade him to act. It is possible to persuade a person to do something without convincing him of the necessity of doing it. *Persuade* may be followed by an infinitive, but *convince* may not. Thus the following sentence is wrong: 'The Soviet Union evidently is not able to convince Cairo to accept a rapid cease-fire' (*The New York Times*). Make it either 'persuade Cairo to accept' or 'convince Cairo that it should accept'.

country, nation. It is perhaps a little fussy to insist too strenuously on the distinction, but, strictly, *country* refers to the geographical characteristics of a place and *nation* to the political and social ones. Thus the United States is one of the richest nations, but largest countries.

crass means stupid and grossly ignorant to the point of insensitivity and not merely coarse or tasteless. A thing may be distasteful without necessarily being crass.

creole, pidgin. A pidgin – the word is thought to come from the Chinese pronunciation of the English 'business' – is a simplified and rudimentary language that springs up when two or more cultures come in contact. If that contact is prolonged and generations are born for whom the pidgin is their first tongue, the language usually will evolve into a more formalized creole (from the French for 'indigenous'). Most languages that are commonly referred to as pidgins are in fact creoles.

crescendo. 'David English, whose career seemed to be reaching a crescendo this month when he took over editorship of the stumbling Mail on Sunday ...' (*Sunday Times*). *Crescendo* is frequently misused, though only rarely trampled on in quite the way it has been here. It does not mean reaching a milestone, as was apparently intended in the quotation, or signify a loud or explosive noise, as it is more commonly misused. Properly, it should be used to describe a gradual increase in volume or intensity.

criteria, criterion. One criterion, two criteria. See also DATA.

criterion. See CRITERIA, CRITERION.

culminate. 'The company's financial troubles culminated in the resignation of the chairman last June' (*The Times*). *Culminate* does not mean simply the result or outcome. It indicates the arrival at a high point. A series of battles may culminate in a final victory, but financial troubles do not culminate in a chairman's resignation.

current, currently. It is a rare reader of newspapers these days who can venture all the way through an article without bumping into one or other of these – and very often a whole community of them. On one page of *The Times* in 1982 there were fourteen *current*s in residence, most of them conspicuously idle. At about the same time, *The New York Times* was providing sanctuary for six *current*s and a *currently* on one of its inside pages.

When there is a need to contrast the present with the past, *current* has its place. But all too often its inclusion is lazy and gratuitous, as in this example from one of the worst of the abusers, *Time* magazine: 'The Government currently owns 740 million acres, or 32·7% of the land in the U.S.'. Nothing would be lost if *currently* were deleted. Or take this sentence from the same article: 'Property in the area is currently fetching $125 to $225 per acre'. Why not save twelve characters and make it: 'Property in the area fetches [or, if necessary, 'now fetches'] $125 to $225 per acre'?

currently. See CURRENT, CURRENTLY.

cut back. 'Losses in the metal stamping division have forced the group to cut back production' (*Daily Telegraph*). It would be more succinct to say 'have forced the group to cut production'. *Cutback* is often similarly pleonastic. 'Spending cutbacks' can almost always be shortened to 'spending cuts'. See PHRASAL VERBS.

◦ D ◦

dais. See LECTERN, PODIUM, DAIS, ROSTRUM.

dangling modifiers are one of the more complicated and disagreeable aspects of English usage, but at least they provide some compensation by being frequently amusing. Every authority has a stock of illustrative howlers. Fowler, for instance, gives us 'Handing me my whisky, his face broke into an awkward smile' (that rare thing, a face that can pass whisky), while Bernstein offers 'Although sixty-one years old when he wore the original suit, his waist was only thirty-five' and 'When dipped in melted butter or Hollandaise sauce, one truly deserves the food of the gods'.

Most often, dangling modifiers are caused by unattached present participles. But they can also involve past and perfect participles, appositive phrases, clauses, infinitives or simple adjectives.* Occasionally the element to be modified is missing altogether: 'As reconstructed by the police, Pfeffer at first denied any knowledge of the Byrd murder' (cited by Bernstein). It was not, of course, Pfeffer that was reconstructed by the police, but the facts or story or some other noun that is only implied.

Regardless of the part of speech at fault, there is in every dangling modifier a failure by the writer to say what he means because of a simple mispositioning of words. Consider this example: 'Slim, of medium height and with sharp features, Mr Smith's technical skills are combined with strong leadership qualities' (*The New York Times*). As written, the sentence is telling us that Mr Smith's technical skills are slim and of medium height. It needs to be recast as 'Slim, of medium height and with sharp features, he combines technical skills with strong leadership qualities' or words to that effect (but see NON SEQUITUR).

Or consider this sentence from *Time* magazine: 'In addition to being cheap and easily obtainable, Crotti claims that the bags have several advantages over other methods'. We can reasonably assume that it

---

* Strictly speaking, only adverbs modify; nouns and adjectives qualify. But because the usage problems are essentially the same for all the parts of speech, I have collected them under the heading by which they are most commonly, if not quite accurately, known.

is not Crotti that is cheap and easily obtainable, but the bags. Again, recasting is needed: 'In addition to being cheap and easily obtainable, the bags have several advantages over other methods, Crotti claims' (but see CLAIM).

William and Mary Morris offer a simple remedy to the problem of dangling modifiers – namely that after having written the modifying phrase or clause, you should make sure that the next word is the one to which the modifier pertains. That is sound enough advice, but, like so much else in English usage, it will take you only so far.

There are, to begin with, a number of participial phrases that have the effect of prepositions or conjunctions, and you may dangle them as you will without breaking any rules. They include *generally speaking*, *concerning*, *regarding*, *judging*, *owing to*, *failing*, *speaking of* and many others. There are also certain stock phrases and idiomatic constructions that flout the rule but are still acceptable, such as 'putting two and two together' and 'getting down to brass tacks'.

It is this multiplicity of exceptions that makes the subject so difficult. If I write, 'As the author of this book, let me say this', am I perpetrating a dangling modifier or simply resorting to idiom? It depends very much on which authority you consult.

It is perhaps also worth noting that opprobrium for the dangling modifier is not universal. The Evanses, after asserting that the problem has been common among good writers at least since Chaucer, call the rule banning its use 'pernicious' and add that 'no one who takes it as inviolable can write good English'. They maintain that the problem with sentences such as 'Handing me my whisky, his face broke into a broad grin' is not that the participle is dangling, but rather that it isn't. It sounds absurd only because 'his face' is so firmly attached to the participial phrase. But when a note of absurdity is not sounded, they say, the sentence should be allowed to pass.

They are certainly right to caution against becoming obsessed with dangling modifiers, but there is, I think, a clearer need than they allow to watch out for them. Certainly if you find yourself writing a phrase that permits the merest hint of incongruity, it is time to recast your sentence.

data. Many careful users of English continue to insist that we treat data as a plural. Thus 'Data from the 1980 census is unavailable' (*Los Angeles Times*) should read 'are unavailable'. To be sure, the purists have etymology on their side: in Latin, data is unquestionably a plural. The problem is that in English usage etymology doesn't always count for much. If it did, we would also have to write, 'My stamina aren't what they used to be', or, 'I've just paid two insurance premia'.

The fact is, of course, that for centuries we have been adapting Latin words to fit the needs and patterns of English. Museums, agendas, stadiums, premiums and many others are freely – and unexceptionably – inflected in ways that would have confounded Cicero. It may be time that we did the same for data.

There is a tendency these days to treat all Latin plurals as singulars, most notably criteria, media, phenomena, strata and data. With the first four of these the impulse is better resisted, partly as a concession to convention, but also because there is a clear and useful distinction to be made between the singular and plural forms. In stratified rock, for instance, each stratum is clearly delineated. In any list of criteria, each criterion is distinguishable from every other. Media suggests – or ought to suggest – one medium and another medium and another. In each case the elements that make up the whole are invariably distinct and separable.

But with data such distinctions are much less evident. This may be because, as Prof. Randolph Quirk suggests, there is a natural tendency to regard data as an aggregate – that is, as a word in which we perceive the whole more immediately than the parts. Just as we see a bowlful of sugar as a distinct entity rather than as a collection of granules (which is why we don't say, 'Sugar are sweet'), so we tend to see data as a complete whole rather than as one datum and another datum and another. In this regard it is roughly synonymous with 'news' (which, incidentally, was treated by some nineteenth-century purists as a plural) and 'information'.

There is probably no other usage in English that more neatly divides the authorities. About half accept the word as a singular, though some only grudgingly. And about half are opposed to it, a few of them implacably. Fowler merely notes the existence of the singular usage but passes no judgement on it.

The shift is clearly in the direction of treating data as a singular, and a generation from now anyone who says, 'The data are here', may seem as fussy as the nineteenth-century newspaper editor* who sent one of his reporters a telegram asking, 'Are there any news?'

* The inquiry has been variously attributed to John Thaddeus Delane of *The Times* and to Horace Greeley of the *New York Tribune*.

(to which reportedly came the reply: 'No, not a single damn new'). But for now you are as likely to be castigated for your ignorance as you are to be applauded for your far-sighted liberalism. I vote for the singular, but until a consensus emerges, you are probably better advised to keep data plural, at least in formal writing.

decimate. Literally, the word means to reduce by a tenth (from the ancient practice of punishing the mutinous or cowardly by killing every tenth man). By extension it may be used to describe the inflicting of heavy damage, but it should never be used to denote annihilation, as in this memorably excruciating sentence cited by Fowler: 'Dick, hotly pursued by the scalp-hunter, turned in his saddle, fired, and literally decimated his opponent'. Equally to be avoided are contexts in which the word's use is clearly inconsistent with its literal meaning, as in 'Frost decimated up to 80 per cent of the crops'.

deduce, deduct. Occasionally confused. *Deduce* means to make a conclusion on the basis of evidence. *Deduct* means to subtract.

deduct. See DEDUCE, DEDUCT.

defective, deficient. To distinguish these two, it is necessary only to think of their noun forms: *defect* and *deficit*. When something is not working properly, it is defective; when it is missing a necessary part, it is deficient. *Defective* applies to quality, *deficient* to quantity.

deficient. See DEFECTIVE, DEFICIENT.

definite, definitive. *Definite* means precise and unmistakable. *Definitive* means final and conclusive. A definite offer is a clear one; a definitive offer is one that permits of no haggling.

definitive. See DEFINITE, DEFINITIVE.

demean. Some authorities, among them Fowler, object to the word in the sense of to debase or degrade, pointing out that its original meaning had to do with conduct and behaviour (by way of which it is related to *demeanour*). But, as Bernstein notes, the looser usage has been with us since 1601, which suggests that it may be just a bit late to try to hold the line now.

47

demise. 'The group has also been badly hit by the demise of the British shipbuilding industry' (*The Times*). *Demise* does not mean decline, as was intended here and occasionally elsewhere. Originally, *demise* described the transfer of an estate or title, usually as a consequence of a sovereign's death. By extension it came to be a synonym for death itself, but as such it is generally an unnecessary euphemism.

deplete, reduce. Though their meanings are roughly the same, *deplete* has the additional connotation of injurious reduction. As the Evanses note, a garrison may be reduced by administrative order, but depleted by sickness.

deplore. You may deplore a thing, but not a person. Thus 'We may deplore him for his conceit' (cited by Partridge) should be 'We may deplore his conceit' or 'We may condemn him for his conceit'.

deprecate. '. . . but he deprecated the significance of his achievement' (*Los Angeles Times*). *Deprecate* does not mean to play down or disparage or show modesty, as is often intended. It means to disapprove of strongly or to protest against.

de rigueur. Often misspelled, as here: 'A few decades ago when dinner jackets were de rigeur . . .' (*Daily Telegraph*).

derisive, derisory. Something that is derisive conveys ridicule or contempt. Something that is derisory invites it. A derisory offer is likely to provoke a derisive response.

derisory. See DERISIVE, DERISORY.

derogate. See ABDICATE, ABROGATE, ABJURE, ADJURE, ARROGATE, DEROGATE.

despite, in spite of. There is no distinction between the two. A common construction is seen here: 'But despite the fall in sterling, Downing Street officials were at pains to play down any suggestion of crisis' (*Daily Telegraph*). Because *despite* and *in spite of* indicate a change in emphasis, a shifting of gears, by the writer, 'but' is generally superfluous with either. It is enough to say: 'Despite the fall in sterling, Downing Street officials . . .'.

destroy is an incomparable – almost. If a house is consumed by fire, it is enough to say that it was destroyed, not that it was 'totally destroyed' or 'completely destroyed'. But what if only part of it burns down? Is it wrong to say that it was partly destroyed? The answer, contradictory though it may be, must be no. There is no other way of putting it without resorting to more circuitous descriptions. That is perhaps absurd and inconsistent, but ever thus was English.

diagnosis, prognosis. To make a diagnosis is to identify and define a problem, usually a disease. A prognosis is a projection of the course and likely outcome of a problem. *Diagnosis* applies only to conditions, not to people. Thus 'Asbestos victims were not diagnosed in large numbers until the 1960s' (*Time*) is not quite right. It was the victims' conditions that were not diagnosed, not the victims themselves.

dialect, patois. There is no difference in meaning between the two. Both describe the form of language prevailing in a region, though patois obviously is better reserved for contexts involving French or its variants. 'He spoke in the patois of Yorkshire' is at best jocular. The plural of patois, incidentally, is also patois.

differ, diverge. 'There now seems some hope that these divergent views can be reconciled' (*Daily Telegraph*). Linguistically, that is unlikely. When two things diverge, they move further apart (just as when they converge they come together). It is not a word that should be applied freely to any difference of opinion, but only to those in which a rift is widening.

different. Often used unnecessarily. 'The phenomenally successful Rubik Cube, which has 43,252,003,274,489,856,000 different permutations but only one solution . . .' (*Sunday Times*); 'He plays milkmaid to more than 50 different species of poisonous snake' (*Observer*); '[He] published at least five different books on grammar' (Simon, *Paradigms Lost*). Frequently, as in each of these examples, it can be excised without loss.

different from, to, than. There is a continuing belief among some writers and editors that *different* may be followed only by *from*. At least since 1906, when the Fowler brothers raised the issue in *The King's English*, many authorities have been pointing out that there is no real basis for this belief, but still it persists.

Different from is, to be sure, the usual form in most sentences and the only acceptable form in some, as when it precedes a noun or pronoun ('My car is different from his', 'Men are different from women'). But when different introduces a clause, there can be no valid objection to following it with a *to* (though this usage is chiefly British) or *than*, as in this sentence by John Maynard Keynes: 'How different things appear in Washington than in London'. You may, if you wish, change it to 'How different things appear in Washington from how they appear in London', but all it gives you is more words, not better grammar.

dilemma. 'Indeed this was the dilemma facing the Bank of England. How could it coax people to help Laker?' (*Sunday Times*). The use of *dilemma* to signify any difficulty or predicament, as here, weakens the word. Strictly speaking, *dilemma* applies only when someone is faced with two clear courses of action, both of them unsatisfactory. Fowler accepts its extension to contexts in which there are more than two alternatives, but the number of alternatives should be definite and the consequences of each should be unappealing.

disassemble, dissemble. 'It would almost have been cheaper to dissemble the factory and move it to Wales' (*Sunday Times*). No it wouldn't. Unlike 'dissociate' and 'disassociate', which mean the same thing, *dissemble* and *disassemble* have quite separate meanings. *Dissemble* means to conceal. If someone close to you dies, you may dissemble your grief with a smile. The word wanted in the example above was *disassemble*, which means to take apart.

disassociate, dissociate. The first is not incorrect, but the second has the virtue of brevity.

discomfit, discomfort. 'In this she is greatly assisted by her husband ... who enjoys spreading discomfiture in a good cause as much as she does' (*Observer*). The writer here, like many before him, apparently meant *discomfort*, which has nothing in common with *discomfiture* apart from a superficial resemblance. *Discomfit* means to overwhelm, rout, defeat utterly.

discomfort. See DISCOMFIT, DISCOMFORT.

discreet, discrete. The first means circumspect, careful, showing good judgement ('a discreet inquiry'). The second means unattached or un-related ('discrete particles').

discrete. See DISCREET, DISCRETE.

disinterested, uninterested. 'Gerulaitis, after appearing almost dis-interested in the first set, took a 5–1 lead in the second' (*The New York Times*). A participant in a tennis match might appear un-interested, but he could never be disinterested, which means neutral and impartial. A disinterested person is one who has no stake in the outcome of an event; an uninterested person is one who doesn't care.

disorientated. *Disoriented* is shorter and usually preferable.

disposal, disposition. If you are talking about getting rid of, use *disposal* ('the disposal of nuclear wastes'). If you mean arranging, use *disposition* ('the disposition of troops on the battlefield').

disposition. See DISPOSAL, DISPOSITION.

dissemble. See DISASSEMBLE, DISSEMBLE.

dissociate. See DISASSOCIATE, DISSOCIATE.

distrait, distraught. The first means abstracted in thought, absent-minded. The second means deeply agitated.

distraught. See DISTRAIT, DISTRAUGHT.

disturb, perturb. The first is better applied to physical agitation, the second to mental agitation.

diverge. See DIFFER, DIVERGE.

double negatives. Most people know that you shouldn't say, 'I haven't had no dinner', but some writers, probably more out of haste than ignorance, sometimes perpetrate sentences that are scarcely less jarring, as here: 'The rest are left to wander the flat lowlands of West Bengal without hardly a trace of food or shelter' (*The New York*

Times). Since 'hardly', like 'scarcely', has the grammatical effect of a negative, it requires no further negation. Make it 'with hardly'.

Some grammarians condemn all double negatives, but there is one kind – in which a negative in the main clause is paralleled in a sub-ordinate construction – that we might view more tolerantly. Evans cites this sentence from Jane Austen: 'There was none too poor or remote not to feel an interest'. And Shakespeare wrote: 'Nor what he said, though it lacked form a little, was not like madness'. But such constructions must be considered exceptional. More often the intrusion of a second negative is merely a sign of fuzzy writing. At best it will force the reader to pause and perform some verbal arithmetic, adding negative to negative, as here: 'The plan is now thought unlikely not to go ahead' (*The Times*). At worst it may leave the reader darkly baffled, as here: 'Moreover ... our sense of linguistic tact will not urge us not to use words that may offend or irritate' (Quirk, *The Use of English*).

doubt if, that, whether. Idiom demands some selectivity in the choice of conjunction to introduce a clause after *doubt* and *doubtful*. The rule is simple: *doubt that* should be reserved for negative contexts ('There is no doubt that ...'; 'It was never doubtful that ...') and interrogative ones ('Do you doubt that ...?' 'Was it ever doubtful that ...?'). *Whether* or *if* should be used in all others ('I doubt if he will come'; 'It is doubtful whether the rain will stop').

doubtless, undoubtedly, indubitably. 'Tonight he faces what is doubt-lessly the toughest and loneliest choice of his 13-year stewardship of the Palestine Liberation Organization' (*Washington Post*). Since *doubtless* can be an adverb as well as an adjective, there is no need to add -*ly* to it. *Undoubtedly*, however, would have been a better choice still because, as the Evanses note, it has a less concessive air. *Doubtless* usually suggests a tone of reluctance or resignation: 'You are doubtless right'. *Undoubtedly* carries more conviction: 'You are undoubtedly right'. *Indubitably* is a pretentious synonym for either.

due to. Most authorities continue to accept that *due* is an adjective only and must always modify a noun. Thus, 'He was absent due to illness' would be wrong. We could correct it either by saying, 'He was absent because of [or owing to] illness', or by recasting the sentence in such a way as to give *due* a noun to modify, e.g., 'His absence was due to illness'.

The rule is mystifyingly inconsistent – no one has ever really explained why 'owing to' used prepositionally is correct, while *due to* used prepositionally is not – but it should perhaps still be observed, at least in formal writing, if only to avoid a charge of ignorance.

◉ E ◉

each is not always an easy word – even, it seems, for some authorities. Here are William and Mary Morris writing in *The Harper Dictionary of Contemporary Usage*: 'Each of the variants indicated in boldface type count as an entry'. As the Morrises no doubt knew but failed to note, when *each* is the subject of a sentence the verb should be singular – in this case 'counts'.

A plural verb is correct only when the sentence has another subject and *each* is a mere adjunct. Thus this sentence is also wrong: 'The Wimbledon and United States Open men's tournaments each has [make it 'have'] a first round of 128 players . . .' (*The New York Times*).

Deciding whether to use a singular or plural verb isn't so difficult. When *each* precedes the noun or pronoun to which it refers, the verb should be singular: 'Each of us was . . .'. When it follows the noun or pronoun, the verb should be plural: 'They each were . . .'.

Each not only influences the number of the verb, it also influences the number of later nouns and pronouns. Simply put, if *each* precedes the verb, subsequent nouns and pronouns should be plural; if each follows the verb, the nouns and pronouns should be singular. Thus it should be: 'They each are subject to sentences of five years', but, 'They are each subject to a sentence of five years' (Bernstein).

each and every is at best a trite way of providing emphasis, at worst redundant and often both, as here: 'Each and every one of the 12 songs on Marshall Crenshaw's debut album is breezy and refreshing' (*Washington Post*). Equally to be avoided is *each individual*, as in, 'Players do not have to face the perils of qualifying for each individual tournament' (*The New York Times*). In both cases *each* alone would have been sufficient.

each other, one another. A few arbiters of usage (Simon, for instance) continue to insist on *each other* for two things and *one another* for more than two. There is no harm in observing such a distinction, but also little to be gained from it, and, as Fowler notes, the practice has no basis in historical usage.

economic, economical. If what you mean is cheap, thrifty, not expensive, use *economical*. For every other meaning use *economic*. An economic rent is one that is not too cheap for the landlord. An economical rent is one that is not too expensive for the tenant.

economical. See ECONOMIC, ECONOMICAL.

effect. See AFFECT, EFFECT.

effete. 'Nor is it a concern only to the highly educated, or the effete Northeast, or to city folk' (Edwin Newman, *A Civil Tongue*). *Effete* does not mean affectedly intellectual or sophisticated, as was apparently intended here, or effeminate and weak, as it is sometimes used. It means exhausted and barren. An effete poet is not necessarily either intellectual or foppish, but rather someone whose creative impulses are spent.

e.g., i.e. The first is an abbreviation of *exempli gratia* and means 'for example', as in 'Some words are homonyms, e.g., blue and blew'. The second is the abbreviation for *id est* and means 'that is' or 'that is to say', as in 'He is pusillanimous, i.e., lacking in courage'.

egoism, egotism. The first pertains to the philosophical notion that a person can prove nothing beyond the existence of his own mind. It is the opposite of altruism and is better left to contexts involving metaphysics and ethics. If all you wish to suggest is inflated vanity or preoccupation with the self, use *egotism*.

egotism. See EGOISM, EGOTISM.

either. 'But in every case the facts either proved too elusive or the explanations too arcane to be satisfactory' (Julian and Zelda Boyd, *The State of the Language*). *Either* should be placed before 'the facts' or deleted; for a discussion, see BOTH ... AND. For a discussion of errors of number involving *either*, see NEITHER.

eke. 'After a series of fits and starts yesterday the stock market eked out a gain' (cited by Bernstein). *Eke* means to add to or supplement in a meagre way. It does not mean to squeeze out, as was intended in the example above. You eke out an original supply – either by adding to it or by consuming it frugally – but you do not eke out a result.

elemental, elementary. *Elemental* refers to things that are basic or primary: 'Physiology is an elemental part of a medical student's studies'. *Elementary* means simple or introductory: 'This phrase book provides an elementary guide to Spanish'.

elementary. See ELEMENTAL, ELEMENTARY.

elicit, extract, extort. These three are broadly synonymous, but are distinguished by the degree of force that they imply. *Elicit*, the mildest of the three, means to draw or coax out, and sometimes suggests craftiness: you can elicit information without the informant being aware that he has divulged it. It shouldn't be confused with *illicit* ('unlawful'). *Extract* suggests a stronger and more persistent effort, possibly involving threats or importuning. *Extort* is stronger still and suggests clear threats of violence or physical harm.

empathy, sympathy, compassion, pity, commiseration. *Empathy* denotes a very close understanding of the feelings or problems of another. It is often employed as no more than a pretentious variant of *sympathy* and on the whole is better left to the psychologists. *Compassion* suggests a deeply felt understanding of the problems of others. *Pity* is rather more condescending; it suggests understanding of a problem intellectually but not emotionally. *Commiseration* falls roughly between compassion and pity, suggesting less emotion than compassion but more emotion than *pity*. *Sympathy* can cover all of these.

end result. Inescapably redundant.

enormity. 'The impression of enormity produced by the building ...' (cited by Fowler). *Enormity* does not, as is often thought, indicate size, but refers to something that is wicked, monstrous and outrageous ('The enormity of Hitler's crimes will never be forgotten'). In the example above, the writer should have said 'enormousness' – or, better still, found a less ungainly synonym.

enquiry. See QUERY, INQUIRY, ENQUIRY.

enthuse. '[They] are unlikely to enthuse over the news that the casino licensing appeal is due to start a week tomorrow' (*Observer*). *Enthuse* is a back formation – that is, a word coined from an existing word on the erroneous assumption that the new word forms the root of the old word. At some time in the past, someone seeing the noun *enthusiasm* assumed, wrongly, that it was formed from a verb *enthuse*. There is nothing inherently wrong with back formations – 'scavenge', 'laze', 'grovel' and even 'pea' (back formed from 'pease') were all usefully added to the language as a consequence of ignorance. But many other back formations – among them 'commentate', 'sculpt' and 'emote' – have failed to win complete acceptance because they are thought to be unnecessary or ungainly or to have too strong an air of novelty. As such they are better avoided.

envisage, envision. Both words suggest the calling up of a mental image. *Envision* is slightly the loftier of the two. You might envision a better life for yourself, but if all you are thinking about is how the dining room will look when the walls have been repainted, *envisage* is the better word. If there is no mental image involved, neither word is correct. A rough rule is that if you find yourself following either word with 'that' you are using it incorrectly, as here: 'He envisaged that there would be no access to the school from the main road' (cited by Gowers).

envision. See ENVISAGE, ENVISION.

epidemic. Strictly speaking, only people can suffer an epidemic (the word means 'in or among people'). An outbreak of disease among animals is epizootic. It may also be worth noting that *epidemic* refers only to outbreaks. When a disease or other problem is of long standing, it is endemic.

epitome is sometimes used as if it meant ultimate or unparalleled. In fact, it means typifying. 'The epitome of bad writing' is not writing that is quintessentially bad; it is writing that is representative of bad writing.

equable, equitable. Most dictionaries define *equable* as meaning steady and unvarying, but it should also convey the sense of being remote from extremes. A consistently hot climate is not equable, no matter how unvarying the temperature. Similarly, someone whose outlook is invariably sunny cannot be described as having an equable temperament. *Equitable*, with which *equable* is occasionally confused, means fair and impartial. An equitable settlement is a just one.

equally as is illiterate. 'This is equally as good' should be 'This is equally good' or 'This is as good'.

equitable. See EQUABLE, EQUITABLE.

equivocal. See AMBIGUOUS, EQUIVOCAL.

escalate is a useful word to describe an upward movement that is happening in stages, as in 'escalating taxes' or 'escalating warfare'. But many writers use it needlessly when they mean no more than increasing or accelerating. One writer, apparently uncertain just what he meant, referred to 'the increasing and rapidly escalating militarization of outer space' (*Time*). Since an escalating militarization must also be increasing, the phrase is redundant.

estimated at about. 'The crowd was estimated at about 50,000' (*Los Angeles Times*). Because *estimated* contains the idea of an approximation, *about* is superfluous. Delete it.

et cetera (etc.). 'Thousands competed, thousands watched and thousands also served – volunteers all of them – who only pinned numbers, massaged muscles, supplied water, charted positions, screamed encouragement, etc'. (*Los Angeles Times*). In lexicography and other more technical types of writing, *etc.* has its place. But in newspapers and magazines its use tends to suggest that the writer either didn't know what else he meant or, as in the foregoing example, was too lazy to tell us. Almost always it is better avoided.

evangelical, evangelistic. *Evangelical* is better reserved for contexts strictly pertaining to the Christian gospel. If you need a word to describe militant zeal, use *evangelistic*, e.g., 'The evangelistic fervour of the Campaign for Nuclear Disarmament'.

evangelistic. See EVANGELICAL, EVANGELISTIC.

eventuate. 'Competition for economic interest, power and social esteem can eventuate in community formation only if ...' (*British Journal of Sociology*, cited by Hudson). A pompous synonym for 'result'.

ever. 'On Wall Street, a late rally provided shares with their largest ever one-day rise' (*The Times*). Some people object to *ever* in the sense used here on the grounds that it covers the future as well as the past, and we cannot possibly know what Wall Street shares, or anything else, will be doing tomorrow.

Such an interpretation is a trifle short-sighted for two reasons. First, it fails to acknowledge that the usage has been established in Britain for almost sixty years and in America for nearer eighty; even if we accepted the purists' reasoning, we could defend the usage on grounds of idiom. But there is a more important consideration: to suggest that *ever* must always include the future is – or ought to be – clearly absurd. As an adverb, *ever* can indicate a span of time only to the extent that the verb will allow it – and a simple past-tense verb cannot push *ever*'s sense beyond the present. If I say, 'Have you ever been to Paris?' obviously I do not mean, 'Have you ever been to Paris or will you be going there sometime before you die?'

There may be a case for using *ever* sparingly. But to ban it arbitrarily is fussy and unidiomatic and can easily lead to ambiguity.

everybody. See NUMBER (4).

everyone. See NUMBER (4).

exception proves the rule, the. As a moment's thought should tell us, it isn't possible for an exception to confirm a rule – but then that isn't the sense in which the expression was originally intended. *Prove* here is a 'fossil' – that is, a word or phrase that is now meaningless except within the confines of certain common sayings ('hem and haw', 'rank and file' and 'to and fro' are other fossils). Originally, *prove* meant test (it comes from the Latin *probo*, 'I test'), so the sentence above meant – and really still ought to mean – that the exception tests the rule. It is bad enough to perpetuate a cliché without perpetuating it inaccurately. The original meaning of *prove* is preserved a bit more clearly in two other expressions: 'proving ground' and 'the proof of the pudding is in the eating'.

exigent, exiguous. The first means urgent and pressing or exacting and demanding; the second means scanty and slender. But both have a number of synonyms. If, like me, you weren't sure of the distinction until a moment ago, think how your readers will feel when you put them in the same position.

exiguous. See EXIGENT, EXIGUOUS.

exorbitant. There is a perplexing impulse among many writers on both sides of the Atlantic to put an 'h' into the word, as here: 'This is on the argument that they are troubled by exhorbitant interest charges' (*The Times*). Inhexcusable.

expatriate. Occasionally misspelled, as here: 'Kirov and other Russian expatriots . . .' (*Daily Mail*). Not to be confused with compatriot.

expectorate, spit. The distinction between these two is not, it must be conceded, often a matter of great moment, but still it is worth noting that there is a distinction. To spit means to expel saliva; to expectorate is to dredge up and expel phlegm from the lungs. *Expectorate* therefore is not just an unnecessary euphemism for *spit*, it is usually an incorrect one.

extort. See ELICIT, EXTRACT, EXTORT.

extract. See ELICIT, EXTRACT, EXTORT.

⊡ **F** ⊡

fable, parable, allegory, myth. Fables and parables are both stories intended to have instructional value. They differ in that parables are always concerned with religious or ethical themes, while fables are usually concerned with more practical considerations (and usually have animals as the characters). An allegory is an extended metaphor – that is, a narrative in which the principal characters represent things that are not explicitly stated. Orwell's *Animal Farm* is an allegory. Myths originally were stories designed to explain some belief or phenomenon, usually through the exploits of superhuman beings. Today, of course, the word can signify any popular misconception or invented story.

facade. 'Above the pilasters, on the front facade, is a five-story-high keystone ...' (*Time*). Although most dictionaries allow that *facade* can apply to any side of a building, it normally indicates the front (or face), and thus gives 'front facade' a ring of redundancy.

facile is usually defined as easy, smooth, without much effort. But the word should contain at least a suggestion of derision. Facile writing isn't just easily read or written, it is also lacking in substance or import. Unless a pejorative meaning is intended, the use of *facile* is, to quote Fowler, 'ill-judged'.

factious, factitious, fractious. *Factious* applies to factions; it is something that promotes internal bickering or disharmony. *Factitious* applies to that which is artificial or a sham; applause for a despotic ruler may be factitious. *Fractious* is that which is unruly or disorderly, as in 'a fractious crowd'.

factitious. See FACTIOUS, FACTITIOUS, FRACTIOUS.

farther, further. Insofar as the two are distinguished, *farther* usually appears in contexts involving literal distance ('New York is farther from Sydney than from London') and *further* in contexts involving figurative distance ('I can take this plan no further') or the idea of moreover or additionally ('a further point'). But there is, as *The OED* notes, 'a large intermediate class of instances in which the choice between the two forms is arbitrary'.

faze, meaning to disturb or worry, is sometimes confused with 'phase', as here: 'Christmas doesn't phase me' (*New York Review of Books* headline).

feasible. 'We ourselves believe that this is the most feasible explanation of the tradition' (cited by Fowler). Feasible does not mean probable or plausible. It means capable of being done. Its principal value, as Fowler notes, is as a substitute for 'possible' where the use of 'possible' might lead to ambiguity.

feet, foot. 'First, take a 75-feet hole ...' (*Daily Mail*); 'Twelve Para-guyan Anaconda snakes, each two foot long ...' (*The Times*). It shouldn't need pointing out that both of those sentences border on the illiterate.

We do not have 75-feet holes for the same reason that we do not have teethbrushes or necksties or horses races. In English, when one noun qualifies another, the first is almost always singular. There are exceptions – 'systems analyst', 'singles bar' – but usually they appear only when the normal form would produce ambiguity. When a noun is not being made to function as an adjective (as in the *Times* quotation above), the plural is the usual form. Thus a wall that is six feet high is a six-foot-high wall (for a discussion of the punctuation distinction, see HYPHEN in the appendix).

fever, temperature. You often hear sentences like, 'John had a tempera-ture yesterday', when in fact John has a temperature every day. What he had yesterday was a fever. The distinction is not widely observed, even by some medical authorities. Bernstein cites the instance of a Massachusetts hospital that issued an official bulletin saying: 'Everett has no temperature'. Fowler excuses the usage as a 'sturdy inde-fensible', but, even so, it is better avoided in careful writing.

fewer, less. 'In the first four months of the year Rome's tourists were 700,000 less than in the corresponding period last year' (*Guardian*). Probably no other pair of words causes more problems, and with less justification, than *less* and *fewer*. The generally cited rule is that *less* applies to quantity and *fewer* to number. A rougher but more helpful guide is to use *less* with singular nouns (less money, less sugar) and *fewer* with plural nouns (fewer houses, fewer doctors). Thus the quotation above could be made either 'Rome's tourists [plural noun] were 700,000 fewer' or 'the number [singular noun] of tourists was 700,000 less'.

A particularly common error is the construction 'no less than', as here: 'There are no less than six bidders for the group' (*The Times*). This construction is so common, in fact, that it might be regarded as now having the force of idiom. Philip Howard for one allows it when he writes in *Weasel Words*: 'The watch with hands is an analogue device in no less than three different ways'.

Another problem worth noting occurs in this sentence: 'Representatives have offered to produce the supplements on one fewer press than at present ...' (*The Times*). Idiom, according to Bernstein, doesn't allow 'one fewer press'. You must make it either 'one press fewer', which is more grammatical, or 'one less press', which is more idiomatic.

A final type of problem occurs in this sentence: '... but some people earn fewer than $750 a year' (*The Times*). The difficulty here is that $750 is being thought of as a total sum and not as 750 units of $1. Make it 'less than $750'. Similarly it would not be incorrect to write, 'He lives less than fifty miles from London' because fifty miles is being thought of as a total distance and not as fifty individual miles.

finalize. 'But Cardin is, I gather, about to finalize plans for his China breakthrough' (*The Times*). An ugly and unnecessary word. What's wrong with 'complete' or 'conclude' or 'finish'?

first, firstly. The question of whether to write *firstly ... secondly* or *first ... secondly* or *first ... second* constitutes one of the more bizarre and inane, but most hotly disputed, issues in the history of English usage. Most of the animus has focused on *firstly* (De Quincey called it 'a ridiculous and most pedantic neologism'), though what makes it so objectionable has never been entirely clear. Fowler, ever the cool head, should perhaps be allowed the final word on the matter: 'The preference for *first* over *firstly* in formal enumerations is one of the harmless pedantries in which those who like oddities because they are odd are free to indulge, provided that they abstain from censuring those who do not share the liking'.

first and foremost. Choose one.

firstly. See FIRST, FIRSTLY.

flagrant. See BLATANT, FLAGRANT.

flak. Often misspelled, as here: 'Japanese women take a lot of flack from foreigners for their alleged docility' (*Observer*). The word, for what it's worth, is a contraction of the German *Fliegerabwehrkanone* ('anti-aircraft gun'), which contains nineteen letters, not one of them a 'c'.

flammable, inflammable. It is an apparent inconsistency of English that 'incombustible' describes an object that won't burn, while *inflammable* describes an object that will. Because the meaning of *inflammable* is so often misapprehended, there is an increasing tendency to use the less ambiguous *flammable*. In other cases this might be considered a regrettable concession to ignorance. But it would be even more regrettable to insist on linguistic purity at the expense of human safety.

flank. 'A Special Report on Finland tomorrow looks at the only Western nation that has to live with the Soviet Union as its neighbour on two flanks' (*The Times*). Two points to note here: the first is that a thing can have only two flanks, so the usage above would be tautological if it weren't inaccurate; the second point is that flanks fall on either side of a body. If I am flanked by people, they are to my right and left. Finland is flanked by the Soviet Union and Sweden, and not by the Soviet Union alone, which is to the east and south.

flaunt, flout. The confusion over these two is so widespread that at least two American dictionaries have granted them legitimacy as synonyms. The misusage is illustrated in this statement by President Jimmy Carter: 'The Government of Iran must realize that it cannot flaunt, with impunity, the expressed will and law of the world community'. To flaunt means to display ostentatiously, to show off. To flout, the word the President wanted, means to treat with contempt, to smugly disregard. There is every reason for keeping these meanings distinct.

floor. See CEILING, FLOOR.

flotsam and jetsam. In the increasingly unlikely event that you have need to distinguish these two, jetsam is that part of a shipwreck that has been thrown overboard (think of *jettison*) and flotsam that which has floated off of its own accord. Wreckage found on the sea floor is – or at least once was – lagan. There was, of course, a time when the distinction was important: flotsam went to the crown and jetsam to the lord of the manor on whose land it was washed up.

flounder, founder. *Founder* means to sink, either literally (as with a ship) or figuratively (as with a project). *Flounder*, which is thought to be a portmanteau word formed from *founder* and *blunder*, means to flail helplessly. It too can be used literally (as with someone struggling in deep water) or figuratively (as with a nervous person making an extemporaneous speech).

flout. See FLAUNT, FLOUT.

following, used carelessly, all too often results in unintentional absurdities, as here: 'The plumber was arrested in Virginia on a fugitive warrant following a 39-count indictment ...' (*The New York Times*). The plumber was following the indictment that was following him? I think not. Here we have a doctor who is darting from tree to tree in pursuit of a medical inquiry, apparently while invisible: 'A family doctor has vanished from his home and surgery following an inquiry into his medical qualifications' (*Daily Mail*). What ever happened to 'after'?

foot. See FEET, FOOT.

forbid, prohibit. The words have the same meaning, but the construction of sentences often dictates which should be used. *Forbid* may be followed only by *to* ('I forbid you to go'). *Prohibit* may not be followed by *to*, but only by *from* ('He was prohibited from going') or by an object noun ('The law prohibits the construction of houses without planning consent'). 'They are forbidden from uttering any public comments' (*The New York Times*) could be corrected by making it 'They are prohibited from uttering [or forbidden to utter] any public comments'.

forced. See FORCEFUL, FORCIBLE, FORCED.

forceful, forcible, forced. *Forcible* indicates the use of brute force ('forcible entry'). *Forceful* suggests a potential for force ('forceful argument', 'forceful personality'). *Forced* can be used for *forcible* (as in 'forced entry'), but more often is reserved for actions that are involuntary ('forced march') or occurring under strain ('forced laughter', 'forced landing').

forcible. See FORCEFUL, FORCIBLE, FORCED.

forego, forgo. Commonly confused, as here: 'West Germans are proving unwilling to forego what many regard as their right to two or three foreign holidays a year' (*Financial Times*). *Forego* means to go before, to precede. To do without is to *forgo*.

forever, for ever. In American usage, *forever* is always one word. In Britain, traditionally it has been two words (Fowler insists on it), but more and more dictionaries now give *forever* as their first choice. *The OED* makes a distinction between *for ever* (meaning for all time) and *forever* (meaning continually).

for ever. See FOREVER, FOR EVER.

forgather. 'Wherever people foregather, one hears two kinds of talk ...' (John Simon, *Paradigms Lost*). Although *foregather* is not incorrect, the more usual spelling is *forgather*. A separate question is whether *forgather* adds anything that *gather* alone wouldn't say, apart from a creak of antiquity.

forgo. See FOREGO, FORGO.

former, latter. *Former* should refer only to the first of two things and *latter* only to the second of two things. Thus this extract is incorrect: 'There will be delegates from each of the EEC countries, plus Japan, Singapore, South Korea and Taiwan. Representatives from the latter ...' (*The Times*). Both words, since they require the reader to hark back to a previous reference, should be used sparingly and only when what they refer to is immediately evident. Few things are more annoying to a reader than to be made to re-cover old ground.

fortuitous. Not to be confused with fortunate, as it was here: 'If Mr Perella's merger assignment was mostly chance, it nevertheless was fortuitous' (*The New York Times*). *Fortuitous* means accidental or by chance, so the sentence above is telling us that Mr Perella's assignment was not only mostly chance, it was nevertheless entirely chance. A fortuitous occurrence may or may not be a fortunate one.

founder. See FLOUNDER, FOUNDER.

fraction. 'The gold recovered so far may represent only a fraction of the total hoard' (*Sunday Times*). A few purists continue to maintain that *fraction* in the sense of a small part is loose: $\frac{99}{100}$ is also a fraction but hardly a negligible part. The looser usage, however, has been with us for at least 300 years (Shakespeare employs it in *Troilus and Cressida*) and is unlikely to be misunderstood in most contexts. Even so, it would be more precise to say 'a small part' or 'a tiny part'. (See also PERCENTAGE, PROPORTION.)

fractious. See FACTIOUS, FACTITIOUS, FRACTIOUS.

frisson. 'A slight frisson went through the nation yesterday' (*The Times*). There is no other kind of frisson than a slight one. The word means shiver or shudder.

fruition has nothing to do with fruit. It derives from the Latin *frui* ('to enjoy') and formerly meant enjoyment. The sense in which it is most often used today – to describe the ripening or realizing of plans or the attainment of an end – is based on a misconception that took hold in the nineteenth century and reached its fruition (if you will) in this one. Today, Fowler alone rejects the word in its modern sense. No dictionary condemns it and most authorities consider it a useful addition to the language.

fulsome is one of the most frequently misused words in English. The sense that is usually accorded it – of being copious or lavish or un-stinting – is almost the opposite of the word's dictionary meaning. *Fulsome* is related to *foul* and means odious and overfull, offensively insincere. 'Fulsome praise', properly used, isn't a lavish tribute; it is unctuous and insincere toadying.

further. See FARTHER, FURTHER.

future. As an adjective, the word is often used unnecessarily: 'He refused to say what his future plans were' (*Daily Telegraph*); 'The parties are prepared to say little about how they see their future prospects' (*The Times*). In both sentences *future* adds nothing and should be deleted.

▣ G ▣

gambit is often misused in either of two ways. First, it sometimes appears as 'opening gambit', which is redundant. Second, it is often incorrectly employed to mean no more than ploy or opportunity or tactic. Properly, a gambit is an opening move that involves some strategic sacrifice or concession. All gambits are opening moves, but not all opening moves are gambits.

gendarmes. Some dictionaries (*Collins*, for example) define *gendarmes* as French policemen. In fact, gendarmes are soldiers employed in police duties, principally in the countryside. Policemen in French cities and towns are just that – policemen.

gender. 'A university grievance committee decided that she had been denied tenure because of her gender' (*The New York Times*). *Gender*, originally strictly a grammatical term, became in the nineteenth century a euphemism for the convenience of those who found 'sex' too disturbing a word to utter. As such, its use today is disdained by most authorities.

germane, relevant, material. *Germane* (often misspelled 'germaine') and *relevant* are synonymous. Both indicate a pertinence to the matter under discussion. *Material* has the additional connotation of being necessary. A material point is one without which an argument would be incomplete. A germane or relevant point will be worth noting but may not be essential to an argument.

gerunds are verbs made to function as nouns, as in 'I don't like *dancing*' and '*Cooking* is an art'. There are two problems with gerunds:
  1. Sometimes the gerund is unnecessarily set off by an article and preposition, as here: 'They said that *the* valuing *of* the paintings could take several weeks' (*Daily Telegraph*). Deleting the italicized words would make the sentence shorter and more forceful.
  2. Problems also occur when a possessive noun or pronoun (called a 'genitive') qualifies a gerund. A common type of construction is seen here: 'They objected to him coming'. Properly, it should be: 'They

69

objected to his coming'. Similarly, 'There is little hope of Smith gaining admittance to the club' should be 'There is little hope of Smith's gaining admittance . . .'.

The possessive form is, in short, the preferred form, especially with proper nouns and personal pronouns. For Fowler (who treated the matter under the heading 'fused participle') the possessive was virtually the only form. He insisted, for instance, on 'We cannot deny the possibility of anything's happening' and 'This will result in many's having to go into lodgings'. Most other authorities regard this as a Fowler idiosyncrasy and none would insist on the possessive for words that do not normally have a possessive form.

gift (as a verb). 'She talked easily of her own successes – a six-figure income, two wonderful children and the ability to gift her mother with a mink coat . . .' (*Los Angeles Times*). A useful facet of English is its ability to turn nouns into verbs – we can man a boat, pocket some money, mother a child, people the earth – but is this one really necessary? No. (See CHAIR.)

gild the lily. The passage from Shakespeare's *King John* is: 'To gild refined gold, to paint the lily . . ./Is wasteful and ridiculous excess'. Nobody has ever gilded a lily.

glean. Originally the word applied to the act of going over a field after a harvest to gather the pieces that had escaped the reaper. Enough of its original meaning lingers that it should still convey the idea of gathering thoroughly and arduously, which the following sentence clearly does not: 'We can glean an indication of his vast wealth from the fact that he owns houses in London, Switzerland and California, with new or newish Rolls-Royces gracing each' (*Observer*).

glutton. See GOURMET, GLUTTON, GOURMAND.

gourmand. See GOURMET, GLUTTON, GOURMAND.

gourmet, glutton, gourmand. A gourmet is someone who takes a great deal of interest in, and trouble over, his food. A glutton is someone who enjoys food to excess and is not notably discriminating about what he shoves in his mouth. A gourmand falls between the two: he may be no more than a slightly greedier gourmet or no less than a glutton with some pretence of taste. In all instances, though, *gourmand* should convey at least a suggestion of disdain.

graffiti. 'There was graffiti in glorious abundance' (*Daily Mail*). *Graffiti*, meaning drawings or messages scrawled on walls and monuments, is a plural. Thus it should be 'There were graffiti ...'. If all you mean is a single embellishment, the word is *graffito*.

grammatical error is sometimes objected to on the grounds that a word or phrase cannot be simultaneously grammatical and erroneous, but must be either one or the other. In fact, the primary meaning of *grammatical* is 'of or relating to grammar', which includes errors of grammar, and in any case the expression is well established.

greater. 'The cost for a 17-year-old living in the greater London area ...' (*The Times*). 'In greater London' or 'the London area' says the same thing as 'the greater London area', but says it more simply.

grievous, not *grievious*.

grisly, grizzly. Occasionally confused. The first means horrifying or gruesome. The second means grey, especially grey-haired, and is a cliché when applied to old men.

grizzly. See GRISLY, GRIZZLY.

growth. Often used contrarily by economists and those who write about them, as here: 'It now looks as if growth will remain stagnant until spring' (*Observer*); '... with the economy moving into a negative growth phase' (*The Times*). Economists on the whole have had about as much beneficial effect on our language as they have had on our economies. *Growth* indicates expansion. If a thing is shrinking or standing still, *growth* isn't the word to describe it.

guttural. Often misspelled *gutteral*. Note the middle 'u'.

◉ H ◉

habits. 'As was his usual habit ...' (*Sunday Express*); 'The customary habits of the people of the South Pacific ...' (*Daily Telegraph*). Habits are always customary and always usual. That is, of course, what makes them habitual.

hail. See HALE, HAIL.

hale, hail. *Hale* means robust and vigorous, or to drag or forcibly draw (as in 'haled into court'), in which sense it is related to *haul*. *Hail* describes a greeting, a salute or a downpour. The expressions are 'hale and hearty' and 'hail-fellow-well-met'.

hamlet. 'Police searched his house in the tiny hamlet of Oechtringen ...' (*Observer*). It is in the nature of hamlets to be tiny.

hangar. All too often misspelled. The place where aircraft are kept is a hangar, not a hanger.

hanged. 'It was disclosed that a young white official had been found hanged to death in his cell ...' (*The New York Times*). 'Hanged to death' is redundant. So too, for that matter, are 'starved to death' and 'strangled to death'. The writer was correct, however, in saying that the official had been found hanged and not hung. People are hanged; pictures and the like are hung.

harangue, tirade. Each is sometimes used when the other is intended. A tirade is always abusive and can be directed at one person or at several. A harangue, however, need not be vituperative, but may merely be prolonged and tedious. It does, however, require at least two listeners. One person cannot, properly speaking, harangue another.

hare-brained. Occasionally misspelled, as here: 'The 22-year-old police constable dreamed up a "hair-brained and dangerous scheme ..."' (*Standard*).

72

head over heels is not just a cliché; it is also, when you think about it, a faintly absurd one. Our heads are usually over our heels.

healthful. See HEALTHY, HEALTHFUL, SALUTARY.

healthy, healthful, salutary. It is sometimes maintained that *healthy* should apply only to those things that possess health and *healthful* to those that promote it. Thus we could have 'healthy children', but 'healthful exercise' and 'healthful food'. There is no harm in observing the distinction, but there is little to be gained from insisting on it. If we are to become resolute, it would be better to focus on *healthy* in the sense of big or vigorous, as in 'a healthy wage increase', which is both imprecise and overworked.

Salutary has a wider meaning than either of the other words. It too means conducive to health, but can also apply to anything that is demonstrably beneficial ('a salutary lesson in etiquette'). Most often, however, it is used to describe actions or properties that have a remedial influence: 'The new drug has a salutary effect on arthritis'.

Hebrew, Yiddish. The two languages have nothing in common except that they are spoken primarily by Jewish people. Yiddish (from the German *jüdisch*, 'Jewish') is a modified German dialect and thus a part of the Indo-European family of languages. Hebrew is a Semitic tongue and therefore is more closely related to Arabic. Yiddish writers sometimes use the Hebrew alphabet, but the two languages are no more closely related than, say, English and Urdu.

historic, historical. 'The Landmarks Preservation Commission voted yesterday to create a historical district on a gilded stretch of Manhattan's East Side' (*The New York Times*). Something that makes history or is part of history, as in the example above, is historic. Something that is based on history or describes history is historical ('a historical novel'). A historic judicial ruling is one that makes history; a historical ruling is one based on precedent. There are, however, at least two exceptions to the rule – in accountancy ('historic costs') and, curiously, in grammar ('historic tenses'). (See also A, AN.)

historical. See HISTORIC, HISTORICAL.

hitherto. 'In 1962, the regime took the hitherto unthinkable step of appropriating land' (*Daily Telegraph*). *Hitherto* means 'until now'. The writer meant 'thitherto' ('until then'), but 'theretofore' would have been better and 'previously' better still.

hoard, horde. Sometimes confused. The first describes an accumulation (usually hidden) of valuables. The second originally described nomadic tribes, but now applies to any crowd, particularly to a thronging and disorganized one ('hordes of Christmas shoppers').

Hobson's choice is sometimes taken to mean a dilemma or difficult decision, but in fact it means no choice at all. It derives from a sixteenth-century Cambridge stable-keeper named Thomas Hobson, who hired out horses on a strict rotation. The customer was allowed to take the one nearest the stable door or none at all.

hoi polloi. Two problems here. The first is that *hoi polloi* means the masses, the common populace and not the elite as is sometimes thought. The second problem is that in Greek *hoi* means 'the', so to talk of 'the hoi polloi' is tantamount to saying 'the the masses'. The best answer to both problems is to avoid the expression altogether.

holocaust. A holocaust is not just any disaster, but one involving fiery destruction. (In Greek the word means 'burnt whole'.)

hopefully. 'To travel hopefully is a better thing than to arrive'. Fifty years ago that sentence by Robert Louis Stevenson would have suggested only one interpretation: that it is better to travel filled with hope than to actually reach your destination. Today, however, it could also be read as meaning: 'To travel is, I hope, better than arriving'.

This extended sense of *hopefully* has been condemned with some passion by many authorities, among them Philip Howard, who calls it 'ambiguous and obscure, as well as illiterate and ugly'. Many others, notably Bernstein and Gowers, accept it, though usually only grudgingly and often with provisos attached.

Most of those who object to *hopefully* in its looser sense do so on the argument that it is a misused modal auxiliary – that is to say, that it fails to modify the elements it should. Consider this sentence: 'Hopefully the sun will come out soon'. Taken literally, it is telling us that the sun, its manner hopeful, will soon emerge. Even if we accept the sentence as meaning 'I hope [or *we hope* or *it is hoped that*] the sun will come out soon', it is still considered grammatically amiss. Would you say, 'Thinkingly the sun will come out soon' if you thought it might, or 'Believably it will come out' if you believed as much, or 'Hopelessly . . .' if you hoped it wouldn't?

The shortcoming of that argument is that those writers who scrupulously avoid *hopefully* do not hesitate to use at least a dozen other words – apparently, presumably, happily, sadly, mercifully, thankfully and many others – in precisely the same way. In *Paradigms Lost*, John Simon disdains the looser *hopefully*, yet elsewhere he writes: 'Marshall Sahlins, who professes anthropology at the University of Chicago, errs some 15 times in an admittedly long piece'. That 'admittedly' is as unattached as any *hopefully* ever was. But Simon and others of his view would argue that 'admittedly' there is an absolute or sentence modifier – a word that can modify a whole clause or sentence and not just a single element in it.

To accept the one while excluding the other is, I think, curious and illogical and more than a little reminiscent of those Victorian purists who insisted that 'laughable' should be 'laugh-at-able' and that virtue would be served by turning 'reliable' into 'relionable'. All that distinguishes 'admittedly' and 'mercifully' and the others from *hopefully* is that the members of the first group have a pedigree. Yet feelings on the matter continue to run high. One American commentator recently said that acceptance of the looser *hopefully* would mark 'the final descent into darkness for the English language'. That's silly.

There are, however, two more compelling reasons for regarding *hopefully* with suspicion. The first is that, as in the Stevenson quotation at the beginning of this entry, it opens a possibility of ambiguity. Gowers cites this sentence: 'Our team will start their innings hopefully immediately after tea'. It isn't possible to say with any certainty whether *hopefully* refers to the team's frame of mind or to the time it will start batting.

A second objection is to the lameness of *hopefully*. If a newspaper article says, 'Hopefully the miners' strike will end today', who exactly is doing the hoping? The writer? The miners? All right-thinking people? All too often the word is used as no more than an easy escape from having to claim responsibility for a sentiment and as such is to be deplored.

But the real issue with *hopefully* has more to do with fashion than with linguistic rectitude. As *The American Heritage Dictionary* observes, the looser usage of *hopefully* is 'grammatically justified by analogy to similar uses of "happily" and "mercifully". However, this usage is by now such a bugbear to traditionalists that it is best avoided on grounds of civility, if not logic'.

horde. See HOARD, HORDE.

horribly. See TERRIBLY, AWFULLY, HORRIBLY, ETC.

host. As a verb ('He hosted the conference'), the word is a casualism that is not much needed and even less liked and is better avoided.

◉ I ◉

I, me. In 1981 *The Times* ran a series of articles under the heading 'Christmas and me'. Me cringed. Such lapses are not as uncommon as we might hope them to be. Consider, for instance: 'It was a bizarre little scenario – the photographer and me ranged on one side, the petulant actor and his agent on the other' (*Sunday Times*). At least the next sentence didn't begin: 'Me turned to the actor and asked him ...'.

Probably the most common problem with *I* and *me*, and certainly the most widely disputed, is deciding whether to write 'It was I' or 'It was me'. The more liberal authorities are inclined to allow 'It was me' on the argument that it is more colloquial and less affected, while the prescriptivists lean towards 'It was I' on the indisputable grounds that it is more grammatical. A point generally overlooked by both sides is that 'It is I' and like constructions are usually a graceless and wordy way of expressing a thought. Instead of writing 'It was he who was nominated' or 'It is she whom I love', why not simply say, 'He was chosen' and 'I love her'?

Things become more troublesome still when a subordinate clause is influenced contradictorily by a personal pronoun and a relative pronoun, as here: 'It is not you who is [are?] angry'. 'Is' is grammatically correct, but again the sentence would be less stilted if recast as 'You are not the one who is angry' or 'You aren't angry'. (See also IT.)

idiosyncrasy. Not idiosyncracy.

i.e. See E.G., I.E.

if. Problems often arise in deciding whether *if* is introducing a subjunctive clause ('If I were ...') or an indicative one ('If I was ...'). Simply put, when *if* introduces a notion that is clearly untrue or hypothetical or improbable, the verb should be in the subjunctive: 'If I were king ...'; 'If he were in your shoes ...'. But when the *if* is introducing a thought that is true or could well be true, the mood should be indicative: 'If I was happy then, I don't remember it now'. One small hint may help: if the sentence contains a *would* or its variants, the mood of the sentence is subjunctive, as in 'If I were you, I wouldn't take the job'. (See also SUBJUNCTIVES.)

if and when. Almost always unnecessary. Choose one or the other.

ilk. 'And it was because Oskar could play the part of brother to Amon and his ilk ...' (*Sunday Times*). The authorities are virtually – and perhaps a little curiously – unanimous in condemning *ilk* in the sense of type or kind, as it is used above. A Scots word, it means 'same'. 'McFarlan of that ilk' means 'McFarlan of McFarlan'. But in condemning the word the authorities fail to acknowledge that there is very little need for the word in its stricter sense inside Britain and no need at all outside. If we are to allow the broader meaning, we should at least not employ it redundantly, as it was here: 'Politicians of all stripes and ilks ...' (William Safire in *The New York Times*).

immoral. See AMORAL, IMMORAL.

impel. See COMPEL, IMPEL.

imply, infer, insinuate. The first two are all too often confused. *Imply* means to suggest: 'He implied that I was a fool'. *Infer* means to deduce: 'We inferred that he wasn't coming'. A speaker implies, a listener infers. *Inference* and *implication* are also sometimes confused, as here: 'Asked if he meant that the Russians were bluffing, the Secretary said ... that that was "a fair implication"' (cited by Bernstein). The Secretary meant 'a fair inference'.

   Insinuate is similar to *imply* in that it describes an action not explicitly stated. But unlike *imply*, which can be neutral, *insinuate* always has pejorative connotations.

important, importantly. 'But more importantly, his work was instrumental in eradicating cholera' (*Sunday Telegraph*). Some authorities condemn *importantly* here on the argument that the sentence involves an ellipsis of thought, as if it were saying, 'But [what is] more important...'. Others contend that *importantly* is being used as a sentence adverb, modifying the whole expression, in much the same way as 'happily' in 'Happily, it didn't rain'. Both points are grammatically defensible, so the choice of which to use must be entirely a matter of preference.

importantly. See IMPORTANT, IMPORTANTLY.

impracticable. See IMPRACTICAL, IMPRACTICABLE, UN-PRACTICAL.

impractical, impracticable, unpractical. If a thing could be done but isn't worth doing, it is impractical or unpractical (the words mean the same thing). If it can't be done at all, it's impracticable.

in, into, in to. *In* normally indicates a fixed position: 'He was in the house'. *Into* indicates movement towards a fixed position: 'He went into the house'. There are, however, many exceptions (e.g., 'He put it in his pocket'). *In to* (two words) is correct when *in* is an adverb: 'He turned himself in to the police'.

It is perhaps also worth noting that *in* is the first word in a number of expressions that usually do no more than consume space: in connection with, in terms of, in respect of, in the event that, in view of the fact that, in the course of, in order to and in excess of. In the following two examples the italicized words would be better replaced by the word or words in parentheses: 'Profits were *in excess of* (more than) £12 million' (*Guardian*); 'Rationalization measures *in respect of* (at) the timber merchanting division . . .' (*The Times*).

inchoate. Probably because of the similarity in spelling to *chaotic* and in pronunciation to *incoherent*, the word is sometimes used in the sense of disorderly or disorganized. In fact, it means incipient, undeveloped, just starting. An inchoate enterprise is likely to be disorganized, but the disorderliness is not what makes it inchoate.

incline. As a verb, *incline* indicates a conscious decision, as in 'He was inclined to go to Greece for the summer'. When there is no choice involved, *incline* is incorrect, as it was here: 'Roads are inclined to deteriorate during bad weather' (*Daily Telegraph*).

include indicates that what is to follow is only part of a greater whole. To use it when you are describing a totality is sloppy: 'The company's three main operating divisions, which include hotels, catering and package holidays . . .' (*Guardian*); 'The 630 job losses include 300 in Redcar and 330 in Port Talbot' (*The Times*).

inculcate means to persistently impress a habit upon or a belief into another person. You inculcate an idea, not a person. 'My father inculcated me with a belief in democracy' should be 'My father inculcated in me a belief in democracy'. A simple guide: If you cannot substitute 'implant', then *inculcate* is not being used correctly.

indefinitely. 'The new structures should, by contrast, last almost indefinitely' (*Newsweek*). *Indefinitely* in the sense of 'for a very long time' is better avoided. The word means only 'without prescribed limits'. Thus, strictly speaking, the sentence above is telling us that the structures may last for a million years or they may collapse after ten minutes. 'Almost indefinitely', incidentally, is impossible.

indexes, indices. Both *The Concise Oxford* and *The American Heritage* prefer *indexes*. *The Concise Oxford* suggests, however, that *indices* is better for technical applications. *The American Heritage* takes no stand on usage.

indices. See INDEXES, INDICES.

individual is acceptable when you are contrasting one person with an organization or body of people ('How can one individual hope to rectify the evils of society?'). But as a synonym for person ('Do you see that individual standing over there?') it is otiose.

indubitably. See DOUBTLESS, UNDOUBTEDLY, INDUBITABLY.

infectious. See CONTAGIOUS, INFECTIOUS.

infer. See IMPLY, INFER, INSINUATE.

inflammable. See FLAMMABLE, INFLAMMABLE.

inflation has spawned a number of variants, all of which need to be used with care if they are to be used at all. *Inflation* itself means that the money supply and prices are rising. *Hyper-inflation* means that they are rising rapidly (at an annual rate of at least 20 per cent). *Deflation* means that they are falling and *reflation* that they are being pushed up again after a period of deflation. *Disinflation*, the ugliest and most frequently misused of the words, means that prices are rising, but at a slower rate, and *stagflation* means that prices are rising while output is stagnant. The last two in particular are better avoided. There is a separate point worth noting: if the rate of inflation was 8 per cent last month and 6 per cent this month, it does not mean that prices are falling; it means they are rising at a slower rate.

ingenious, ingenuous. The first means clever, the second means frank, unsophisticated, naive. Problems also sometimes occur with the negative form *disingenuous*, which means crafty or not straight-forward.

ingenuous. See INGENIOUS, INGENUOUS.

innocent. 'She and four other inmates have pleaded innocent to the tax charges' (*Boston Globe*). Under the British and American judicial systems, people do not plead innocent. They plead guilty or not guilty.

input, output. Gowers writes of a man who, every time he saw *input* and *output*, wanted to upstand and outwalk. The spread of computers and their attendant argot is now inescapable, but the use of *input*, at least outside contexts involving the processing of data, is better resisted. *Output* has gained wider acceptance and can be used to describe industrial and economic production, but elsewhere is still better replaced.

inquiry. See QUERY, INQUIRY, ENQUIRY.

insidious, invidious. *Insidious* indicates the stealthy spread of something undesirable ('an insidious leak in the roof'). *Invidious* means offensive or inviting animosity ('an invidious remark').

insinuate. See IMPLY, INFER, INSINUATE.

in spite of. See DESPITE, IN SPITE OF.

intense, intensive. *Intense* should describe things that are heavy or extreme or occur to a high degree ('intense sunlight', 'intense down-pour'). *Intensive* implies a concentrated focus ('intensive care'). Although the two words often come to the same thing, they needn't. An intense bombardment, as Fowler points out, is a severe one. An intensive bombardment is one directed at a small area.

intensive. See INTENSE, INTENSIVE.

interface. To a scientist an interface is the meeting place of two regions, systems or processes. For the rest of us it should suggest no more than a misguided attempt by the writer to impress his readers. 'Our social services group provides an interface for the different specialists concerned with the subject' (cited by Howard) is merely pretentious.

internecine. For more than 200 years writers have been using *internecine* quite wrongly in the sense of a prolonged or costly internal conflict. For this small error we can thank Samuel Johnson, who was misled by the prefix *inter-* and defined the word as 'endeavouring mutual destruction'. In its proper sense the word does denote extermination, slaughter or a bloody quarrel, but contains no sense of being mutually destructive. It has, however, been misused for so long that it would be pedantic, and wildly optimistic, to try to enforce its original meaning. As Philip Howard notes: 'The English language cannot be regulated so as to avoid offending the susceptibilities of classical scholars'. He does suggest, however, that the word should be reserved for bloody and violent disputes and not mere squabblings.

interpretative. See INTERPRETIVE, INTERPRETATIVE.

interpretive, interpretative. Either is correct.

interval. '. . . the training period was still three years, an interval widely regarded in the industry as being unrealistically long' (cited by Gowers). An interval is the period *between* two events.

into. See IN, INTO, IN TO.

in to. See IN, INTO, IN TO.

intrigue. Originally *intrigue* signified underhanded plotting and nothing else. The looser meaning of 'arousing' or 'fascinating' ('We found the lecture intriguing') is now established. It is, however, greatly overworked and almost always better replaced by a more telling word.

invariably does not mean frequently or usually, as was intended here: 'Supersede is yet another word that is invariably misspelled' (*Chicago Tribune*). *Invariable* and *invariably* mean fixed, constant, not subject to change. Night invariably follows day, but no word is invariably misspelled.

inveigh, inveigle. Occasionally confused. The first means to speak strongly against ('He inveighed against the rise in taxes'). The second means to entice or cajole ('They inveigled an invitation to the party').

inveigle. See INVEIGH, INVEIGLE.

invidious. See INSIDIOUS, INVIDIOUS.

irony, sarcasm. *Irony* is the use of words to convey a contradiction between the literal and intended meanings. *Sarcasm* is very like irony except that it is more stinging. Where the primary intent behind irony is to amuse, with sarcasm it is to wound.

irregardless. *The Oxford English Dictionary* contains 414,825 words. *Irregardless* is not one of them. (There is, however, a perfectly good word 'irrespective'.) Make it *regardless*.

it. Sentences that begin with *it* are always worth a second look. Oftentimes an anticipatory or 'dummy' *it* is unobjectionable or even unavoidable ('It seems to me', 'It began to rain', 'It is widely believed that'), but perhaps just as often it is no more than a sign of circuitous and tedious writing. The two following examples came from one article in *The New York Times*: 'It was Mr Bechtel who was the more peripatetic of the two'; 'It was under his direction that the annual reports began'. Both sentences would be shorter and more forceful if 'It was' and the relative pronouns (respectively 'who' and 'that') were removed, making them 'Mr Bechtel was the more peripatetic of the two' and 'Under his direction the annual reports began'.

its, it's. The distinction between these two ought not to trouble a ten-year-old, but one article in the *Washington Post* in 1981 managed to confuse them five times: 'Its the worst its been in the last five years'; 'Its awful'; 'Its come full circle'; 'Its nice to see the enemy'.

It's

Its is the possessive form of *it*: 'Put each book in its place'. *It's*, which was intended in each of the examples above, is the contraction of *it is*.

it's. See ITS, IT'S.

▣ J ▣

jargon, argot, lingua franca. At a conference of sociologists in America in 1977, love was defined as 'the cognitive-affective state characterized by intrusive and obsessive fantasizing concerning reciprocity of amorant feelings by the object of the amorance'. That is jargon – the practice of never calling a spade a spade when you might instead call it a manual earth-restructuring implement. So long as it circulates only among a given profession, jargon is usually unobjectionable and frequently useful, since every profession needs its own form of short-hand. But all too often it escapes into the wider world, so that we have schools in Dallas sending parents a manual called 'Terminal Behaviour Objectives for Continuous Progression Modules in Early Childhood Education' (cited by Newman) and a critic who describes an artist as having 'the courage to monumentalize the polymorphous-perverse world of his inner quickenings' in a painting that contains 'the tall duration of a muralizing necessity that strains to leap its pendulum's arc while carrying a full weight on iconographic potency' (cited by Bernstein). This vacuous pretentiousness, this curious urge to speak of 'attitudinal concepts' when we mean attitudes and 'opti-mally consonant patterns of learning constructs' when we mean a sound education, is probably the greatest linguistic sin of the century.

Argot was originally the language of thieves, but has, like *jargon*, come to mean a way of communicating peculiar to a particular group. *Lingua franca* (literally 'the Frankish tongue') is any language or mixture of languages that serves as a common means of communica-tion among diverse parties. English, for instance, is the lingua franca of international air travel.

join together, link together. The Bible and marriage ceremonies not-withstanding, *join together* is almost always tautological. Similarly *linked together*, even when written by as eminent a man as C. T. Onions: 'The first members of a group linked together by one of the above conjunctions ...' (in *Modern English Syntax*).

Jonson, Ben. The English dramatist and poet (1573–1637) has pro-bably the most frequently misspelled surname in the literary world.

Even Bernstein calls him Ben Johnson (in *Dos, Don'ts and Maybes of English Usage*).

just deserts. Not *just desserts*. The expression has nothing to do with the sweet course after dinner. It comes from the French for 'deserve', which may help you to remember that it has just one middle 's'.

▪ K ▪

key. After 'major' (which see), *key* is perhaps the lazy writer's best friend. It can be appended to a multiplicity of nouns ('key decisions', 'key elections', 'key proposals') and made to cover a range of meanings from notable to essential. It spares the writer the annoyance of having to think of a more precise word and the challenge of making his writing interesting.

Khrushchev, Nikita. 'The man who adored Khruschev' (*Daily Telegraph* headline). Khrushchev may have been adored by one man, but he has been misspelled by many. Note that the name has three 'h's.

kind. 'Those are the kind of numbers that easily solve the mystery ...' (*New York Daily News*). There should be what grammarians call concord between *kind* and *kinds* and their antecedents. Just as we say 'this hat' but 'those hats', so the writer above should have said, 'Those are the kinds of numbers' or 'This is the kind of number'. Shakespeare, for what it's worth, didn't always observe the distinction. In *King Lear* he wrote: 'These kind of knaves'.

kith and kin. Your kin are your relatives. Your kith are your relatives and acquaintances. Individually the words are antiquated. Together they are redundant and hackneyed.

knot. 'The yacht was doing about nine knots an hour, according to Mr Starr' (*The New York Times*). Because *knot* means nautical miles an hour, the time element is implicit in it. The sentence above is telling us that the yacht was progressing at a speed of nine nautical miles an hour an hour. Either delete 'an hour' or change 'knots' to 'nautical miles'.

koala bears is wrong. Koalas are marsupials, not bears. Just call them koalas.

krona, krone. The currencies of the Scandinavian nations cause occasional confusion, as in this *Times* headline: 'Sweden devalues kroner by 10 per cent'. The Swedes call it a *krona* (plural *kronor*). In Denmark and Norway it is a *krone* (plural *kroner*). In Iceland it is also a *krona*, but the plural is *kronur*.

krone. See KRONA, KRONE.

Krugerrand. Often misspelled, as here: 'The premium on Krugerands was just over 3 per cent' (*Guardian*). Note the two 'r's in the middle.

kudos. 'He did not feel he had received the kudos that were his due' (*Washington Post*). *Kudos*, a Greek word meaning fame or glory, is singular. Thus it should be 'the kudos that was his due', which rather helps to expose the word as the pompous pretender that it is. There is no such thing, incidentally, as one kudo.

▪ L ▪

languid, limpid. Not to be confused. *Limpid* means clear, calm, untroubled ('a limpid stream'). It has nothing to do with being limp or listless – meanings that are covered by *languid*.

last, past, latest. Various authorities have issued various strictures against using *last* when you mean *latest*. Generally speaking, *last* should not be used when it might be interpreted as meaning final, as in 'the last issue of the newspaper' when you mean 'the latest issue'. The chances of ambiguity, however, are probably not as great as some authorities would have us believe, and in any case the choice of word is dictated as often by idiom as by sense. We must, for instance, say, 'I last saw him a week ago' or 'I spoke to him last night', even when there is no suggestion of it being a final meeting. Some newspapers make a similar distinction between *last* and *past*, though here the likelihood of confusion can generously be called remote.

latest. See LAST, PAST, LATEST.

latter. See FORMER, LATTER.

laudable, laudatory. Occasionally confused. *Laudable* means deserving praise. *Laudatory* means expressing praise.

laudatory. See LAUDABLE, LAUDATORY.

lay, lie. A constant source of errors. There are no simple rules for this pair. You must either commit their forms to memory or avoid them altogether. The forms are:

	lay	*lie*
Present:	I lay the book on the table.	I lie down; I am lying down.
Past:	Yesterday I laid the book on the table.	Last night I lay down to sleep.
Present perfect:	I have already laid the book on the table.	I have lain in bed all day.

The most common type of error is to say: 'If you're not feeling well, go upstairs and lay down'. It should be 'lie down'.

lectern, podium, dais, rostrum. The first two are frequently confused. A lectern is the stand on which a speaker places his notes. A podium is the raised platform on which he and the lectern stand. A podium can hold only one person. A platform for several people is a dais. A rostrum is any platform; it may be designed for one speaker or for several.

legend, legendary. Lytton Strachey described Florence Nightingale as 'a living legend in her own lifetime' (as opposed, apparently, to a dead legend in her own lifetime) and thereby gave the world a cliché it could do without. Properly, a legend is a story that may have some basis in fact, but is mostly fanciful. King Arthur and Robin Hood are legendary figures. The word can be fairly extended to those people or things whose fame is such as to inspire myths (Babe Ruth, Rolls-Royces), but the word is often used far too loosely, as here: 'Doctors call it Munchhausen's syndrome, after the legendary ... Baron Hieronymous Karl Friedrich von Munchhausen, who spun fantastic and exaggerated stories about his experiences as a German cavalry officer ...' (*The New York Times*). To attach the word to a man whose history is well documented and whose fame exists almost exclusively within medical circles is to use it loosely.

legendary. See LEGEND, LEGENDARY.

lend, loan. *Loan* as a verb ('He loaned me some money') is common in America, probably because *lent* sounds affected to most American ears, and is appearing increasingly in Britain as here: 'They have agreed to loan the fund more than $4,000 million' (*The Times*). However, most British authorities and two leading American ones (Bernstein and *The American Heritage Dictionary*) continue to urge that the usage be resisted.

less. See FEWER, LESS.

level, mark are often empty words. 'Share prices once again fell below the 600 level' (*Guardian*) says no more than 'fell below 600'. Similarly *mark*, as in 'This year attendances have been hovering around the 25,000 mark' (*Sunday Times*). Make it 'hovering around 25,000'.

liable, likely, apt, prone. All four indicate probability, but there are distinctions worth noting. *Apt* is better reserved for general probabilities ('It is apt to snow in January') and *likely* for specific ones ('It is likely to snow today'). *Liable* and *prone* are better used to indicate a probability arising as a regrettable consequence: 'People who drink too much are prone to fall down'; 'If you don't pay your taxes, you are liable to get caught'. Fowler says that *prone* should apply only to people, but he appears to be alone in this view and the 1982 *Concise Oxford Dictionary* cites 'strike-prone industries' as an acceptable usage.

A separate problem with *likely*, more common in America than elsewhere, is seen in this sentence: 'Cable experts say the agreement will likely strengthen the company's position' (*Washington Post*). When used as an adverb, *likely* needs to be accompanied by a 'very', 'quite', 'more', or 'most'. Thus the sentence should say 'will very likely strengthen'. A greater improvement still would be to rework the phrase entirely: 'Cable experts say the agreement is likely to strengthen the company's position'. (See also INCLINE.)

licence, license. In British usage the first is the noun, the second the verb ('a licence to sell wines and spirits' but 'licensed premises'). In America *license* is preferred for both noun and verb, although with the exception of 'practice' (which see) the distinction is elsewhere preserved, as in device/devise, advice/advise and prophecy/prophesy.

license. See LICENCE, LICENSE.

lie. See LAY, LIE.

lifelong. 'Jesse Bishop was a lifelong drug addict who had spent 20 of his 46 years in prison' (*Guardian*). You might be a lifelong resident of New York or a lifelong church-goer or, at a stretch, a lifelong lover of music. But unless the unfortunate Mr Bishop had turned to drugs at a remarkably early age, *lifelong* is much too literal a word to describe his addiction.

lighted, lit. Either is correct. *Lighted*, however, is more usual when the word is being used as an adjective ('a lighted torch').

light years. 'So protracted have the discussions been that their progress should almost be measured not in years but in light years' (*Guardian*).

like

Though the intention above was obviously facetious, it is as well to remember that light years are a measure of distance, not time.

like, as. Problems often arise in choosing between *like* and *as*. Here are two examples, both from *The New York Times* and both wrong: 'Advertising agencies may appear as [make it *like*] homespun enterprises to the American public ...'; 'On the surface it looks like [*as if*] all of the parties are preparing for serious bargaining'.

The rule is, on the face of it, simple: *as* and *as if* are always followed by a verb; *like* never is. Therefore we would say, 'He plays tennis like an expert' (no verb after *like*), but, 'He plays tennis as if his life depended on it' (verb *depended*).

Although that is the rule, there may be times when you wish to suspend it. Except in the most formal writing, sentences like the one you are now reading and the two that follow should not be considered objectionable: 'She looks just like her mother used to'; 'He can't dance like he used to'. There is also one apparent inconsistency in the rule in that *like* may be used when it comes between 'feel' and an '-ing' verb: 'He felt like walking'; 'I feel like going abroad this year'.

A separate problem with *like* is that it often leads writers to make false comparisons, as here: 'Like the Prime Minister, his opposition to increased public spending is fierce' (*Daily Telegraph*). The writer has inadvertently likened 'Prime Minister' to 'opposition'. In order to liken person with person, the sentence needs to be recast: 'Like the Prime Minister, he is fiercely opposed to increased public spending', or words to that effect. Phythian cites this example: 'It is believed that this strike, like last year, could go on for several weeks'. As written, the sentence is telling us that last year could go on for several weeks. Make it 'this strike, like last year's ...'.

likely. See LIABLE, LIKELY, APT, PRONE.

limit means constrained, set within bounds. Unless there is the idea of a limit being imposed, the word is being used loosely, as it was here: 'Information about his early life is limited' (cited by Fowler). It should not be used as a simple synonym for small, brief, rare, meagre or other more precise words.

limpid. See LANGUID, LIMPID.

92

lingua franca. See JARGON, ARGOT, LINGUA FRANCA.

link together. See JOIN TOGETHER, LINK TOGETHER.

lion's share is better avoided unless there is some suggestion of a greedy or selfish accumulation, a sense not intended here: 'The Territory, which controls the lion's share of Australia's high-grade uranium reserves . . .' (*Australian*).

liquefy. Frequently misspelled, as here: 'Indonesia intends to double its exports of liquified gas to Japan' (*The Times*).

lit. See LIGHTED, LIT.

literally. All too often used as a kind of disclaimer by writers who mean – literally – the opposite of what they're saying. The result is generally painful: 'Hetzel was literally born with a butcher's knife in his mouth' (*Chicago Tribune*); 'After a slow start, they literally sliced up the Wildcats with their stunning last-half onslaught' (*San Francisco Chronicle*); 'Our eyes were literally pinned to the curtains' (cited by Fowler).

It shouldn't need saying, but if you don't wish to be taken literally, don't use *literally*. The word means actually, not figuratively. It is acceptable only when it serves to show that an expression usually used metaphorically is to be taken at its word, as in: 'He literally died laughing'.

livid. There is an uneasy compromise between the two meanings of the word. Originally *livid* indicated a bluish, leaden shade of the sort associated with bruising. It has since been extended to mean furious and argumentative, and in that sense is now well established. But the word has nothing to do with redness, as is often assumed, or with brightness, as was apparently thought here: 'For the sun room she chose a bold, almost livid, array of patterns and textures' (*Chicago Tribune*). Unless the sun room was decorated in a dullish blue, the word the writer wanted was 'vivid'.

loan. See LEND, LOAN.

local residents. 'The proposals have upset many local residents' (*Guardian*). Residents generally are local.

luxuriant, luxurious. The words are not interchangeable, though the meanings sometimes overlap. *Luxuriant* indicates profuse growth ('luxuriant hair'). *Luxurious* means sumptuous and expensive ('a luxurious house'). A luxuriant carpet is a shaggy one. A luxurious carpet is a very expensive one.

luxurious. See LUXURIANT, LUXURIOUS.

⊡ M ⊡

major. On the day in 1982 that *The New York Times* was telling its readers about a major initiative, a major undertaking, a major speech, two major changes, a major operation and a major cause, *The Times* of London was offering its readers a major scandal, a major change, two major improvements and two major steps, a major proposal, a major source of profits and a major refurbishment. *Major*, it seems, has become a major word. Generally imprecise, frequently fatuous and always grossly overworked, it is in almost every instance better replaced by a more expressive term.

majority, like *major*, has been wearied by overuse, particularly in the expression 'the vast majority of', as in the three following examples, all from authorities: 'The vast majority of conditional sentences ...' (Partridge); 'In the vast majority of instances ...' (Bernstein); 'The vast majority of such mistakes ...' (Fowler). Even when written by the most discriminating writers, 'the vast majority of' seldom says more in four words than 'most' says in one.

  Majority should be reserved for describing the larger of two clearly divisible things, as in 'The majority of the members voted for the resolution'. But even then a more specific description is usually better: 52 per cent, almost two thirds, more than 70 per cent, etc. When there is no sense of a clear contrast with a minority (as in 'The majority of his spare time was spent reading'), *majority* is better avoided.

marginal is unobjectionable when used to describe something falling near a lower limit ('a marginal profit'). But it is a poor choice when all you mean is small or slight, as it was here: 'There has been a marginal improvement in relations between police and blacks in the community' (*Guardian*).

mark. See LEVEL, MARK.

masterful, masterly. Most authorities continue to insist that we observe a distinction between these two – namely that *masterly* should apply to that which is adroit and expert and *masterful* to that which is imperious and domineering. So in the following quotation *masterly* would have been the better word: 'Leroy (Satchel) Paige, a masterful pitcher and baseball showman . . .' (*Washington Post*). There are two difficulties with that argument. The first is that none of the leading dictionaries insist on the distinction and most don't even indicate that such a distinction exists. The second is that *masterly* makes a clumsy adverb. Although it is grammatically correct to write, 'He swims masterly' or even 'He swims masterlily', who would want to? *Masterly* should perhaps be your first choice when you mean in the manner of a master, but to insist on it at the expense of euphony is to be overfussy.

masterly. See MASTERFUL, MASTERLY.

material. See GERMANE, RELEVANT, MATERIAL.

materialize is usually no more than a pompous synonym for occur, develop or happen. If the urge to use it is irresistible, at least try to ensure that it is not qualifying the wrong noun, as it was here: 'Hopes of an improvement in the second half of the year have not materialized' (*The Times*). The hopes had not been realized; what had not materialized was the improvement.

may. See CAN, MAY.

me. See I, ME.

mean, median, average. Imagine that we have five people with IQs of 100, 110, 120, 130 and 150. The average IQ would be the sum of the IQs divided by the number of people – in this case 122. The mean IQ would be the number falling midway between the high of 150 and low of 100 – or 125. Both average and mean are notional numbers: they needn't correspond (and in this case don't) to any actual IQs. The median, however, is the actual number that falls midway in a given series. In this case it is 120 because there are two numbers that are higher and two that are lower. Except in technical writing, *mean* and *median* are almost always better avoided because hardly anyone will know what you are really talking about.

media. 'Is the media – that offensive word – being fair?' (*The New York Times*). One medium, two media. See DATA.

median. See MEAN, MEDIAN, AVERAGE.

mediate. See ARBITRATE, MEDIATE.

metal, mettle. What Samuel Johnson gave the world in lexicography, he sometimes took away in spelling. It is him we can thank for the fact that we have 'deign' but 'disdain', 'moveable' but 'immovable', and 'deceit' but 'receipt', among many others. With *metal* and *mettle*, however, his inconsistency of spelling was intentional. Though both come from the Greek *metallon* (meaning 'a mine') and historically were often spelled the same, their meanings today are normally distinguished, as Johnson intended them to be. *Metal*, of course, describes one of the basic elements, such as gold, silver or copper. *Mettle* means courage or spirit. To be on your mettle is to show the world that you are ready to do your best. A common misspelling is seen here: 'Market conditions have put the hoteliers on their metal' (*Observer*).

metaphors. Enough has been written on the perils of mixed metaphors that it probably requires no more comment than to say that constructions such as the following are profoundly bad: 'This is a virgin field pregnant with possibilities' (cited by Fowler); 'Yet the President has backed him to the hilt every time the chips were down' (cited by Bernstein). The difficulty with such sentences usually is not so much that they mix metaphors as that they mix clichés. When neither of the metaphors in a sentence is hackneyed, you might just get away with it – as Shakespeare clearly did when he wrote, 'Or to take arms against a sea of troubles'.

It should also be noted that it isn't necessary to have two metaphors to botch a sentence. One will do if it is sufficiently inappropriate, as it was here: 'Indiana, ranked the No. 1 swimming power in the nation, walked away with the Big Ten championships tonight' (Associated Press).

meticulous. 'The story has been published in meticulously researched weekly parts . . .' (*Observer*). *Meticulous* does not merely mean careful or thorough; it means fussily thorough and overcareful. Correctly used, it has a pejorative tone. The word today is so often misused by respected writers (the example above comes from Germaine Greer) that to object is itself perhaps a somewhat meticulous act. Meanings change and it is usually futile and occasionally retrograde to try to stand in their way. But there are at least two reasons to regard *meticulously* meticulously. First, because the earlier meaning is so obviously contrary to the meaning often intended, it is subject to misinterpretation. More importantly, there is no need for the word in its broader sense. In the example above, Ms Greer might have chosen in its stead carefully, scrupulously, thoroughly, painstakingly, punctiliously or any of a score of other words. In its earlier sense only fastidious begins to approach it in meaning. Why then debase it?

mettle. See METAL, METTLE.

militate, mitigate. Often confused. To militate is to operate against or, much more rarely, for something: 'The news of the scandal militated against his election prospects'. To mitigate means to assuage, soften, make more endurable: 'His apology mitigated the insult'. *Mitigate against* frequently appears and is always wrong.

millennium. The plural can be *millennia* or *millenniums*. In either case note the double 'n'.

minimize. 'He minimized speculation that a boardroom reshuffle was on the way' (*Observer*). *Minimize* does not mean to play down or depreciate. It means to reduce to an absolute minimum.

minuscule. Frequently misspelled, as here: 'It is a market which was miniscule only five years ago' (*Guardian*). Think of *minus*, not *mini-*.

minute detail. Almost always redundant: 'The cube will be split into little pieces and its components examined in minute detail' (*Sunday Times*). Delete *minute*.

mishap. Dictionaries generally define *mishap* as an unlucky accident, but most people give it a more narrow meaning than that – and one that would rule out this headline from *The Times*: '30 die in mishap'. Used carefully, a mishap should suggest no more than a not very serious accident. It isn't possible to say at what point it becomes an inadequate description for a misfortune, but it is unlikely to involve more than superficial injuries and certainly not multiple fatalities.

mitigate. See MILITATE, MITIGATE.

modus vivendi. Although *modus vivendi* is frequently used to mean 'way of life' (which is its literal meaning), a few authorities maintain that it should describe only a truce between disputing parties pending settlement of their disagreement. The best way to avoid offending the learned or perplexing the ignorant is to find an English equivalent.

moribund. 'Problems in the still-moribund oil tanker business mean there is little sign of recovery on the horizon' (*The Times*). *Moribund* does not mean troubled or struggling or dormant, as was intended above and frequently elsewhere. It means dying, on the point of death.

motiveless. 'French police have intensified their search for the killer in the motiveless murder of a Parisian housewife and her three children yesterday' (*The Times*). *Motiveless* is an impudent word, and under English law a possibly dangerous one, in such contexts. Who is to say at an early stage of an investigation that a murder was committed without motive?

multilateral. See UNILATERAL, BILATERAL, MULTILATERAL.

mutual, common. Most authorities continue to insist, with varying degrees of conviction, that *mutual* should be reserved for describing reciprocal relationships between two or more things and not loosely applied to those things that are shared in common. Thus, if you and I like each other, we have a mutual friendship. But if you and I both like Shakespeare, we have a common admiration. The use of *mutual* in the sense of *common* has been with us since the sixteenth century and was given a much noted boost in the nineteenth with the appearance of the Dickens novel *Our Mutual Friend*. Most authorities accept it when *common* might be interpreted as a denigration ('our common friend'), but, even so, in its looser sense the word is better avoided. It is, at all events, more often than not superfluous, as here: 'They hope to arrange a mutual exchange of prisoners' (*Daily Telegraph*). An exchange of anything could hardly be other than mutual.

myself. Except when it is used for emphasis ('I'll do it myself') or reflexively ('I cut myself while shaving'), *myself* is almost always timorous. In the following two examples, the better word is inserted

myth

in parentheses: 'Give it to John or myself (me)'; 'My wife and myself
(I) would just like to say . . .'.

myth. See FABLE, PARABLE, ALLEGORY, MYTH.

◾ N ◾

nation. See COUNTRY, NATION.

nauseous. 'It made me feel quite nauseous' is increasingly common, especially in America. Make it *nauseated*. As Bernstein very neatly puts it, people who are nauseated are no more nauseous than people who are poisoned are poisonous.

near disaster. 'His quick thinking saved an R A F jet pilot from a near disaster' (*The Times*). Not quite. The pilot was saved from a disaster. A near disaster is what he had.

needless to say. Then why say it? Similarly fatuous is 'it goes without saying'.

neither. Writers have been curiously confounded by the word for centuries; even Samuel Johnson bungled his grammar with *neither* at least once. Things have not improved noticeably since his day, as these two sentences show: 'Neither he nor his agent were available for comment' (*Standard*); 'But maybe neither Churchill nor Chamberlain were as gullible as these remarks suggest' (*Sunday Times*). In both the verb should be 'was'.

When a *neither . . . nor* conjunction is used, the verb should agree with the noun nearest it. In the examples above, the nouns nearest the verb (respectively 'agent' and 'Chamberlain') are both singular, so the verb should be as well. When the noun nearest the verb is plural, the verb should be plural: 'Neither the Prime Minister nor her ministers were available for comment'.

It should be noted that a *neither . . . or* combination is always wrong, as here: '[The] movie mixes horror with science fiction to make something that is fun as neither one thing or the other' (*The New York Times*). Make it *nor*. The following sentence makes the same error and the additional one of failing to provide a grammatical balance between the *neither* phrase and the *nor* phrase: 'Borrowing which allows a country to live beyond its means serves neither the interests of the borrower or the financial community' (*The Times*). Make it *nemesis*

'serves the interests of neither the borrower nor the financial community'. (For a fuller discussion of the problem, see BOTH ... AND.)

When *neither* is used on its own without the *nor*, the verb should always be singular: 'Neither of the men was ready'; 'Neither of us is hungry'.

nemesis. 'Instead, the unions directed their wrath toward another nemesis, the European Community's Executive Commission ...' (*Time*). This will come as a blow to thousands of sportswriters, and at least one writer at *Time* magazine, but a nemesis (from Nemesis, the Greek goddess of vengeance) is one who extracts retributive justice or is utterly unbeatable, and not merely a rival of long standing.

new. 'New chairman named at Weir Group' (*Financial Times* headline); 'Medical briefing: the first in an occasional series on new developments in the sciences' (*Times* headline); 'The search for new breakthroughs seems to have spurred extra spending in recent years' (*Newsweek*). As an adjective, *new* is frequently superfluous. The Weir Group would hardly be appointing an old chairman, nor scientists searching for old breakthroughs, nor *The Times*, let us hope, running a series on old developments in the sciences. In each instance it could be deleted without loss.

no. See YES, NO.

nobody. See NUMBER (4).

noisome has nothing to do with noise or noisiness. It is related to *annoy* and means offensive or objectionable and is most often used to describe unpleasant smells.

none. The widely held belief that *none* must always be singular is a myth. Since Fowler, Bernstein, Howard, Gowers, Partridge, the Evanses, the Morrises, Follett, *The Oxford English Dictionary*, *The American Heritage*, *Random House* and *Webster's New World* dictionaries and many others have already made this point, I do not suppose that the addition of my own small voice to the chorus will make a great deal of difference.

Whether you treat *none* as a singular or a plural, you should at least be consistent throughout the sentence, as this writer was not:

'None of her friends, she says, would describe themselves as a feminist' (*Guardian*). Make it either 'would describe themselves as feminists' or 'would describe herself as a feminist'.

A more notable inconsistency, if only because it comes from a respected authority, is seen here: 'The total vocabulary of English is immense and runs to about half a million items. None of us as individuals, of course, knows more than a fairly limited number of these, and uses even less ...' (Quirk, *The Use of English*). 'None of us ... uses even less'? Though the sense of the sentence is clear enough in the context, grammatically it is telling us that nobody uses fewer words than he knows – which is, unfortunately, the opposite of what the author intended. It would be better, I think, if we made it 'and we use even less' (and better still if we made it 'and we use even fewer').

non sequitur is the Latin for 'it does not follow' and means the combination of two or more unrelated statements. Non sequiturs are most commonly encountered in American newspapers in sentences like the following (which was also cited under *dangling modifiers*): 'Slim, of medium height and with sharp features, Mr Smith's technical skills are combined with strong leadership qualities' (*The New York Times*). What, we might ask, do Mr Smith's height and features have to do with his leadership qualities? The answer, of course, is not a damn thing. When non sequiturs are not intrusive and annoying, they are often just absurd, as here: 'Dyson's catch of Clarke was unbelievable, the best catch I've seen. And the one before it was just as good' (*Sydney Daily Telegraph*, cited in *Punch*).

no one. See NUMBER (4).

normalcy is widely, and wrongly, believed to have been coined by Warren G. Harding, the American president. It is in fact much older. Although most dictionaries accept it as standard, it is still derided by many authorities, who suggest *normality* instead.

not. Sometimes when writers invert the normal word order of a sentence to place greater emphasis on *not*, they present the reader with a false parenthesis. Consider this sentence by John Simon in *Paradigms Lost*: 'Could not that lingua franca be, not Esperanto, Volupük, or even English, but humour?' As punctuated, 'not Esperanto, Volupük, or even English' is parenthetical. But if we deleted it (as we should be able to do with all parenthetical expressions, including this one), the sentence would say: 'Could not that lingua franca be but humour?' The first comma should be removed. Except when the sentiment is pithy ('Death be not proud') such sentences are usually clumsy, which may account for the urge to embellish them with unnecessary punctuation.

not all. 'For some time now tales have been circulating that all was not well in the Goldsmith empire' (*The Times*). What the writer really meant was that not all was well in the empire, not that everything was unwell. The authorities are curiously, and almost unanimously, tolerant on this point. The Evanses are rather vehement about it: 'Distinctions such as this, between *all is not* and *not all is*, appeal to a fictitious logic and seem to have been invented for the purpose of proving other people in the wrong. They are not good for much else'.

I'm afraid the authorities and I are at odds here – or, as the Evanses might put it, all of us don't agree. It seems to me difficult to justify a sentence that so blatantly contradicts what it means to say, especially when the solution is as simple a matter as moving the *not* back two places. Setting aside any considerations of grammatical tidiness and rectitude, if we accept the Evanses' position, how do we make ourselves clear when we really do mean that all is not well? There are a few expressions that we must accept as idiomatic ('All is not lost', 'All that glisters is not gold'), but on the whole I think the construction is better avoided. Certainly I wouldn't want to have to defend the New York clothing store that advertised: 'All items not on sale' (cited by William Safire in *The New York Times*).

not only ... but also. The rule of correlative conjunctions (discussed under BOTH ... AND) applies equally here. That is, there should be a grammatical balance in the sentence. Thus, 'Not only does the fall in the birth-rate vary from city to city but also from area to area' (cited by Phythian) should be: 'The fall in the birth-rate varies not only from city to city but also from area to area'.

not so much is often followed by 'but' when the word should be 'as', as here: 'He was not so much a comic actor, consciously presenting an amusing part, but [make it as] a real comedian ...' (J. B. Priestley, cited by Partridge).

number. Errors of number – the failure to maintain agreement between the subject and verb in a sentence – are probably the most common grammatical fault in English and often the least excusable. In a language where so much is so complicated, the rule is gratifyingly simple: a singular subject takes a singular verb and a plural subject takes a plural verb. As Bernstein says, anyone who can distinguish between one and more than one shouldn't find that too sophisticated a challenge. Yet errors abound – even, as we shall see, among those who should know better. Many of the causes of errors are treated separately throughout the book, but five in particular are worth noting here:

1. *Errors involving 'and'.* When two nouns or pronouns joined by *and* form a compound subject, a plural verb is required. 'Impatience and anger in political and editorial circles has been sharply mounting ...' (*Los Angeles Times*). Make it 'have'. 'She told the meeting that the disorder and despair of the Conservative Party was not self-evident' (*The Times*). Make it 'were'.

The error is especially common when the normal subject-verb order is reversed, as here: 'Why, you may ask, is correct speech and writing important, as long as the writing is clear?' (Simon, *Paradigms Lost*). Speech and writing 'are' important.

Simon might argue – indeed, he would have to – that 'speech' and 'writing' are so closely related that they form a single idea. When that is the case a singular verb is unobjectionable. But such exceptions are better kept for things that are routinely combined – fish and chips, ham and eggs, law and order, the long and the short of it, etc. – and even then a plural verb would not be wrong.

2. *Errors involving 'or'.* Whereas *and* draws diverse elements together, *or* keeps them separate. When all the elements are singular, the verb should be singular too. Thus this sentence is wrong: 'A nod, wink or even a discreet tug of the ear aren't [make it 'isn't'] going to be the only sign language at the auction ...' (*Observer*). When all the elements are plural, the verb should be plural. When there is a mixture of singulars and plurals, the rule is to make the verb agree with the noun or pronoun nearest it. Consider: 'No photographs or television footage have been transmitted from the fleet for almost a week' (*The New York Times*). Because the nearest noun (footage) is singular, the verb should be 'has'. Had the two nouns been reversed, 'have' would have been correct.

The need to maintain agreement can sometimes lead to awkward constructions, particularly with pronouns. 'Is he or we wrong?' is grammatically perfect but perfectly awful. The solution would be to recast the sentence: 'Is he wrong or are we?'

A final point to note is that *or* influences not only the verb, but also subsequent nouns and pronouns. In the following sentence the correct forms are given in parentheses: 'While Paris, Mexico City, Hong Kong or Munich have (has) shown how their (its) underground systems (system) can become part of the pride of their (its) city ...' (*Observer*). A better alternative with that sentence, however, would be to change the *or* to *and* and leave the rest of it as it is.

3. *Errors caused by failure to keep track of antecedents*. Few people, it sometimes seems, have shorter attention spans than the average writer. All too often he will confidently set out with a plural or singular noun, become distracted by three or four intervening words and finish with a verb of the opposite number. Such was the case in each of the following (the correct forms are given in parentheses): 'Bank mortgages, which now account for most expensive property, is (are) not included in the figures ...' (*The Times*); 'The pressure of living and working on board 24 hours a day have (has) led to some strained relationships' (*Observer*); 'The incident demonstrates the reluctance with which some requests for interviews with ministers and senior officials is (are) met' (*The Times*).

Occasionally the writer does not even have the excuse of intervening matter: 'Meet Allan and Sondra Gotlieb, whose official titles may cause glazed looks but whose frankness have made them among the most popular, and unusual, diplomats in Washington' (*The New York Times*). Frankness 'have'?

And sometimes the intervening matter is so clearly unconnected with the main clause that the error is startling – all the more so when it is committed by as careful a user as Philip Howard: 'Populist (and its generic class of politics, populism) have recently been adopted as vogue words in British politics ...' (from *New Words for Old*). Make it 'has recently been adopted as a vogue word'. For a discussion, see PARENTHESES in the appendix.

4. *Errors involving personal pronouns*. This is a common type and one that points up the inadequacies both of English and of those who use it. Consider. 'If someone is learning a language for their job ...' (*Financial Times*). The problem is that the singular 'someone' and singular 'is' are being attached to the plural 'their'. Grammatically it is equivalent to saying 'No one were there' or 'They is studying French'.

The convention is to make the second pronoun 'his': 'If someone is learning a language for his job ...'. The obvious shortcoming is that this slights women. To avoid offending either them or grammar, you could make it 'his or her job', which is often cumbersome, or you could recast the sentence with a plural subject: 'People who are learning a language for their job ...'. I recommend recasting.

Too strict an application of the rule can result in incongruities – a point that evidently occurred to Philip Howard when he penned the following sentence in *Words Fail Me*: 'Nobody pretends any more (if they ever did) that economics is an exact science'. 'If they ever did' is strictly incorrect, but to change it to 'if he ever did' would unbalance the sense of the sentence. One way of preserving the grammar would be to make the subject plural: 'Few people pretend any more ...'. Another would be to replace 'they' with a singular pronoun: 'Nobody pretends any more (if anyone ever did) that economics is an exact science'. These solutions are not perhaps entirely satisfactory – but then neither, I think, is a grammatical error.

Whichever tack you take, you should at least be consistent throughout the sentence. Here is one in which the writer went to some lengths to get his pronouns right before abruptly self-destructing just short of home: 'Anyone who does confess to being a Sedaka fan does so with the guarded reluctance of one edging out of the closet, fearing he or she will be made immediate targets of fun' (*Sunday Times*). It should be 'an immediate target of fun'.

5. *Errors involving the word 'number'*. There is frequent confusion over whether to use a plural or singular verb with the noun *number*. Both of the following examples come from the same issue of *The Times*. Both are wrong. 'Mr Isaacs said a substantial number of households was inhabited today not by the conventional family group, but by single tenants'; 'A small, but increasing number of individuals is apparently buying secondhand British Rail coaches'. There is an easy way out of the confusion. Always make it 'The number was ...' but 'A number were ...'. The same rule applies to TOTAL.

▣ O ▣

oblivious. Both Fowler and Partridge insist that *oblivious* can mean only forgetful; you cannot be oblivious of something that you were not in the first place aware of. But in its broader sense of merely being unaware or impervious or unconscious, *oblivious* is now accepted by most dictionaries.

obsolescent. See OBSOLETE, OBSOLESCENT.

obsolete, obsolescent. Things that are no longer used or needed are *obsolete*. Things that are becoming obsolete are *obsolescent*.

obviate does not mean reduce, as is sometimes thought: 'A total redesign of the system should obviate complaints about its reliability' (*The Times*). It means to make unnecessary.

occur, take place. *Take place* is better reserved for scheduled events. When what is being described is accidental, *occur* is the better word, as it would have been here: 'The accident took place in driving rain' (*Guardian*).

oculist. See OPHTHALMOLOGIST, OCULIST, OPTOMETRIST, OPTICIAN.

on, upon. Although some journalists think there is, or ought to be, a distinction between these two, there isn't. The choice is sometimes dictated by idiom ('upon my word', 'on no account'), but in all other instances it is a matter of preference.

one. 'The makers claim that one in 14 people in the world are following the exploits of this new hero' (*Sunday Times*). In such constructions *one* should be singular. In effect the sentence is saying: 'Out of every 14 people in the world, one is following the exploits of this new hero'. A slightly trickier case appears here: 'An estimated one in three householders who are entitled to rate rebates are not claiming' (*The Times*). The first 'are' is correct, but the second is wrong. Again, it may help to invert the sentence: 'Of those householders who are entitled to rate rebates, one in every three is not claiming'.

one another. See EACH OTHER, ONE ANOTHER.

one of the, one of those. The problem here is similar to that discussed in the previous entry, but with the difference that here *one* does not govern the verb. Consider: 'Nott is actually one of those rare politicians who really doesn't mind what he says' (*Observer*). The operative word here is not *one* but *those*, as can be seen by inverting the sentence: 'Of those politicians who do not [not 'does not'] mind what they say, Nott is one'.

The mistake is a common one. Even Fowler makes it in his *Dictionary of Modern English Usage* when he writes: 'Prestige is one of the few words that has had an experience opposite to that described in "Worsened Words"'. It should be 'have had'. Just sixty pages earlier Fowler calls the error a frequent blunder. Which only goes to show.

It should also be noted that *one of the* is often verbose, as here: 'One of the reasons for all the excitement ...' (*Sunday Telegraph*); 'One of the members said he would almost certainly abstain' (*Guardian*). Why not simply make it 'one reason' and 'one member'?

one or more is plural. 'Inside each folder is one or more sheets of information' (cited by Bernstein) should be 'are one or more'.

only. Most of us when speaking, and too many of us when writing, are not notably discriminating about the positioning of *only* in sentences. In general, *only* ought to be attached to the word or phrase it is modifying and not set adrift, as here: 'The A Class bus only ran on Sundays' (*Observer*). As written, the sentence suggests that on other days of the week the bus did something else – perhaps flew? The writer would better have said that the bus 'ran only on Sundays' or 'on Sundays only'. The versatility of *only* can be seen in the fact that she might have placed it in any of five positions, four of which would have given the sentence quite separate meanings.

Oftentimes clarity and idiom are better served by bringing *only* to a more forward position ('This will only take a minute'; 'The victory can only be called a miracle'). But while those considerations might

109

grant us some latitude in the positioning of *only*, they shouldn't excuse ambiguity or sloppiness.

onstream. A pretentious variant for 'begin' or 'open', as in 'The factory will come onstream in 1983' (*Guardian*).

ophthalmologist, oculist, optometrist, optician. *Ophthalmologist* can frequently be seen misspelled – including on the windows of one very upmarket optical shop on Sloane Street in London. Note that it begins *oph-* and not *opth-* and that the first syllable is pronounced *off*, not *op*. Thus it is similar in both pronunciation and spelling to diphtheria, diphthong and naphtha, all of which are frequently misspelled and more frequently mispronounced.

Ophthalmologist and *oculist* both describe doctors who specialize in diseases of the eye. An *optometrist* is one who is trained to test eyes but is not a doctor. An *optician* is one who makes or sells corrective lenses.

opine. Quaint, stilted and better avoided.

opposite. See CONTRARY, CONVERSE, OPPOSITE, REVERSE.

opt, choose. Safire suggests that *opt* would be a more expressive word if we used it only to describe impulsive choices, and he is right. But it must be said that none of the leading dictionaries note or encourage such a distinction.

optician. See OPHTHALMOLOGIST, OCULIST, OPTOMETRIST, OPTICIAN.

optimistic, pessimistic. Both words are better used to describe a general outlook rather than a specific view, particularly with regard to the inconsequential. 'He was optimistic that he would find the missing book' would be better as 'was hopeful' or 'was confident'.

optimum does not mean greatest or fastest or biggest, as is sometimes thought. It describes the point at which conflicting considerations are reconciled. The optimum take-off speed of an aircraft, for instance, is the fastest speed at which it can take off without becoming unsafe or uncomfortable or wasteful of fuel.

optometrist. See OPHTHALMOLOGIST, OCULIST, OPTOMETRIST, OPTICIAN.

or. A frequent source of errors, even sometimes among the authorities, as here: 'Short words rather than long ones are naturally used in headlines: "investigation" becomes "probe"; "questioning" or "interrogation" become "quiz"; "examination" becomes "test" ' (Frederick T. Wood, *Current English Usage*). It should be 'becomes' all three times. For a discussion, see NUMBER (2).

oral, verbal. 'The 1960 understanding ... was a verbal understanding that was never written down' (*The New York Times*). Because *oral* can apply only to the spoken word, it would have been a better choice. *Verbal*, which can apply to both spoken and written words, is more usefully employed to distinguish between words and gestures or between words and substance. In the example above, however, neither word is necessary. It would be enough to say, 'The 1960 understanding was never written down'.

orientate is not incorrect, but it has nothing to recommend it over the shorter and simpler *orient*.

output. See INPUT, OUTPUT.

over. The notion that *over* is incorrect for 'more than' (as in 'over 300 people were present') is a widely held superstition. The stricture has been traced to Ambrose Bierce's *Write It Right* (1909), a usage book teeming with quirks and quiddities, most of which have since been discarded. There is no harm in preferring 'more than', but also no basis for insisting on it.

overly. 'Even granting that some past environmental arguments have been overly alarmist, the evidence against acid rain cannot be ignored' (*Chicago Tribune*). Making *over* into *overly* is a little like turning 'soon' into 'soonly'. Adding an -*ly* does nothing for *over* that it couldn't already do before. The convention in America is to attach *over* directly to the word it is modifying (overalarmist, overearnest), though in Britain hyphens are often used (over-careful, over-eager). When this becomes overinelegant or even over-inelegant, the alternative is to find another adverb: 'excessively' or 'unnecessarily' or even the admirably concise 'too'.

overweening. Arrogant or presumptuous expectations are overweening ones. There is no word *overweaning*.

ozone. Those people who like to refer to fresh air as ozone indulge in an expression that is not only a cliché but also a grossly inaccurate one. Although ozone is present in the air we breathe, it is a noxious substance and in all but the smallest quantities is lethal.

◉ P ◉

panacea is a universal remedy, a cure for all woes, and is not properly applied to a single shortcoming, as it was here: 'One of the best panaceas for the styling similarity of many modern cars seems to be the removal of the roof' (*Observer*).

parable. See FABLE, PARABLE, ALLEGORY, MYTH.

parameter. If you need a word to describe the relationship between a diameter and its conjugate in a conic section, or the points on a crystal at which the axes intercept a given plane, or a neat way of describing an aggregation of curves that are constant in one case but are otherwise varied, then *parameter* is the very thing. In all other instances I would venture that you were merely trying to impress us, like the US government official who called his study 'Evaluation and Parameterization of Stability and Safety Performance Characteristics of Two and Three Wheeled Vehicular Toys for Riding' (cited by Bernstein, who provides this translation: 'Why Children Fall Off Bicycles'). If all you mean is boundary or limit or perimeter, don't use *parameter*.

partially. See PARTLY, PARTIALLY.

partly, partially. Although they are often interchangeable, their meanings are slightly different. *Partially* means incompletely and *partly* means in part. 'The house was made partially of brick and partially of stone' would be better as 'partly of brick and partly of stone'. A separate danger with *partly* can be seen here: 'He was partly educated at Eton' (*The Times*), which prompted more than one wag to ask, 'Which part of him?'

past. See LAST, PAST, LATEST.

past history. 'The Tristan islanders talk of their past history with great pride' (*Sunday Times*). Hopelessly redundant, as are past records, past experience, past achievements and past precedents.

pastiche. 'This provided the occasion for a successful pastiche of that great Fonda film, Twelve Angry Men' (*The Times*). A pastiche is a work inspired by a variety of sources. The word the writer was groping for here was parody.

patois. See DIALECT, PATOIS.

peaceable, peaceful. *Peaceful* means tranquil and serene. *Peaceable* is a disposition towards the state of peacefulness.

peaceful. See PEACEABLE, PEACEFUL.

pedagogue. See PEDANT, PEDAGOGUE.

pedant, pedagogue. The two are synonyms. They describe someone who makes an ostentatious show of his learning or is dogmatically fussy about rules. Some dictionaries still give pedagogue as a synonym for teacher or educator, but its pejorative sense has effectively driven out the neutral one.

per. Generally, it is better not to use Latinisms when English phrases are available. 'Ten tons a year' is better than 'ten tons per annum'. It is also generally better not to mix Latin and English, as in 'ten tons per year'. But when avoidance of the Latin would result in clumsy constructions such as 'output a man a year', don't hesitate to use *per*.

percentage, proportion. The words are used inexactly when the relationship between two numbers isn't specified. 'This drug has proved of much value in a percentage of cases' (cited by Gowers) tells us next to nothing; it could mean 2 per cent or 98 per cent. Similarly, 'a ship of large proportions' would be better replaced by 'a ship of large dimensions' or simply 'a large ship'.

perpetrate, perpetuate. Occasionally confused. To perpetrate is to commit or perform. To perpetuate is to prolong or, literally, to make perpetual. Jack the Ripper perpetrated a series of murders. Those who write about him perpetuate his notoriety.

perpetuate. See PERPETRATE, PERPETUATE.

personal, personally. When it is necessary to indicate that a person is acting on his own rather than as a spokesman or that he is addressing people individually rather than collectively, *personal* and *personally* are unobjectionable. But usually the context makes that clear and the word is used without purpose, particularly in the expression 'personal friend'. Here the writer considerately draws our attention to the gratuitous use of the word by setting it off with equally gratuitous punctuation: 'He said that he "personally" wished that Princeton had selected a less harsh penalty' (*Chicago Tribune*).

personally. See PERSONAL, PERSONALLY.

perspicacity, perspicuity. *Perspicacity* means shrewdness and applies to people ('a perspicacious judge of character'). *Perspicuity* means easily understood and applies to things ('a perspicuous explanation'). But 'shrewd' for the first and 'clear' for the second are both briefer and more widely understood.

perspicuity. See PERSPICACITY, PERSPICUITY.

persuade. See CONVINCE, PERSUADE.

perturb. See DISTURB, PERTURB.

peruse. 'Those of us who have been idly perusing the latest flock of holiday brochures . . .' (*Guardian*). *Peruse* does not mean to look over. It means to read carefully. You cannot do it idly.

pessimistic. See OPTIMISTIC, PESSIMISTIC.

Philippines. Often misspelled. Note: one 'l', double 'p'. A native is a Filipino.

phrasal verbs. One of the more versatile aspects of English is its ability to give new shades of meaning to verbs by attaching adverbial particles to them to form what are called phrasal verbs. Thus we can *break up, break off, break down, break in, break into* and *break away from,* or *take to, take off, take in, take up, take down* or *take away.* Each expression conveys a nuance that would not be possible without the particle. But this capacity to grace a verb with a tail sometimes leads writers to add a particle where none is needed. Thus we get *head up, check out, lose out, pay off, try out, cut back, meet with, trigger off* and countless others. Sometimes such expressions, though strictly unnecessary, gain the force of idiom (*stand up, sit down, beat up*), but just as often they are merely a sign of verbosity or carelessness. In the following examples, the italicized words do nothing but consume space: 'Now the bureau proposes to sell *off* 280 acres ...' (*Time*); 'The time will be cut *down* to two hours within two years' (*Daily Telegraph*); 'A light snowfall did little to slow *down* the British advance' (*Sunday Times*).

pidgin. See CREOLE, PIDGIN.

Pittsburgh. Often misspelled *Pittsburg* outside North America. Since 1894, when Pittsburgh refused to comply with an order by the US Board on Geographic Names that all *-burghs* in America should become *-burgs* and all *-boroughs* should become *-boros*, it has been almost the only community in the country whose name ends with a *-gh*. There are Pittsburgs in California, Kansas, Kentucky, New Hampshire, Oklahoma and Texas, but the city in Pennsylvania is exceptionally and defiantly Pittsburgh.

pity. See EMPATHY, SYMPATHY, COMPASSION, PITY, COMMISERATION.

plan ahead. '[The] keys to success are to plan ahead, to choose manageable recipes and to cook in batches' (*The New York Times*). Always tautological. Would you plan behind?

pleonasm. See TAUTOLOGY, REDUNDANCY, PLEONASM, SOLECISM.

plethora is not merely a lot, it is an excessive amount, a superabundance. For a word that is often similarly misused, see SPATE.

plus. 'The end of the holiday season plus the fact that London banks remained closed were cited as factors contributing to the quiet trading day' (Associated Press). *Plus* is a preposition, equivalent to 'with the addition of', and not a conjunction, and therefore does not influence the number of the verb. Two and two are four, but two plus two is four. The example above should say 'was cited as a factor' or *plus* should be changed to 'and'.

podium. See LECTERN, PODIUM, DAIS, ROSTRUM.

pore, pour. Occasionally *pour* appears where *pore* is intended. As a verb, *pore* means to examine carefully ('He pored over the documents') or, more rarely, to meditate. *Pour* indicates a flow, either literally ('He poured the water down the drain') or figuratively ('The rioters poured through the streets').

position. Often a sign of verbosity. 'They now find themselves in a position where they have to make a choice' (*Daily Telegraph*) would be immeasurably better as 'They now have to make a choice'.

possible is wrongly followed by 'may' in constructions such as the following: 'It is possible that she may decide to go after all' (*Daily Telegraph*). Make it either 'It is possible that she will decide to go after all' or 'She may decide to go after all'. Together the two words are unnecessary.

pour. See PORE, POUR.

practicable. See PRACTICAL, PRACTICABLE.

practical, practicable. Anything that can be done *and* is worth doing is practical. Anything that can be done, whether or not it is worth doing, is practicable.

practically. See VIRTUALLY, PRACTICALLY.

practice, practise. 'U.S. usage ... spells both noun and verb *practise*, as with *license*' (Harry Fieldhouse, *Everyman's Good English Guide*). That is a common misconception outside North America. In the United States, *practice* is in fact always spelled with a 'c': *practice, practiced, practicing.* In British usage, the noun is spelled *practice* ('Practice makes perfect') and the verb *practise* ('You must practise your piano lessons').

practise. See PRACTICE, PRACTISE.

precautionary measure. Why not simply *precaution*?

precipitant, precipitate, precipitous. All three come from the Latin *praecipitare* ('to throw headlong'). *Precipitous* means very steep; cliff faces are precipitous. *Precipitant* and *precipitate* both indicate a headlong rush and are almost indistinguishable in meaning. But *precipitant* tends to emphasize the abruptness of the rush and *precipitate* the rashness of it. The most common error is to use *precipitous* to describe actions ('his precipitous departure from the Cabinet'). *Precipitous* can describe only physical characteristics.

precipitate. See PRECIPITANT, PRECIPITATE, PRECIPITOUS.

precipitous. See PRECIPITANT, PRECIPITATE, PRECIPITOUS.

precondition. 'There are, however, three preconditions to be met before negotiations can begin' (*Guardian*). *Pre-* adds nothing to the meaning of *condition* and should be excised. *Preplanning* is similarly superfluous.

premises. 'His business premises was raided by environmental health officers and police' (*Daily Telegraph*). *Premises* is plural. There is no such thing as a business premise.

prepositions at end of sentences. Anyone who believes that it is wrong to end a sentence with a preposition – and there are still some who do – is about a century out of touch. The 'rule' was enshrined by one Robert Lowth, an eighteenth-century Bishop of London and gentleman grammarian. In his wildly idiosyncratic but curiously influential *Short Introduction to English Grammar*, Lowth urged his readers not to end sentences with prepositions if they could decently avoid it. Too many people took him too literally and for a century and a half the notion held sway. Today, happily, it is universally condemned as a ridiculous affectation. Indeed, there are many sentences where the preposition could scarcely come anywhere but at the end: 'This bed hasn't been slept in'; 'What is the world coming to?'; 'I don't know what you are talking about'.

prescribe, proscribe. *Prescribe* means to set down as a rule or guide. *Proscribe* means to denounce or prohibit. If you get bronchitis, your doctor may prescribe antibiotics and proscribe smoking.

present, presently. Like 'current' and 'currently', these two are often vacuous, as here: 'A new factory, which is presently under construction in Manchester, will add to capacity' (*The Times*). *Presently* adds nothing and should be deleted.

presently. See PRESENT, PRESENTLY.

pressurize. 'Esso accused him of trying to pressurize the Prime Minister into bailing out his petrochemical plant ...' (*The Times*). Gases, liquids and foods can be pressurized (i.e., compacted into containers under pressure). People are pressed or pressured.

prestigious. Some writers continue to insist that *prestigious* can properly describe only that which is deceptive or illusory because the word comes from the Latin *praestigeae*, meaning 'juggler's tricks'. That meaning has in fact been dying since the early nineteenth century.

To try to defend the stricter meaning now on grounds of etymology is rather like insisting that 'silly' must, because of its derivation, mean happy and holy or that a villain is someone who works in a villa or that 'nice' should describe only those who are ignorant and unaware. Meanings change. When those changes appear to be for the worse, we might fairly try to get in their way. But with *prestigious* that would be neither practical nor desirable. People have been broadening its sense for almost 200 years, not as an act of defiance against the grammarians, but simply because the newer meaning was felt to be needed and the older was not. Today the original sense of the word is effectively dead everywhere but in the hearts of a scattering of purists. Most dictionaries now give the broader sense of 'worthy of esteem' as the only one, including (since 1976) one of the word's last defenders, *The Concise Oxford*.

presumptive, presumptuous. The first is often used when the second is intended. *Presumptuous* means impudent and inclined to take liberties, or excessively bold and forthright. *Presumptive* means giving grounds to presume and is primarily a technical term. The wrong use is seen here: 'She considered the question with the equanimity of someone who has long since become immune to presumptive prying' (*Sunday Telegraph*). It should be *presumptuous*.

presumptuous. See PRESUMPTIVE, PRESUMPTUOUS.

prevaricate, procrastinate. Curiously, but frequently, confused. *Prevaricate* means to speak or act evasively, to stray from the truth. *Procrastinate* means to put off doing.

prevent often appears incorrectly in sentences such as this: 'They tried to prevent him leaving'. It should be: 'They tried to prevent his leaving' or 'they tried to prevent him from leaving'. (See GERUNDS (2).)

preventative is not incorrect, but *preventive* is preferred.

prima facie. See A PRIORI, PRIMA FACIE.

principal, principle. *Principle* means fundamental and is usually applied to fundamental beliefs or truths ('It's not the money, it's the principle') or to fundamental understandings ('They have signed an agreement in principle'). It is always a noun. *Principal* can be a noun meaning chief or of first importance ('He is the school's principal') or an adjective with the same meaning ('The principal reason for my going ...').

principle. See PRINCIPAL, PRINCIPLE.

prior to. See BEFORE, PRIOR TO.

pristine. '... the campaign waged by the anti-repeal forces was pristine clean' (cited by Kingsley Amis in *The State of the Language*). *Pristine* does not mean spotless, as was apparently intended above, or brand new, as is frequently intended elsewhere. It means original or primeval or in a state virtually unchanged from the original.

procrastinate. See PREVARICATE, PROCRASTINATE.

prodigal does not mean wandering or given to running away, a sense sometimes wrongly inferred from the Biblical story of the Prodigal Son. It means recklessly wasteful or extravagant.

prognosis. See DIAGNOSIS, PROGNOSIS.

prohibit. See FORBID, PROHIBIT.

prone, prostrate, recumbent, supine. *Supine* means lying face upwards (it may help to remember that a supine person is on his spine). *Prone* and *prostrate* are regarded by most authorities – but by no means all – as meaning lying face downwards. *Prostrate* should, in any case, suggest throwing oneself down, either in submission or for protection; someone who is merely asleep shouldn't be called prostrate. *Recumbent* means lying flat in any position, but, like repose, it should indicate a position of ease and comfort.

For the other sense of *prone*, see LIABLE, LIKELY, APT, PRONE.

proper nouns. Many writers are strangely at a loss when confronted with the challenge of finding a plural form for a proper noun, as in the two following examples, both from *The Times* and both wrong: 'This is the first of a new series about the Rush's'; 'The two Germanies are hoping to establish closer links at the summit'. The rule is simple. An *s* should be added to those names that will take it: the Smiths, the Browns, the Lowes, the two Germanys. Names that end in *s*, *sh*, *ch* or *x* should be given an *es*: the Foxes, the Joneses, the Rushes. The rule is invariable with Anglo-Saxon surnames, but there are a few exceptions with other proper nouns, among them *Mercuries*, *Ptolemies*, *Rockies* and *Alleghenies*.

prophecy, prophesy. The first is the noun, the second the verb: 'I prophesy war; that is my prophecy'.

prophesy. See PROPHECY, PROPHESY.

proportion. See PERCENTAGE, PROPORTION.

proscribe. See PRESCRIBE, PROSCRIBE.

prostrate. See PRONE, PROSTRATE, RECUMBENT, SUPINE.

protagonist. Literally the word means 'first actor' (from the Greek *protos* and *agonistes*) and by extension may be applied to the principal person in any affair. But it cannot properly apply to more than one person, as was thought here: 'During the anomalous decade of the 1930s the three protagonists of this book each played out important – if somewhat ephemeral – roles ...' (*The New York Times*). The word is not the opposite of *antagonist*, of which there can be any number.

Nor does it have anything to do with the Latin *pro-* (meaning 'for' or 'on behalf of'). A protagonist may champion a cause – and in practice often does – but that isn't implicit in the word.

prototype is the word for an original that serves as a model for later products of its type. Thus first prototype, experimental prototype and model prototype are all usually redundant.

proved, proven. 'Sizewell – a case not proven' (*New Scientist* headline). *Proved* is the preferred past participle, but there are two exceptions. One is in references to Scottish law, where there is a verdict of *not proven*, and the other is in the expression *proven reserves*, as in 'The company has proven reserves of 20 million barrels of oil in the Brent field'.

proven. See PROVED, PROVEN.

proverbial is wrongly used when there is no connection with a proverb, as here: 'He stuck up the proverbial two fingers' (*Daily Mail*).

provided, providing. Most authorities consider the first preferable to the second in constructions such as 'He agreed to come provided he could get the day off work', but either would be correct. 'If' is often better still.

providing. See PROVIDED, PROVIDING.

purport means to give the appearance or idea of. Two points need to be noted when using it:
    1. It should not be used passively. 'The relics are purported to come from Etruria' should be 'The relics purport to come from Etruria'.
    2. It should apply only to things or, more rarely, to a person or persons considered as a phenomenon. Fowler cites this as a legitimate use: 'The Gibeonites sent men to Joshua purporting to be ambassadors from a far country'. And he cites this as an illegitimate one: 'She purports to find a close parallel between the Aeschylean Trilogy and The Ring ...'.

purposefully. See PURPOSELY, PURPOSEFULLY.

purposely, purposefully. The first means intentionally; the second means with an objective in mind. 'He purposely nudged me' means it was no accident. 'He purposefully nudged me' means he did it for a purpose – perhaps to draw my attention to something.

put an end to is an expression to which we should do just that. Make it 'stop'.

pyrrhic victory is not, as is sometimes thought, a hollow triumph. It is one won at great cost.

▣ Q ▣

quandary. Not *quandry*.

quantum. '"It gives us the opportunity to make a quantum leap in the growth of our business," he said yesterday' (*The Times*). A quantum jump is not, as is often thought, a huge one. It is almost the opposite. It describes a significant but really rather small advance from one plane to another. If we use the analogy of a man standing at the foot of a stairway, if he made a quantum leap, he would not bound to the top, but would merely hop on to the first step. Anyone who understands theoretical physics will no doubt consider that a hopelessly simplistic interpretation, but then anyone who understands theoretical physics is unlikely to misuse quantum. For the rest of us, it is enough to say that the word is much too technical to be employed casually.

query, inquiry, enquiry. A query is a single question. An inquiry or enquiry may be a single question or an extensive investigation. Either spelling is correct, but *inquiry* is preferred by most dictionaries in both Britain and America.

question, leading and **begging the.** Both expressions are commonly misunderstood. A leading question is not a challenging or hostile one, but rather the opposite. It is one designed to help the person being questioned make the desired response. A lawyer who says to a witness, 'You didn't see the murder, did you?' has asked a leading question.

Begging the question does not mean evading a straight answer, as was thought here: 'But to say that comedians don't tell spouse jokes simply because they're not married begs the question to a large extent' (*Boston Globe*). It means to use as a basis of proof something that itself needs proving. If I say that the House of Lords should be abolished because it is a worthless institution, I must first prove that it has no worth. The expression means arguing in a circle.

question mark has become an overworked embellishment of the expression 'a question hanging over', which is itself tattered from overuse. Consider: 'The case of Geoffrey Prime ... has raised a question mark over the competence of British security' (*The Times*). Would you say of a happy event that it had raised an exclamation mark over the proceedings or that a pause in negotiations had a comma hanging over them?

quite. Because *quite* means positively or completely, some authorities object to its use where it creates a redundancy, as in 'quite all right' and 'quite similar'. Such expressions are perhaps a little quaint and certainly better avoided in formal writing, but equally they could be defended as idiomatic.

quorum. The plural is *quorums*, not *quora*.

quoting in fragments is often a timid and needless affectation, as here: 'He said that profits in the second half would be "good"' (*The Times*). Quoted matter, especially when in fragments, should have some justification. When the word or words being quoted are unusual or unexpected or particularly descriptive ('It was, he said, a "lousy" performance') or are otherwise notable, the use of punctuation marks is always unobjectionable and usually advisable. But to set off a neutral and workaday word like 'good' in the example above is un-warranted. Here is a sentence in which the second set of quotation marks is as unobjectionable as the first is fatuous: 'Dietz agreed that loneliness was a "feature" of Hinckley's life but he added that studies have shown that "loneliness is as common as the common cold in winter"' (*Washington Post*).

A separate, grammatical danger of quoting in fragments is seen here: 'Although he refused to be drawn on the future of the factory, Sir Kenneth said that the hope of finding a buyer "was not out of the question"' (*The Times*). Sir Kenneth would have said, 'That *is* not out of the question', not 'That *was* not out of the question'. In quoted material, even when fragmentary, the tense must be preserved.

A final problem is the tendency of some writers to put the words of one person into the mouths of many, as here: 'Witnesses at the scene said that there was "a tremendous bang and then all hell broke loose"' (*Guardian*). The comment should be paraphrased or attributed to just one witness.

▣ R ▣

rack, wrack. 'It noted that its reserves constituted a very slender margin of safety in a world increasingly wracked by political risks' (*The Times*). *Wrack* means wreck and almost never appears except in the expression 'wrack and ruin' – which is, incidentally, both a redundancy and a cliché. *Rack*, the word intended in the quotation above, means to put under strain. The expressions are 'nerve-racking' and 'to rack one's brains'.

raining cats and dogs. No one knows what inspired this expression, but it is worth noting that in 1738, when Swift condemned it, it was already hackneyed.

rapt, wrapped. 'Rapt in thought' occasionally appears as 'wrapped in thought', which is incorrect. *Rapt* is the past participle of an extinct verb, *rap*. It means engrossed, absorbed, enraptured.

razed. 'Zurich's Autonomous Youth Centre was razed to the ground yesterday' (*The Times*). The ground is the only place that a building can be razed to. It is enough to say: 'Zurich's Autonomous Youth Centre was razed yesterday'.

razzamatazz. See RAZZMATAZZ, RAZZAMATAZZ.

razzmatazz, razzamatazz. Often misspelled, as here: 'For them the promotional razamataz is much more about holding on to what they have' (*The Times*). *The Concise Oxford* gives either of the above spellings. *The American Heritage Dictionary* curiously does not treat the word at all.

reaction is better reserved for spontaneous responses ('He reacted to the news by fainting'). It should not be used to indicate responses marked by reflection, as it was here: 'He said he could give no reaction until he had had time to consider the proposal' (*Daily Telegraph*). Response, reply or answer would be better words.

reason. A few authorities are oddly inconsistent – unreasonable even – on the uses of *reason*. Fowler, for instance, maintains that 'reason is because' is a tautology. Thus, 'The reason he went inside is because it was raining' should be 'The reason he went inside is it was raining' or, preferably, 'He went inside because it was raining'. On this Fowler is undoubtedly right. Yet he raises no objection to 'reason why', which often looks equally tautological, and in fact frequently employs the expression himself, as here: 'No doubt the reason why we substitute the definite article for the indefinite ...'. So does Gowers in *The Complete Plain Words*: 'Perhaps the reason why it is so difficult to restrain the word to its "correct" meaning ...'. The Evanses defend both 'reason why' and 'reason is because' as idiomatic, but it does bear pointing out that 'why' in the previous two quotations could be deleted without loss, just as 'the reason' could be dispensed with here: 'If they don't, great bands of shareholders will want to know the reason why' (*Daily Mail*).

rebut, refute. 'Banks refute Lever arguments' (*Times* headline, first edition); 'Banks rebut Lever arguments' (*Times* headline, second edition). The writer of the first headline, like many other people, thought that *refute* means simply to deny or oppose an allegation. He was wrong. Someone else, aware that *refute* is a contentious word and carries a more specific meaning, changed it to *rebut*. He too was quite wrong. *Refute* means to show conclusively that an allegation is wrong. *Rebut* means to disprove an allegation and to answer in kind. If I call you an uneducated bumpkin and you show me your university diploma, then you have refuted my charge. If in addition you say, 'But you, sir, are stupid beyond measure', you have rebutted it. If all you do is deny the allegation, then neither word applies.

reconstruction. 'The play is a dramatic reconstruction of what might happen when a combination of freak weather conditions threatens to flood London' (*The Times*). It shouldn't need saying, but you cannot reconstruct an event that has not yet happened. *Re-* is often prefixed to words where it adds no meaning, most notably 'recopy' and 'reduplicate'.

recumbent. See PRONE, PROSTRATE, RECUMBENT, SUPINE.

reduce. See DEPLETE, REDUCE.

redundancy. See TAUTOLOGY, REDUNDANCY, PLEONASM, SOLECISM,

refute. See REBUT, REFUTE.

regretfully, regrettably. The first means with feelings of regret: 'Regretfully they said their farewells'. The second means unfortunately: 'Regrettably I didn't have enough money to buy it'.

regrettably. See REGRETFULLY, REGRETTABLY.

reiterate. Since *iterate* means repeat, *reiterate* ought to mean re-repeat, but it doesn't. It too just means repeat. That is perhaps fortunate; otherwise the following sentence would in effect be saying re-re-repeat: 'She hopes her message to the markets, reiterated again at the weekend, will be enough to prevent the pound sliding further' (*The Times*). 'Again' is always superfluous with *re-* words (reiterate, repeat, reaffirm) and should be deleted.

relatively, like comparatively, should not be used unless there is some indication of a comparison or relationship. As often as not, the word can be removed without loss, as here: 'The group has taken the relatively bold decision to expand its interests in Nigeria' (*The Times*).

relevant. See GERMANE, RELEVANT, MATERIAL.

relieve. See ALLAY, ALLEVIATE, ASSUAGE, RELIEVE.

repel, repulse. Not to be confused. *Repulse* means to drive back: 'The army repulsed the enemy's attack'. It shouldn't be confused with *repulsive*, meaning to cause repugnance. *Repel* is the word for causing squeamishness or distaste: 'The idea of eating squid repelled her'.

replica. In art, a replica is a duplicate made by the original artist. In other contexts it means an almost exact copy – one built to the same dimensions and using the same materials. To use the word when you might better use model, miniature, copy or reproduction devalues it, as here: 'Using nothing but plastic Lego toy bricks, they have painstakingly constructed replicas of some of the world's most famous landmarks' (*Sunday Times*).

repulse. See REPEL, REPULSE.

restaurateur, not *restauranteur*.

restive. Originally the word meant balky, refusing to move or budge, but through confusion has come more and more to be used as a synonym for restless. Most dictionaries now recognize both meanings, but if the word is to have any value it should contain at least some suggestion of resistance. A crowd of protesters may grow restive upon the arrival of mounted police, but a person sleeping fitfully would be better described as restless.

revenge. See AVENGE, REVENGE.

reverse. See CONTRARY, CONVERSE, OPPOSITE, REVERSE.

revert back is always redundant: 'If no other claimant can be found, the right to the money will revert back to her' (*Daily Telegraph*). Delete *back*.

rostrum. See LECTERN, PODIUM, DAIS, ROSTRUM.

◉ S ◉

sacrilegious. Sometimes misspelled *sacreligious* on the mistaken assumption that *religious* is part of the word. It isn't.

salutary. See HEALTHY, HEALTHFUL, SALUTARY.

sarcasm. See IRONY, SARCASM.

scrutiny. The word is a magnet for superfluous adjectives, as here: 'Mr Shultz's activities are expected to attract close scrutiny' (*The New York Times*). *Scrutiny* means to give careful attention, so close or careful scrutiny is redundant. Bernstein, who often cautioned against the solecism, actually commits it himself in *The Careful Writer* when he says: 'Under close scrutiny, many constructions containing the word "not" make no sense ...'. In the same volume he unwittingly underlines the point by urging writers to 'scrutinize thoughtfully every phrase that eases itself almost mechanically onto the paper'. Had he followed his own advice, he no doubt would have deleted 'thoughtfully' there.

scurrilous, which is most often encountered in the expression 'a scurrilous attack', does not mean specious or disreputable, though those senses are often intended. It means grossly obscene or abusive. An attack must be exceedingly harsh to be scurrilous.

second largest and other similar comparisons often lead writers astray: 'Japan is the second largest drugs market in the world after the United States' (*The Times*). Not quite. It is the largest drugs market in the world after the United States or it is the second largest drugs market in the world.

self-confessed, as in 'a self-confessed murderer', is tautological. *Confessed* alone is enough.

sensual, sensuous. The words are only broadly synonymous. *Sensual* applies to a person's baser instincts as distinguished from reason. It

130

should always hold connotations of sexual allure and lust. *Sensuous* was coined by Milton to avoid those connotations and to suggest instead the idea of being alive to sensations. It should be used when there is no suggestion of sexual arousal.

sensuous. See SENSUAL, SENSUOUS.

servicing. See SERVING, SERVICING.

serving, servicing. 'Cable TV could be servicing half the country within five years' (*Daily Mail*). Bulls service cows; mechanics service faulty machinery. But cable TV systems serve the country. *Servicing* is better reserved for the idea of installation and maintenance. *Serve* is the better word for describing things that are of general and continuing benefit.

shall, will. Authorities have been trying to pin down the vagaries of *shall* and *will* since the seventeenth century, and most have come a cropper. In *The King's English*, the Fowler brothers devote twenty pages to the distinctions. The gist of what they have to say is that either you understand the distinctions instinctively or you don't; that if you don't, you probably never will; and that if you do, you don't need to be told anyway.

The rule most frequently propounded is that to express simple futurity you should use *shall* in the first person and *will* in the second and third persons, and to express determination (or volition) you should do the reverse. But by that rule Churchill committed a grammatical blunder when he vowed: 'We shall fight in the fields and in the streets, we shall fight in the hills; we shall never surrender'. As did MacArthur when he said at Corregidor: 'I shall return'. As have all those who have ever sung 'We Shall Overcome'.

The simple fact is that whether you use *shall* or *will* in a given instance depends very much on your age and your birthplace and the emphasis with which you mean to express yourself. The English tend to use *shall* more frequently and more specifically than do the Scots or Irish or Americans, but even in England the distinctions are quickly fading and by no means fixed.

To try to formulate rules here would be a dangerous and perhaps impossible exercise for an Englishman. For an American, it would be folly of the first order.

shambles properly describes a scene of carnage (it was formerly a word for a slaughterhouse). We might excuse its more common sense of chaos or disorderliness ('The second act of the play was a shambles') when used conversationally or jocularly, but as a serious and considered term it is otiose when there is no suggestion of bloodshed, as here: 'The Colonial Secretary denied ... that the conference on the future of Malta had been a shambles' (cited by Fowler).

should like. 'I should have liked to have seen it' should be 'I should like to have seen it' or 'I should have liked to see it'. (For American usage read *would* for *should*.)

since. 'She gave strong support to the visions of the late Bernard Kilgore and the other executives and editors who operated the Journal and Dow Jones since World War II' (*Wall Street Journal*); 'Since April the Inland Revenue stopped giving immediate tax refunds to those who were unlucky enough to become unemployed' (*The Times*). *Since* indicates action starting at a specified time in the past and continuing up to the present. The verbs in sentences in which it appears must also indicate action that is still continuing – that is, they should be 'have operated' in the first instance and 'has stopped' in the second. As written, both sentences border on the illiterate.

situation. Residents of Britain owe a great debt to the magazine *Private Eye* for mocking the gratuitous use of *situation* into near obscurity through its Ongoing Situations column. The usage is, however, still common in the United States: 'The exchange ... had failed to be alert to the potential of a crisis situation as it developed' (*The New York Times*). Delete *situation*.

sleight of hand, not slight of hand. *Sleight*, meaning dextrous or deceptive, comes from the Old Norse *sloegdh*, and *slight*, meaning slender or frail, comes from the Old Norse *slettr*, but they have nothing else in common except their pronunciation.

solecism. See TAUTOLOGY, REDUNDANCY, PLEONASM, SOLECISM.

sometime, some time. Most often it is one word: 'They will arrive sometime tomorrow'. But when *some* is used as an adjective equivalent to 'a short' or 'a long' or 'an indefinite', it should be two words: 'The announcement was made some time ago'.

Three considerations may help you to make the distinction:

1. *Some time* as two words is usually preceded by a preposition (for some time, at some time) or followed by a helping word (some time ago).

2. When two words, *some time* can be replaced with an equivalent expression. *Sometime* cannot. 'Some time ago' can be replaced with 'a short time ago', 'a long time ago', etc.

3. When spoken, there is greater stress placed on *time* when *some time* is two words.

In practice the distinctions cause less trouble to users of English than to those who try to explain them.

some time. See SOMETIME, SOME TIME.

sort. 'Mr Hawkins said that Mr Webster was a pretty seasoned operator when it came to dealing with these sort of things' (*The Times*). Make it 'this sort of thing' or 'these sorts of things'.

spate. 'The recent spate of takeover offers has focused attention on the sector' (*Observer*). The reference here was to half a dozen takeover offers – a flurry. *Spate* should be used to describe a torrent. See also PLETHORA.

spit. See EXPECTORATE, SPIT.

split compound verbs. Some writers, apparently inspired by a misguided dread of the split infinitive (which see), are equally fastidious about not breaking up compound verbs, whatever the cost to idiom and clarity. (A compound verb is one made up of two elements, such as *has been*, *will go*, *is doing*.) The practice is particularly rife in America, where sentences like the following are more or less standard on many papers: 'It is yet to be demonstrated that a national magazine effectively can cover cable listings' (*Wall Street Journal*); 'Hitler never has been portrayed with more credibility' (*Boston Globe*); 'It always has stood as one of the last great events in amateur sports' (*Los Angeles Times*).

It cannot be stressed vigorously enough that there is no harm whatever in placing an adverb between the two elements of a compound verb. It contravenes no rule and flouts no authority. It is usually the natural place – and frequently the only place – for an adverb to go.

Those writers who so scrupulously avoid offending the integrity of a compound verb must be unaware that they disregard their self-imposed rule every time they write 'He is not going' or 'Have you been waiting long?' or 'Is it raining?' Otherwise they would almost certainly change those sentences to 'He is going not' and 'Have been waiting long you?' and 'Is raining it?' That would hardly be more illogical and contorted than 'effectively can cover' and 'always has stood'.

There are, of course, many instances in which the adverb can happily stand apart from the compound verb – 'He was working feverishly'; 'You must go directly to bed'; 'The time is passing quickly' – but forcibly evicting it for the sake of making words conform to some arbitrary pattern does a disservice to English.

split infinitives. It is probably safe to say that the number of people who would never split an infinitive is a good deal larger than the number of people who actually know what an infinitive is and does.

That may account for the number of misconceptions that litter the issue. One is the belief that the split infinitive is a grammatical error. It's not. If it is an error at all, it is a rhetorical fault – a question of style – and not a grammatical one. Another is the curiously persistent belief that the split infinitive is widely condemned. That too is untrue. No one would ever argue that a split infinitive is a good thing, but it is certainly no worse than some of the excruciating constructions foisted on us by those who regard it with an almost pathological dread. Consider these three sentences, all from *The Times* and all with a certain ring of desperation about them: 'The agreement is unlikely significantly to increase the average price'; 'It was a nasty snub for the Stock Exchange and caused it radically to rethink its ideas'; 'The education system had failed adequately to meet the needs of industry and commerce, he said'.

The problem in each instance is one of a simple conflict between the needs of the infinitive and the needs of the adverb. The natural position for the two elements of a full infinitive is together: 'He proceeded *to climb* the ladder'. With adverbs the most natural position is, very generally, just before the verb: 'He *slowly* climbed the ladder'. The problem of the split infinitive occurs when the two are brought together: 'He proceeded *to slowly climb* the ladder'.

The authorities are almost unanimously agreed that there is no reason to put the needs of the infinitive above those of the adverb.

In practice the problem can usually be circumvented. Most adverbs are portable and can be moved to a position from which they can perform their function without interfering with the infinitive. In the example above, for instance, we could say: 'He proceeded to climb the ladder slowly' or 'Slowly he proceeded to climb the ladder'. But that is not to say that there is any grammatical basis for regarding the infinitive as inviolable.

When moving the adverb produces ambiguity or, to use Fowler's words, patent artificiality, the cure is at least as bad as the disease. Consider again one of the *Times* sentences: 'The education system had failed adequately to meet the needs of industry, he said'. The adverb here is clearly out of place. As written, the sentence suggests that the education system had set out to fail and had done so adequately. Partridge cites this sentence: 'Our object is to further cement trade relations'. Moving the adverb could only result in clumsiness ('further to cement') or ambiguity ('to cement further'). Bernstein cites these constructions, all crying out to be left alone: 'to more than double', 'to at least maintain', 'to all but insure'.

If you wish you may remain blindly intolerant of the split infinitive, but you should do so with the understanding that you are without the support of a single authority. Even Partridge, that most deeply conservative of scholars, is against you. He says: 'Avoid the split infinitive wherever possible; but if it is the clearest and most natural construction, use it boldly. The angels are on our side'.

spoonfuls, not spoonsful or spoons full. Bernstein cites the following: 'Now throw in two tablespoons full of chopped parsley and cook ten minutes more. The quail ought to be tender by then'. As Bernstein says, 'Never mind the quail; how are we ever going to get those tablespoons tender?'.

stalemate. 'Senators Back Rise in Proposed Oil Tax as Stalemate Ends' (*New York Times* headline). Stalemates don't end. 'Deadlock' would have been better.

stanch, staunch. 'He showed how common soldiers ... had fought their fears, staunched their wounds and met their deaths' (*Newsweek*). Although *staunch* is given as an acceptable variant by most dictionaries, *stanch* is the preferred spelling for the verb. As an adjective, *staunch* is the only spelling ('a staunch supporter').

stationary, stationery. The difference in spelling has been observed for centuries, though etymologically there isn't any basis for it. Both words come from the Latin *stationarius* and both originally meant 'standing in a fixed position'. Stationers were tradesmen, usually booksellers, who sold their wares from a fixed spot (as opposed to itinerants). Today in Britain stationery is still sold by stationers, which makes the misspelling there less excusable, if no less frequent. It applies not just to writing paper and envelopes but to all office materials. Strictly speaking, paper clips and pencils are stationery.

stationery. See STATIONARY, STATIONERY.

staunch. See STANCH, STAUNCH.

straitjacket. Often misspelled, as here: 'She was beaten, put into a home-made straightjacket and fed mustard sandwiches' (*Standard*). *Strait* means confined and restricted, as in 'straitened circumstances'. Apart from the pronunciation, it has nothing in common with 'straight'.

strata, stratum. One stratum, two strata. See DATA.

stratum. See STRATA, STRATUM.

strike action has, distressingly and perplexingly, become almost the invariable expression in Britain, as here: 'The report says 2,500 engineers and technicians are threatening strike action because of the crisis' (*Sunday Times*). Why not 'are threatening to strike'?

subjunctives. The subjunctive, one of the four moods of verbs, is falling increasingly into disuse, at least as a recognizable form. Partridge was perhaps its last defender. In *Usage and Abusage* he insisted that 'Although he die now, his name will live' was vastly superior to 'Although he dies now, his name will live'. But constructions of the first sort are almost never encountered now and no other authority argues for them. The subjunctive does survive, however, in three other types of construction. These are:

    1. In certain stock phrases: 'be that as it may', 'God forbid', 'far be it from me', 'come what may', 'so be it', 'as it were' and many others. These are well established as idioms and normally cause no trouble.

2. In expressions involving suppositions or hypotheses: 'If I were you, I wouldn't go'. These are treated under IF and WILL, WOULD.

3. Following verbs of command or request. This problem scarcely exists in America, where this form of the subjunctive has always been part of the native speech, but is endlessly repeated in Britain. In the following instances the correct form is given in parentheses: 'The Senate has now rewritten the contract insisting that the Navy considers (consider) other options' (*Daily Mail*); 'Opec's monitoring committee has recommended that the cartel's output ceiling remains (remain) unchanged' (*The Times*); 'No wonder the Tory Party turned him down as a possible candidate, suggesting he went away (go away) and came back (come back) with a better public image' (*Guardian*). In each of those it might help to imagine placing a 'should' just before the problem verb (e.g., 'suggesting he should go away'). Gowers in fact suggests that such sentences would be better in British usage if 'should' were written in.

substitute can be followed only by 'for'. You substitute one thing for another. If you find yourself following the word with 'by' or 'with' or any other preposition, you should choose another word.

subsume. As Safire notes, the word has a great appeal to those who cannot resist a pretentious variation, but it is also frequently misused. It does not mean to consume or make subordinate, as is often thought. It means to be considered as part of a greater whole. *The Shorter OED* gives this example: 'In the judgment "all horses are animals", the conception "horses" is subsumed under that of "animals"'. Does that sound like a word you really need?

successfully. 'Japanese researchers have successfully developed a semi-conductor chip made of gallium arsenide' (*Associated Press*). It was thoughtful of the writer to tell us that the researchers had not unsuccessfully developed a gallium arsenide chip, but also unnecessary. Delete *successfully*.

supersede. Probably more people visit Antarctica each year than spell *supersede* correctly. Those who habitualy make it *supercede* may take some comfort in knowing that the word caused just as much trouble to the ancient Romans, who often couldn't decide between *supersedere* and *supercedere*. *Supercede* was in early English usage an acceptable variant, but no longer.

supine. See PRONE, PROSTRATE, RECUMBENT, SUPINE.

surrounded. 'Often shrouded by fog and surrounded on three sides by surging seas, the gray stone lighthouse looms like a medieval keep' (*Time*); 'The waterworks is right in the middle of suburban Sutton and completely surrounded by houses' (*Sunday Express*). The first usage is wrong, the second superfluous. If you are not completely encircled, you are not surrounded. *Surrounded* should be changed in the first example to cut off or bordered and 'completely' should be deleted from the second.

sympathy. See EMPATHY, SYMPATHY, COMPASSION, PITY, COMMISERATION.

◉ **T** ◉

take place. See OCCUR, TAKE PLACE.

target. To most people there are really only two things you can do with a target: you can hit it or you can miss it. But for journalists and politicians, targets are things to be achieved, attained, exceeded, expanded, reduced, obtained, met, beaten, overtaken and metaphorically shaken to bits. As a consequence their statements are often a little absurd and more than a little ambiguous, as here: 'More welcome news came with the announcement that the public sector borrowing requirement now appears likely to undershoot its target for the full year' (*The Times*). An archer who undershoots his target will be chagrined. A politician will apparently be pleased. The reader may merely be confused.

To protest too much is quibbling – in practice, target often is the most efficient word for conveying a point concisely, even if the literal meaning is sometimes a bit strained – but it is worth seeing if 'objective' or 'plan' wouldn't work as well.

Even more worth watching are instances in which *target* gets mixed up with other metaphors. Philip Howard cites this curious headline from *The Times*: '£6m ceiling keeps rise in earnings well within Treasury target'.

tautology, redundancy, pleonasm, solecism. Although various authorities detect various shades of distinction between the first three words, those distinctions are always very slight and, on comparison, are frequently contradictory. Essentially all three mean using more words than necessary to convey an idea.

Not all repetition is bad. It may be used for effect, as in poetry, or for clarity, or as a consequence of idiom. 'OPEC countries', 'SALT talks' and 'TUC Congress' are all technically redundant because the second word is already contained in the preceding abbreviation, but only the ultra-finicky would deplore them. Similarly in 'wipe that smile off your face' the last two words are tautological – there is no other place that a smile could be – but the sentence would not stand without them.

On the whole, however, the use of more words than necessary is almost always better avoided, though it occurs among even the most careful writers, as here: 'All writers and speakers of English, including these very grammarians themselves, omit words which will never be missed' (Bergen and Cornelia Evans in *A Dictionary of Contemporary American Usage*). The use of 'these very' ahead of 'grammarians' makes 'themselves' unnecessary. Either delete 'themselves' or delete 'very'.

Finally, *solecism* describes any violation of idiom or grammar. Redundancies, tautologies and pleonasms are all solecisms.

temperature. See FEVER, TEMPERATURE.

temporary respite. 'Even Saudi Arabia's assurance that it would not cut oil prices provided no more than a temporary respite' (*Daily Telegraph*). The expression is common, but redundant. A respite can only be temporary.

terribly, awfully, horribly, etc. The tendency to use words such as these in senses contrary to their literal meanings ('That's terribly good', 'You're awfully funny') is not, as Fowler notes, confined to English. The ancient Greeks abused their word for *awfully* in much the same way. But the habit is better resisted and has no place in formal writing.

than. Three problems here:

1. 'Nearly twice as many people die under 20 in France than in Great Britain' (cited by Gowers). Make it 'as in Great Britain'.

2. 'Hardly had I landed at Liverpool than the Mikado's death recalled me to Japan' (cited by Fowler). Make it 'No sooner had I landed than' or 'Hardly had I landed when'.

3. Should you say, 'She likes tennis more than me' or 'more than I'? It depends on whether you mean that she likes tennis more than she likes me (first example) or that she likes tennis more than I do (second example). In either case, it is better to provide a second verb if there is a chance of ambiguity or a look of overfussiness, e.g., 'She likes tennis more than she likes me' and 'She likes tennis more than I do'. Fowler provides a good example of ambiguity: 'I would rather you shot the poor dog than me'.

that (as a conjunction). Whether you say 'I think you are wrong' or 'I think that you are wrong' is partly a matter of idiom but mostly a matter of preference. Some words usually require *that* (assert, contend, maintain) and some do not (say, think). On the whole it is better to dispense with *that* when it isn't necessary.

that, which. To understand the distinctions between *that* and *which* it is necessary to understand defining and non-defining clauses. Learning these distinctions is not, it must be said, anyone's idea of a good time, but it is one technical aspect of grammar that every professional user of English should understand because it is at the root of an assortment of grammatical errors.

A non-defining clause is one that can be regarded as parenthetical: 'The tree, *which had no leaves*, was a birch'. The italicized words are effectively an aside and could be deleted. The real point of the sentence is that the tree was a birch; its leaflessness is incidental. A defining clause is one that is essential to the sense of the sentence: 'The tree *that had no leaves* was a birch'. Here the leaflessness is a defining characteristic; it helps us to distinguish that tree from other trees.

In correct usage *that* is always used to indicate defining clauses and *which* to indicate non-defining ones. Defining clauses should never be set off with commas and non-defining clauses always should. On that much the authorities are agreed. Where divergence creeps in is on the question of how strictly the distinctions should be observed.

Until relatively recently they were not observed at all. In the King James Bible, for instance, we find: 'Render therefore unto Caesar the things which are Caesar's; and unto God the things that are God's'. The same quotation appears twice more in the Bible – once with *that* in both places and once with *which* in both. Today, *that* is more usual in short sentences or early on in longer ones ('The house that Jack built', 'The mouse that roared'). *Which* often appears where *that* would more strictly be correct, particularly in Britain, as here: 'It has outlined two broad strategies which it thinks could be put to the institutions' (*The Times*).

Although there is ample precedent for using *which* in defining clauses, the practice is on the whole better avoided. There are, at any rate, occasions when the choice of *which* is clearly wrong, as here: 'On a modest estimate, public authorities own 100,000 houses, which remain unoccupied for at least a year' (*Sunday Times*). What the writer meant was that of those houses that are publicly owned, at least 100,000 are left vacant for a year or more. Deleting the comma after 'houses' and changing *which* to *that* would have made this immediately clear.

Another common fault – more a discourtesy to the reader than an error – is the failure to set off non-defining clauses with commas, as here: 'Four members of one of the world's largest drugs rings (,) which smuggled heroin worth £5 million into Britain (,) were jailed yesterday' (*The Times*). That lapse is seen only rarely in America, but is rife in Britain; it occurred five times more in the same article.

Americans, on the other hand, are much more inclined to use *that* where *which* might be preferable, as here: 'Perhaps, with the help of discerning decision-makers, the verb can regain its narrow definition that gave it a reason for being' (William Safire, *On Language*). Had Safire written 'can regain *the* narrow meaning that gave it a reason for being', all would be well. But the use of 'its' gives the final clause the feel of a non-defining afterthought and the sentence might be better rendered as 'can regain its narrow definition, which gave it a reason for being'. The point is arguable.

thinking to oneself. 'Somehow he must have thought to himself that this unfamiliar line needed to be ascribed to someone rather more venerable' (*Sunday Telegraph*); '"Can it be that the Sunday Times Magazine is paying no attention to my book?" Frank Delaney was thinking to himself' (*Sunday Times*). Scrub 'to himself' both times; there is no one else to whom you can think. Similarly vacuous is 'in my mind' here: 'I could picture in my mind where the bookkeeping offices had been . . .' (*Boston Globe*).

though, although. The two are interchangeable except at the end of a sentence, where only *though* is correct ('He looked tired, though') and with the expressions *as though* and *even though*, where idiom precludes *although*.

till. See UNTIL, TILL, 'TIL, 'TILL.

'til. See UNTIL, TILL, 'TIL, 'TILL.

'till. See UNTIL, TILL, 'TIL, 'TILL.

time. Often used superfluously in constructions of this sort: 'The report will be available in two weeks time' (*Guardian*). *Time* adds nothing to the sentence but length and its deletion would obviate the need for an apostrophe after 'weeks'.

tirade. See HARANGUE, TIRADE.

together with, along with. *With* in both expressions is a preposition, not a conjunction, and therefore does not govern the verb. This sentence is wrong: 'They said the man, a motor mechanic, together with a 22-year-old arrested a day earlier, were being questioned' (*The Times*). Make it 'was being questioned'.

A separate danger with such expressions is seen here: 'Barbara Tuchman, the historian, gave $20,000 to the Democrats, along with her husband, Lester' (*The New York Times*). How Lester felt about being given to the Democrats wasn't recorded.

ton, tonne. There are two kinds of tons: a long ton weighing 2,240 pounds and a short ton weighing 2,000 pounds. A tonne is a metric ton weighing 1,000 kilograms, or about 2,204 pounds.

tonne. See TON, TONNE.

tortuous, torturous. *Tortuous* means winding and circuitous ('The road wound tortuously through the mountains'). When used figuratively it usually suggests crookedness or deviousness ('a tortuous tax-avoidance scheme'). The word is thus better avoided if all you mean is complicated or convoluted. *Torturous* is the adjectival form of *torture* and describes the infliction of extreme pain.

torturous. See TORTUOUS, TORTUROUS.

total. There are three points to note here:

1. *Total* is redundant and should be deleted when what it is qualifying already contains the idea of a totality, as here: '[They] risk total annihilation at the hands of the massive Israeli forces now poised to strike at the gates of the city' (*Washington Post*).

2. The expression *a total of*, though common, is also generally superfluous: 'County officials said a total of 84 prisoners were housed in six cells ...' (*The New York Times*). Make it 'officials said 84 prisoners'. An exception is at the start of sentences when it is desirable to avoid spelling out a large number, as in 'A total of 212 sailors were aboard' instead of 'Two hundred and twelve sailors were aboard', though recasting is often better still: 'There were 212 sailors on board'.

3. 'A total of 45 weeks was spent on the study' (*The Times*) is wrong.

As with 'a number of' and 'the number of', the rule is to make it 'the total of . . . was' but 'a total of . . . were'.

toward, towards. The first is the preferred form in America, the second in Britain, but either is correct. *Untoward*, however, is the only accepted form in both.

towards. See TOWARD, TOWARDS.

transatlantic. 'The agreement came just in time to stop the authorities from taking away his permits to operate trans-Atlantic flights' (*Sunday Times*). Most dictionaries prefer *transatlantic*. Similarly, *transalpine, transarctic, transpacific*.

transpire. 'But Mayor Koch had a different version of what transpired [at the hotel]' (*The New York Times*). *Transpire* does not mean occur, as was intended above. Still less does it mean arrive or be received, as was intended here: 'And generally the group found it had too many stocks for the orders that transpired' (*The Times*). It means to leak out (literally in Latin 'to breathe through').

treble. See TRIPLE. TREBLE.

triple, treble. Either word can be used as a noun, verb or adjective. Except in certain musical senses, *triple* is used almost exclusively for all three in America and is becoming increasingly preponderant in Britain. According to Fowler, *treble* is more usual as a verb ('They trebled their profits') and as a noun ('I will give you treble what he offered'). As an adjective, he says, *treble* is preferable for amount and *triple* for kinds. Thus 'treble difficulty' should describe something that is three times as difficult and 'triple difficulty' should describe a difficulty made up of three things.

trivia is a plural. 'All this trivia is a nuisance' should be 'All these trivia are a nuisance'. There is no singular form (the Latin *trivium* now has only historical applications) but there are the singular words *trifle* and *triviality*. The other option is to rework *trivia* into its adjectival form: 'Such a trivial matter is a nuisance'.

true facts. 'No one in the White House seems able to explain why it took such a potentially fatal time to inform the Vice President of the true facts' (*Sunday Times*). *True facts* is always either redundant or incorrect. A fact is not a fact unless it is true.

try and is colloquial and better avoided in serious writing. 'The Monopolies Commission will look closely at retailing mergers to try and prevent any lessening of competition' (*Sunday Times*). Make it 'try to prevent'.

tumult, turmoil. Both describe confusion and agitation. The difference is that *tumult* applies only to people, but *turmoil* applies to both people and things. *Tumultuous*, however, can describe things as well as people ('tumultuous applause', 'tumultuous seas').

turbid. See TURGID, TURBID.

turgid, turbid. It is seldom possible to tell with certainty whether the writer is using *turgid* in its proper sense or is confusing it with *turbid*, but confusion would appear to be the case here: 'She insisted on reading the entire turgid work aloud, a dusk-to-dawn affair that would have tried anyone's patience' (*Sunday Times*). *Turgid* means inflated, grandiloquent, bombastic. It does not mean muddy or impenetrable, which meanings are covered by *turbid*.

turmoil. See TUMULT, TURMOIL.

turpitude. 'As far as Jimmy Carter the man, his integrity, his moral turpitude, his commitment to government, his commitment to family, it is unimpeachable' (cited by William Safire, *On Language*). The man who made that statement – he was a member of the Carter–Mondale Presidential Committee – obviously thought *turpitude* meant rectitude or integrity. In fact, it means baseness or depravity.

▣ U ▣

UCLA. 'A professor of higher education at the University College of Los Angeles has examined the careers of 200,000 students at 350 colleges' (*Sunday Times*). The error is a common one outside North America. UCLA stands for the University of California at Los Angeles.

undoubtedly. See DOUBTLESS, UNDOUBTEDLY, INDUBITABLY.

unexceptionable, unexceptional. Sometimes confused. Something that is unexceptional is ordinary, not outstanding ('an unexceptional wine'). Something that is unexceptionable is not open to objections ('In Britain, *grey* is the preferred spelling, but *gray* is unexceptionable').

unilateral, bilateral, multilateral. These words have become such a standard part of modern political jargon that many people forget they can be replaced by simpler equivalents: one-sided, two-sided and many-sided. In any case, their presence is, as often as not, unnecessary, as here: 'Bilateral trade talks are to take place next week between Britain and Japan' (*The Times*). Trade talks between Britain and Japan could hardly be other than two-sided. Delete *bilateral*.

uninterested. See DISINTERESTED, UNINTERESTED.

unique means the only one of its kind. It is incomparable. One thing cannot be more unique than another, as was thought here: 'Lafeyette's most unique restaurant is now even more unique' (cited by Wood).

unknown is often used imprecisely, as here: 'A hitherto unknown company called Ashdown Oil has emerged as a bidder for the Wytch Farm oil interests' (*The Times*). A company must be known to someone, if only its directors. It would be better to call it a little-known company.

unless and until. One or the other, please.

unlike. When *unlike* is used as a preposition, it should govern a noun or pronoun or a noun equivalent (e.g., a gerund). 'But unlike at previous sessions of the conference . . .' (*The New York Times*) needs to be 'But unlike previous sessions' or 'As was not the case at previous sessions'.

Unlike must also contrast things that are comparable, which was not done here: 'Unlike the proposal by Rep. Albert Gore, outlined in this space yesterday, the President is not putting forth a blueprint for a final treaty' (*Chicago Tribune*). As written, the sentence is telling us that a proposal is unlike the President – which should come as a surprise to no one. It should be: 'Unlike the proposal by Rep. Albert Gore, the President's plan does not put forth a blueprint' or words to that effect.

unpractical. See IMPRACTICAL, IMPRACTICABLE, UNPRACTICAL.

until, till, 'til, 'till. The first two are legitimate and interchangeable. The second two are illiterate.

up. When used as a phrasal verb (which see), *up* is often just a hitch-hiker, joining sentences only for the ride. Sometimes idiom dictates that we include it: we look up a word in a book, we dig up odd facts, we move up in our careers. But often it is needlessly attached to words, as here: 'Plans to tighten up the rules for charging overseas visitors for use of the National Health Service were announced yesterday' (*The Times*); 'Another time, another tiger ate up 27 of Henning's 30 prop animals' (*Washington Post*); 'This could force the banks to lift up their interest rates' (*Financial Times*). *Buoy up, loosen up, ring up, phone up, climb up* and countless others are all generally unnecessary and ought to be avoided. Occasionally in its eagerness *up* moves to the front of words: 'With the continued upsurge in sales of domestic appliances . . .' (*The Times*). Although upsurge is a recognized word, it seldom means more than surge.

upon. See ON, UPON.

usage. See USE, USAGE.

use, usage. *Usage* describes that which is habitual and customary. But *use*, in addition to its other meanings, can also mean that. In practice, *usage* is frowned on by grammarians when it is employed by anyone other than themselves and normally it appears only in the context of languages ('modern English usage').

usual. A common oversight in newspapers – no doubt attributable to haste – is telling readers twice in one sentence that a thing is customary. Both of the following are from *The New York Times*: 'The usual procedure normally involved getting eyewitness reports of one or more acts of heroism'; 'Customarily, such freezes are usually imposed at the end of a fiscal year'. Delete something. See also HABITS.

utilize. In its strictest sense, *utilize* means to make the best use of something that wasn't intended for the job ('He utilized a coat hanger to repair his car'). It can be extended to mean making the most practical possible use of something ('Although the hills were steep, the rice farmers utilized every square inch of the land'). But in all other senses, 'use' is better.

various different is inescapably redundant.

venal, venial. *Venial*, from the Latin *venialis* ('forgivable'), means excusable. A venial sin is a minor one. *Venal* means corruptible. It comes from the Latin *venalis* ('for sale') and describes someone who is capable of being bought.

venerate, worship. Although in figurative senses the words are interchangeable, in religious contexts *worship* should apply only to God. Roman Catholics, for instance, worship God but venerate saints.

venial. See VENAL, VENIAL.

verbal. See ORAL, VERBAL.

very should be made to pay its way in sentences. All too often it is used where it adds nothing to the sense ('It was a very tragic death'), or is inserted in a futile effort to prop up a weak word that would be better replaced by something more descriptive ('The play was very good').

via, meaning 'by way of', indicates the direction of a journey ('A flight from London to Los Angeles via Boston') and not the means by which the journey is achieved. It is used incorrectly here: 'Out at the end of the wharf a man sold tickets [for] "excursion" trips via a speed boat' (cited by Partridge).

viable. 'Such a system would mark a breakthrough in efforts to come up with a commercially viable replacement for internal-combustion vehicles' (*Newsweek*); 'I believe there is a viable market for the Samba Cabriolet in Britain' (*Mail on Sunday*). *Viable* does not mean feasible or workable. It means capable of independent existence and its use really ought to be confined to that meaning. Even when it is correctly used, it tends to make the sentence read like a government document, as here: 'Doing nothing about the latter threatens the viability of the

---

virtually

lakes and woodlands of the northeastern states' (*Chicago Tribune*). Deleting 'the viability of' would shorten the sentence without altering its sense.

virtually, practically. *Practically* means in practice or to all practical purposes. *Virtually* means almost or in effect. In most instances the words are practically/virtually indistinguishable. But there is a slight difference. *Practically* should not be used when you mean almost. As Bernstein notes, to say that you are practically out of coffee when there is enough left for a couple of cups is a bit loose because as a practical matter you are not out of coffee. That, it may be argued, is splitting hairs. But certainly to be avoided are sentences such as 'I practically won the race' when you finished second.

vocal cords have nothing to do with chords of music, as many writers seem to think: 'Understudy Nancy Ringham will play opposite Rex Harrison because Miss Kennedy has problems with her vocal chords' (*Standard*). Make it 'cords'.

vortexes, vortices. For the plural of *vortex*, either is correct. *The Concise Oxford* gives *vortices* first; *The American Heritage* gives *vortexes* first.

vortices. See VORTEXES, VORTICES.

150

⊡ W ⊡

warn. 'British Rail warned that the snow was bound to have a serious effect on its service today' (*Daily Telegraph*). Most British dictionaries continue not to recognize *warn* used intransitively, as it has been above. Accordingly, *warn* needs an expressed personal object – i.e., the sentence must state who or what is being warned. Thus it should be: 'British Rail warned passengers that ...'. In the United States the word may be used with or without an object.

The rule is, I think, more than a little fussy, especially when, as in the example above, a warning is general. If we are to have an expressed personal object for the sake of form, we might equally insist on the inclusion of all the objects for the sake of accuracy. Thus: 'British Rail warned passengers, freight users, people planning to meet passengers, British Rail staff, the Government, the Post Office, the police and ferry operators that snow was bound to have a serious effect on its service today'.

The weight of usage is clearly on the side of accepting the intransitive and I can find no usage authority who argues against it. But if you use it in Britain, you do so at the peril of being called incorrect.

weather conditions. 'Freezing weather conditions will continue for the rest of the week' (*The Times*). Delete *conditions*. Similarly tiresome is the American weather forecasters' fondness for 'activity', as in 'thunderstorm activity over the plains states'.

whence. 'And man will return to the state of hydrogen from whence he came' (*Sunday Telegraph*). Although there is ample precedent for the expression *from whence* – the King James Bible has the sentence 'I will lift up my eyes unto the hills from whence cometh my help' – it is redundant. *Whence* means from where. It is enough to say 'to the state of hydrogen whence he came'.

whether or not. The second two words should be dropped when *whether* is equivalent to 'if', as here: 'It is not yet known whether or not persons who become reinfected can spread the virus to other susceptible individuals' (*The New York Times*). *Or not* adds nothing there and

151

should be deleted. *Or not* is necessary, however, when what is being stressed is an alternative: 'I intend to come whether or not you like it'.

which. The belief that *which* may refer only to the preceding word and not to the whole of a preceding statement is without foundation except where there is a chance of ambiguity. The ridiculousness of the rule – and the impossibility of enforcing it consistently – is illustrated by an anecdote in the *New Yorker* cited by Gowers. A class in Philadelphia had written to a local paper's resident usage expert asking him what was wrong with the sentence 'He wrecked the car, which was due to his carelessness'. Notice how the authority hoists himself with the last three words of his reply: 'The fault lies in using *which* to refer to the statement "He wrecked the car". When *which* follows a noun, it refers to that noun as its antecedent. Therefore in the foregoing sentence it is stated that the car was due to his carelessness, which is nonsense'. See also THAT, WHICH.

who, whom. Shakespeare, Addison, Ben Jonson, Dickens, Churchill, the translators of the King James Bible and I, among many others, have all in our time been utterly flummoxed by the distinction between the relative pronouns *who* and *whom*.

The rule can be stated simply. *Whom* is used when it is the object of a preposition ('To whom it may concern') or verb ('The man whom we saw last night') or the subject of a complementary infinitive ('The person whom we took to be your father'). *Who* is used on all other occasions.

Consider now three extracts in which the wrong choice has been made: 'Mrs Hinckley said that her son had been upset by the murder of Mr Lennon, who he idolized' (*The New York Times*); 'Colombo, whom law enforcement officials have said is the head of a Mafia family in Brooklyn ...' (*The New York Times*); 'Heart-breaking decision – who to save' (*Times* headline). We can check the correctness of such sentences by imagining them as he/him constructions. For instance, would you say 'Hinckley idolized he' or 'idolized him'? Would law enforcement officers say that 'he is the head of a Mafia family' or 'him is the head'? And is it a heart-breaking decision over whether to save he or to save him? When the answer is he, use *who*; when it is him, use *whom*.

Simple, isn't it? Well, not quite. When the relative pronoun follows a preposition in a relative clause, that simple test falls to pieces. Consider this sentence from *Fortune* magazine: 'They rent it to whomever needs it'. Since we know that you say 'for whom the bell tolls' and 'to whom it may concern', it should follow that we would say 'to whomever needs it'. If we test that conclusion by imagining the sentence as a he/him construction – would they 'rent it to he' or 'rent it to him'? – we are bound to plump for *whom*. But we would be wrong. The difficulty there is that the relative pronoun is the subject of the verb 'needs' and not the object of the preposition 'to'. The sentence in effect is saying: 'They rent it to any person *who* needs it'.

Similarly, *whomever* would be wrong in these two sentences: 'We must offer it to whoever applies first'; 'Give it to whoever wants it'. Again, in effect they are saying: 'We must offer it to the person *who* applies first' and 'Give it to the person *who* wants it'. Such constructions usually involve a choice between *whoever* and *whomever* (as opposed to a simple *who* and *whom*), which should always alert you to proceed with caution. But they need not. An exception – and a rather tricky one – is seen here: 'The disputants differed diametrically as to who they thought might turn out to be the violator' (cited by Bernstein). The sentence is saying: 'The disputants differed diametrically as to the identity of the person *who* they thought might turn out to be the violator'.

By performing a little verbal gymnastics it is usually possible to decide with some confidence which case to use. But is it worth the bother? Is it reasonable that we should be required to perform an elaborate grammatical analysis to write our own language? Bernstein, in his later years, thought not. In 1975, he wrote to twenty-five authorities on usage asking if they thought there was any real point in preserving *whom* except when it is directly governed by a preposition (as in 'to whom it may concern'). Six voted to preserve *whom*, four were undecided and fifteen – among them Eric Partridge, Mario Pei, S. I. Hayakawa, William Morris and Bergen Evans – thought it should be abandoned.

English has been shedding its pronoun declensions for hundreds of years; today *who* is the only relative pronoun that is declinable. Preserving the distinction between *who* and *whom* does nothing to promote clarity or reduce ambiguity. It has become merely a source of frequent errors and perpetual uncertainty. Authorities have been tossing stones at *whom* for at least 200 years – Noah Webster was one of the first to call it needless – but the word refuses to go away.

whom

A century from now it may be a relic. But for the moment you ignore it at the risk of being thought ignorant.

For a discussion of *who* in defining and non-defining clauses, see WHOSE.

whom. See WHO, WHOM.

whose. Two small problems here. One is the persistent belief that *whose* can apply only to people. The authorities are unanimous that there is nothing wrong with saying, 'The book, a picaresque novel whose central characters are . . .' rather than the clumsier 'a picaresque novel the central characters of which . . .'.

The second problem arises from a failure to discriminate between defining and non-defining clauses (discussed under THAT, WHICH). Consider: 'Many parents, whose children ride motorbikes, live in constant fear of an accident' (*Observer*). The writer has made the subordinate clause parenthetical. In effect he is saying: 'Many parents (whose children, by the way, ride motorbikes) live in constant fear of an accident'. He meant, of course, that the parents live in fear *because* their children ride motorbikes. The clause is defining; the commas should be removed. Gowers cites this example from a wartime training manual: 'Pilots, whose minds are dull, do not usually live long'. Removing the commas would convert an insult into sound advice.

The same problem often happens with *who*, as in this sentence from the stylebook of *The Times*: '*Normalcy* should be left to the Americans who coined it'. Had the writer meant that 'normalcy' should be left only to those Americans who participated in its coining, the lack of a comma would be correct. But we can assume he meant that it should be left to all Americans, who as a nation (and as an incidental matter) coined it. A comma is therefore required. In fact, however, Americans did not coin the word. It is several hundred years older than the United States and belongs to the English, who coined it. See NORMALCY.

widow, when combined with 'the late', is redundant, as here: 'Mrs Sadat, the widow of the late Egyptian President . . .' (*Guardian*). Make it either 'wife of the late Egyptian President' or 'widow of the Egyptian President'.

will, would. 'The plan would be phased in over 10 years and will involve

extra national insurance contributions . . .' (*The Times*). The problem
here is an inconsistency between what grammarians call the protasis
(the condition) and the apodosis (the consequence). The sentence has
begun in the subjunctive (*would*) and switched abruptly to the indicative (*will*). The same error occurs here: 'The rector, Chad Varah,
has promised that work on the church will start in the New Year
and would be completed within about three years' (*Standard*). In both
sentences it should be either *will* both times or *would* both times.

This is not simply a matter of grammatical orderliness; it is a
question of clarity – of telling the difference between what will happen
and what may happen. Compare these two sentences: 'The plan will
cost £400 million'; 'The plan would cost £400 million'. The first expresses a certainty. The plan either has been adopted or is certain
to be adopted. The second is clearly suppositional. It is saying only
that if the plan were adopted it would cost £400 million.

A common failing of British journalism is to present the suppositional as if it were a certainty. An article in the *Guardian* about
union proposals urging the Prime Minister to spend more on job
creation schemes went on to say: 'The proposals will create up to
20,000 new jobs . . . will be phased in over three years . . . will cost
up to £8 million' and so on. In each instance the sentence should
be qualified: 'The proposals *would* create up to 20,000 jobs' or 'If
they are adopted, the proposals *will* cost up to £8 million'.

For the differences between *will* and *shall*, see SHALL, WILL.

worship. See VENERATE, WORSHIP.

worst comes to worst is the correct expression, not *worse comes to
worst* or *worse comes to worse*, however much more logical they may
be.

would. See WILL, WOULD.

wrack. See RACK, WRACK.

wrapped. See RAPT, WRAPPED.

Y

ye, as in Ye Old Antique Shoppe, is no more pronounced 'yee' than 'lb' is pronounced 'ulb' or 'cwt' is pronounced 'kwut'. It is an abbreviation of *the*, not another word for it. It started as an incorrect transcription of the runic letter called thorn (þ) and was perpetuated by early printers when they needed to abbreviate *the* to justify a line of type. A similar pronunciation error is often made with 'olde worlde'. Those who say 'oldie worldie' should be corrected at once and instructed never to say it again.

yes, no. Writers are often at a loss when deciding what to do with a *yes* or *no* in constructions such as the following: 'Will this really be the last of Clouseau? Blake Edwards says No' (*Sunday Express*). There are two possibilities, neither of which the writer has used. You may make it 'Blake Edwards says no' or you may make it 'Blake Edwards says, "No"'. Capitalizing the word without providing the punctuation is a pointless compromise and should satisfy no one.

yesterday. Anyone not familiar with newspaper offices could be forgiven for assuming that journalists must talk something like this: 'I last night went to bed early because I this morning had to catch an early flight'. That, at any rate, is how many of them write. Consider: 'Their decision was yesterday being heralded as a powerful warning...' (*The Times*); 'Police were last night hunting for...' (*Daily Mail*); 'The two sides were today to consider...' (*Guardian*). Although in newspapers some care must be taken not to place the time element in a position where it might produce ambiguity, a more natural arrangement can almost always be found: 'was being heralded yesterday'; 'were hunting last night for'; 'were to consider today'.

Yiddish, See HEBREW, YIDDISH.

◉ Z ◉

zoom. Strictly speaking, the word should describe only a steep *upward* movement. Almost every authority stresses that point, though how much it is inspired by a desire for precision and how much by the need to find something – anything – to discuss under the letter 'Z' is never easy to say. No one, I think, would argue that zoom lenses should be used only for taking pictures of the sky, nor should the word be considered objectionable when applied to lateral movements ('The cars zoomed around the track'). But for describing downward movements ('The planes zoomed down on the city to drop their bombs') it is better avoided, especially as 'swoop' is available.

Appendix: Punctuation

The uses of punctuation marks, or stops, are so numerous and the abuses so varied that the following is offered only as a very general guide to the most common errors. For those who wish to dig more deeply, I recommend the excellent *Mind the Stop* by G. V. Carey, published by Penguin.

apostrophe. The principal functions of the apostrophe are to indicate omitted letters (*don't, can't, wouldn't*) and to show the possessive (strictly, the genitive) case (*John's book, the bank's money, the people's choice*).

In its more general uses the apostrophe normally causes little trouble to educated writers (though the *Observer* still occasionally devotes a section to 'Childrens Books'). But among advertisers it is endlessly, maddeningly, distressingly neglected. I have before me a holiday brochure offering 'This years holidays at last years prices'. 'Todays Tesco' offers its customers 'mens clothes', 'womens clothes' and 'childrens clothes'. In one thinnish Sunday supplement, nine advertisers clocked up fourteen such errors between them. The mistake is inexcusable and those who make it are linguistic Neanderthals.

Two other types of error occur with some frequency and are worth noting. They involve:

1. *Multiple possessives.* This problem can be seen here: 'This is a sequel to Jeremy Paul's and Alan Gibson's play ...' (*The Times*). The question is whether both of the apostrophes are necessary, and the answer in this instance is no. Because the reference is to a single play written jointly, only the second-named man needs to be in the possessive. Thus it should be: 'Jeremy Paul and Alan Gibson's play'. If the reference were to two or more plays written separately, both names would have to carry apostrophes. The rule is that when possession is held in common, only the nearer antecedent should be possessive; when possession is separate, each antecedent must be in the possessive.

2. *Plural units of measure.* Many writers who would never think of omitting the apostrophes in 'a fair day's pay for a fair day's work' often do exactly that when the unit of measure is increased. Consider:

'Laker gets further 30 days credit' (*Times* headline); 'Mr Taranto, who had 30 years service with the company...' (*The New York Times*). Both 'days' and 'years' should carry an apostrophe. Alternatively we could insert an 'of' after the time elements ('30 days of credit', '19 years of service'). One or the other is necessary.

The problem is often aggravated by the inclusion of excess verbiage, as in each of these examples: 'The scheme could well be appropriate in 25 years time, he said' (*The Times*); 'Many diplomats are anxious to settle the job by the end of the session in two weeks time' (*Observer*); 'The Government is prepared to part with several hundred acres worth of property' (*Time*). Each requires an apostrophe. But that need could be obviated by excluding the superfluous wordage. What is 'in 25 years' time' if not 'in 25 years'? What does 'several hundred acres' worth of property' say that 'several hundred acres' does not?

colon. The colon marks a formal introduction or indicates the start of a series. A colon should not separate a verb from its object in simple enumerations. Thus it would be wrong to say: 'The four states bordering Texas are: New Mexico, Arkansas, Oklahoma and Louisiana'. The colon should be removed. But it would be correct to say: 'Texas is bordered by four states: New Mexico, Arkansas, Oklahoma and Louisiana'.

comma. The trend these days is to use the comma as sparingly as form and clarity allow. But there are certain instances in which it should appear but all too often does not. Equally, it has a tendency to crop up with alarming regularity in places where it has no business. It is, in short, the most abused of punctuation marks and one of the worst offenders of any kind in the English language. Essentially there are three situations where the comma's use is compulsory and a fourth where it is recommended.

1. *When the information provided is clearly parenthetical.* Consider these two sentences, both of which are correctly punctuated: 'Mr Lawson, the Energy Secretary, was unavailable for comment'; 'The ambassador, who arrived in Britain two days ago, yesterday met with the Prime Minister'. In both sentences, the information between the commas is incidental to the main thought. You could remove it and the sentence would still make sense. In the following examples, the writer has failed to set off the parenthetical information. I have provided stroke marks (the proper name, incidentally, is virgules) to show

where the commas should have gone: 'British cars/says a survey/are more reliable than their foreign counterparts' (leader in the *Standard*); 'The new A T & T Tower on Madison Avenue/the first of a new breed/ will be ready by the end of 1982' (*Sunday Times*); 'Operating mainly from the presidential palace at Baabda/southeast of Beirut, Habib negotiated over a 65-day period' (*Time*); 'Mary Chatillon, director of the Massachusetts General Hospital's Reading Language Disorder Unit/maintains: "It would simply appear to be . . ."' (*Time*). It should perhaps be noted that failure to put in a comma is particularly common after a parenthesis, as here: 'Mr James Grant, executive director of the United Nations Children's Fund (UNICEF)/says . . .' (*The Times*).

Occasionally the writer recognizes that the sentence contains a parenthetical thought, but fails to discern just how much of the information is incidental, as here: 'At nine she won a scholarship to Millfield, the private school, for bright children of the rich' (*Standard*). If we removed what has been presented as parenthetical, the sentence would say: 'At nine she won a scholarship to Millfield for bright children'. There should be no comma after 'school' because the whole of the last statement is parenthetical.

A rarer error is seen here: 'But its big worry is the growing evidence that such ostentatious cars, the cheapest costs £55,240, are becoming socially unacceptable' (*The Times*). When the incidental information could stand alone as a sentence, it needs to be set off with stronger punctuation – either dashes or parentheses.

2. *When the information is non-defining.* The problem here – which is really much the same as that discussed in the previous three paragraphs – is illustrated by this incorrectly punctuated sentence from the *Daily Mail*: 'Cable TV would be socially divisive, the chairman of the BBC George Howard claimed last night'. The writer has failed to understand the distinction between (1) 'BBC chairman George Howard claimed last night' and (2) 'The chairman of the BBC, George Howard, claimed last night'. In (1), the name George Howard is essential to the sense of the sentence; it defines it. If we removed it, the sentence would say: 'BBC chairman claimed last night'. In (2), however, the name is non-defining. In effect it is parenthetical. We could remove it without altering the sense of the sentence: 'The chairman of the BBC claimed last night'. When a name or title can be removed, it should be set off with commas. When it cannot be removed, the use of commas is wrong.

Two hypothetical examples may help to clarify the distinction. Both are correctly punctuated. 'John Fowles's novel *The Collector* was a best-seller'; 'John Fowles's first novel, *The Collector*, was a best-seller'. In the first example the name of the novel is defining because *The Collector* is only one of several novels by Fowles. In the second example it is non-defining because only one novel can be the author's first one. We could delete *The Collector* from the second example without spoiling the sense of the sentence, but not from the first.

When something is the only one of its kind, it should be set off with commas; when it is only one of several, the use of commas is wrong. Thus these two sentences, both from *The Times*, are incorrect: 'When the well-known British firm, Imperial Metal Industries, developed two new types of superconducting wires ...'; 'The writer in the American magazine, *Horizon*, was aware of this pretentiousness ...'. The first example would be correct only if Imperial Metal Industries were the only well-known British firm, and the second would be correct only if *Horizon* were America's only magazine. The same error in reverse occurs here: 'Julie Christie knows that in the week her new film *The Return of the Soldier* has opened ...' (*Sunday Times*). Since *The Return of the Soldier* was Julie Christie's only new film of the week, it should have been set off with commas.

The error frequently occurs when a marriage partner is named: 'Mrs Thatcher and her husband Denis left London yesterday' (*Observer*). Since Mrs Thatcher has only one husband, it should be 'and her husband, Denis, left London yesterday'.

3. *With forms of address.* When addressing people, commas are obligatory around the names or titles of those addressed. 'Hit him Jim, hit him' (*Sunday Times*) should be 'Hit him, Jim, hit him'. The BBC television series *Yes Minister* should be *Yes, Minister*. The film *I'm All Right Jack* should have been *I'm All Right, Jack*. The lack of a comma or commas is always sloppy and occasionally ambiguous. In 1981, for instance, the *Sunday Express* illustrated a novel serialization with the heading 'I'm choking Mr Herriot' when what it meant was 'I'm choking, Mr Herriot' – quite another matter.

4. *With interpolated words or phrases.* Words such as *moreover*, *meanwhile* and *nevertheless* and phrases such as *for instance* and *for example* traditionally have taken commas, but the practice has become increasingly discretionary over the years. In Britain they have been more freely abandoned than in America; Fowler, for instance, seldom

uses them. I would recommend using them when they suggest a pause or when ambiguity might result. This is especially true of *however*. Consider these two sentences: 'However hard he tried, he failed'; 'However, he tried hard, but failed'. To keep from confusing the reader, if only momentarily, it is a good idea to set off *however* with commas when it is used as an interpolation. Much the same could be said of *say*: 'She should choose a British Government stock with (,) say (,) five years to run' (*Daily Mail*).

dash. Dashes should be used in pairs to enclose parenthetical matter or singly to indicate a sharp break in a sentence ('I can't see a damn thing in here – ouch!') or to place emphasis on a point ('There are only two things we can count on – death and taxes'). Dashes are most effective when used sparingly and there should never be more than one pair in a single sentence. Fowler insists that when dashes are used in pairs, any punctuation interrupted by the first dash should be picked up after the second (e.g., 'If this is true – and no one can be sure that it is –, we should do something'). But on this, as with so much else to do with punctuation, Fowler is at odds with almost everyone else. There are two common errors with dashes:

1. Failing to mark the end of a parenthetical comment with a second dash: 'The group – it is the largest in its sector, with subsidiaries or associates in 11 countries, says trading has improved in the current year' (*The Times*). Make it 'countries – says'.

2. Allowing a word or phrase from the main part of the sentence to become locked within the parenthetical area, as here: 'There is another institution which appears to have an even more – shall we say, relaxed – attitude to security' (*The Times*). Removing the words between the dashes would give us an institution with 'an even more attitude'. *Relaxed* belongs to the sentence proper and needs to be put outside the dashes: 'There is another institution which appears to have an even more – shall we say? – relaxed attitude to security'. (See also PARENTHESES.)

ellipsis. An ellipsis (sometimes called an ellipse) is used to indicate that material has been omitted. It consists of three full stops (. . .) and not, as some writers think, a random scattering of them. When an ellipsis occurs at the end of a sentence, a fourth full stop is normally added.

exclamation marks are used to show strong emotion ('Get out!') or urgency ('Help me!'). They should almost never be used for giving emphasis to a simple statement of fact: 'It was bound to happen sometime! A bull got into a china shop here' (cited by Bernstein).

full stop (US, period). There are two common errors associated with the full stop, both of which arise from its absence. The first is the run-on sentence (that is, the linking of two complete thoughts by a comma). It is never possible to say when a run-on sentence is attributable to ignorance on the part of the writer or to whimsy on the part of the typesetter, but the error occurs frequently enough that ignorance must play a part. In each of the following I have indicated with a stroke where one sentence should end and the next should begin: 'Although G EC handled the initial contract, much of the equipment is American,/the computers and laser printers come from Hewlett Packard' (*Guardian*); 'Confidence is growing that Opec will resolve its crisis,/however the Treasury is drawing up contingency plans' (*The Times*); 'Funds received in this way go towards the cost of electricity and water supply,/industries, shops and communes pay higher rates' (*The Times*).

The second lapse arises when a writer tries to say too much in a single sentence, as here: 'The measures would include plans to boost investment for self-financing in industry, coupled with schemes to promote investment and saving, alleviate youth unemployment, fight inflation and lower budget deficits, as well as a new look at the controversial issue of reducing working hours' (*The Times*). If the writer has not lost his readers, he has certainly lost himself. The last lumbering flourish ('as well as a new look . . .') is grammatically unconnected to what has gone before; it just hangs there. The sentence is crying out for a full stop – almost anywhere would do – to give the reader a chance to absorb the wealth of information being provided.

Here is another in which the writer tells us everything but his phone number: 'But after they had rejected once more the umpires' proposals of $5,000 a man for the playoffs and $10,000 for the World Series on a three-year contract and the umpires had turned down a proposal of $3,000 for the playoffs and $7,000 for the World Series on a one-year contract, baseball leaders said the playoffs would begin today and they had umpires to man the games' (*The New York Times*).

There is no quota on full stops. When an idea is complicated, break it up and present it in digestible chunks. One idea to a sentence is still the best advice that anyone has ever given on writing.

Appendix

hyphen. Almost nothing can be said with finality about the hyphen. As Fowler says, 'its infinite variety defies description'. Even the word for using a hyphen is contentious: some authorities hyphenate words, but others hyphen them. The principal function of the hyphen is to reduce the chances of ambiguity. Consider, for instance, the distinction between 'the 20-odd members of his Cabinet' and 'the 20 odd members of his Cabinet'. It is sometimes used to indicate pronunciation (de-ice), but not always (coalesce, reissue). Composite adjectives used before a noun are usually given hyphens (a six-foot-high wall, a four-inch rainfall), but again not always. Fowler cites 'a balance-of-payments deficit' and Gowers 'a first-class ticket', but in expressions such as these, where the words are frequently linked, the hyphens are no more necessary than they would be in 'a trade-union conference' or 'a Post-Office strike'. When the phrases are used adverbially, the use of hyphens is wrong, as here: 'Mr Conran, who will be 50-years-old next month ...' (*Sunday Times*). Mr Conran will be 50 years old next month; he will then be a 50-year-old man.

In general, hyphens should be dispensed with when they are not necessary. One place where they are not required by sense but frequently occur anyway is with '-ly' adverbs, as in 'newly-elected' or 'widely-held'. Almost every authority suggests that they should be deleted in such constructions.

parentheses. Parenthetical matter can be thought of as any information so incidental to the main thought that it needs to be separated from the sentence that contains it. It can be set off with dashes, brackets (usually reserved for explanatory insertions in quotations), commas or, of course, parentheses. It is, in short, an insertion and has no grammatical effect on the sentence in which it appears. It is rather as if the sentence does not even know it is there. Thus this statement from *The Times* is incorrect: 'But that is not how Mrs Graham (and her father before her) have made a success of the *Washington Post*'. The verb should be 'has'.

But while the parenthetical expression has no grammatical effect on the sentence in which it appears, the sentence does influence the parenthesis. Consider this extract from the *Los Angeles Times* (which, although it uses dashes, could equally have employed parentheses): 'One reason for the dearth of Japanese-American politicians is that no Japanese immigrants were allowed to become citizens – and thus could not vote – until 1952'. As written the sentence is telling us that 'no Japanese citizens could not vote'. Delete 'could not'.

When a parenthetical comment is part of a larger sentence, the full stop should appear after the second parenthesis (as here). (But when the entire sentence is parenthetical, as here, the full stop should appear inside the final parenthesis.)

question mark. The question mark comes at the end of a question. That sounds simple enough, doesn't it? But it's astonishing how frequently writers fail to include it. Two random examples: '"Why travel all the way there when you could watch the whole thing at home," he asked' (*The Times*); 'The inspector got up to go and stood on Mr Ellis's cat, killing it. "What else do you expect from these people," said the artist' (*Standard*).

Occasionally question marks are included when they are not called for, as in this sentence by Trollope, cited by Fowler: 'But let me ask of her enemies whether it is not as good a method as any other known to be extant?' The problem here is a failure to distinguish between a direct question and an indirect one. Direct questions always take question marks: 'Who is going with you?'. Indirect questions never do: 'I would like to know who is going with you'.

When direct questions take on the tone of a command, the use of a question mark becomes more discretionary. 'Will everyone please assemble in my office at four o'clock?' is strictly correct, but not all authorities insist on the question mark there.

A less frequent problem arises when a direct question appears outside a direct quotation. Fieldhouse, in *Everyman's Good English Guide*, suggests that the following punctuation is correct: 'Why does this happen to us, we wonder?' The Fowler brothers, however, call this an amusing blunder; certainly it is extremely irregular. The more usual course is to attach the question mark directly to the question. Thus: 'Why does this happen to us? we wonder'. But such constructions are clumsy and are almost always improved by being turned into indirect questions: 'We wonder why this happens to us'.

quotation marks (inverted commas). An issue that arises frequently in Britain, but almost never in America, is whether to put full stops and other punctuation inside or outside quotation marks when they appear together. The practice that prevails almost exclusively in America and is increasingly common in Britain is to put the punctuation inside the quotes. Thus: 'He said: "I will not go."' But some publishers prefer the punctuation to fall outside except when it is part of the quotation. Thus the example above would be: 'He said: "I will not go".'

Both systems are marked by inconsistencies – even Americans are forced to put the punctuation outside the quotes in such sentences as 'Which of you said, "Look out"?' – and there is not much to choose between them on grounds of logic. Similarly, the question of whether to use single quotes (') or double quotes (") is entirely a matter of preference except when it is dictated by house-style.

When quotation marks are used to set off a complete statement, the first word of the quotation should be capitalized ('He said, "Victory is ours"') except when the quotation is preceded by 'that' ('He said that "victory is ours"'). Fowler believed that no punctuation was necessary to set off attributive quotations; he would, for instance, delete the commas from the following: 'Tomorrow', he said, 'is a new day'. His argument was that commas are not needed to mark the interruption or introduction of a quotation because the quotation marks already do that. Logically he is correct. But with equal logic we could argue that question marks should be dispensed with on the grounds that the context almost always makes it clear that a question is being asked. The commas are required not by logic but by convention.

semicolon. The semicolon is heavier than the comma but lighter than the full stop. Its principal function is to divide contact clauses – that is, two ideas that are linked by sense but that lack a conjunction. For instance: 'You take the high road; I'll take the low road'. Equally that could be made into two complete sentences or, by introducing a conjunction, into one ('You take the high road and I'll take the low road'). The semicolon is also sometimes used to separate long coordinate clauses. In this role it was formerly used much more extensively than it is today – Fowler, for instance, would often string together a whole series of semicolons. Today its use is almost entirely discretionary. Many good writers scarcely use the semicolon at all.

Bibliography

Throughout the text I have in general referred to the following books by the surname of the author, ignoring the contributions of those who revised the originals. Thus although Sir Ernest Gowers substantially revised *A Dictionary of Modern English Usage* in 1965, that book is referred to throughout the text as 'Fowler'. References to 'Gowers' are meant to suggest Gowers's own book, *The Complete Plain Words*.

Aitchison, Jean, *Language Change: Progress or Decay?*, Fontana, London, 1981.

American Heritage Dictionary, American Heritage Publishing Company, New York, 1969.

Bernstein, Theodore M., *The Careful Writer*, Atheneum, New York, 1967.
   Dos, Don'ts and Maybes of English Usage, Times Books, New York, 1977.

Carey, G. V., *Mind the Stop*, Penguin, Harmondsworth, 1971.

Collins Dictionary of the English Language, Collins, London, 1979.

Concise Oxford Dictionary of Current English, Oxford University Press, Oxford, 1982.

Evans, Bergen and Cornelia, *A Dictionary of Contemporary American Usage*, Random House, New York, 1957.

Fieldhouse, Harry, *Everyman's Good English Guide*, J. M. Dent & Sons, London, 1982.

Fowler, E. G. and H. W., *The King's English*, third edition, Oxford University Press, London, 1970.

Fowler, H. W., *A Dictionary of Modern English Usage*, second edition (revised by Sir Ernest Gowers), Oxford University Press, Oxford, 1980.

Gowers, Sir Ernest, *The Complete Plain Words*, second edition (revised by Sir Bruce Fraser), Penguin, Harmondsworth, 1980.

Howard, Philip, *New Words for Old*, Unwin, London, 1980.
   Weasel Words, Hamish Hamilton, London, 1978.
   Words Fail Me, Hamish Hamilton, London, 1980.

Hudson, Kenneth, *The Dictionary of Diseased English*, Papermac, London, 1980.

Jordan, Lewis (ed.), *The New York Times Manual of Style and Usage*, Times Books, New York, 1976.

Michaels, Leonard, and Ricks, Christopher (ed.), *The State of the Language*, .University of California Press, Berkeley, 1980.

Morris, William and Mary, *Harper Dictionary of Contemporary Usage*, Harper & Row, New York, 1975.

Bibliography

Newman, Edwin, *Strictly Speaking*, Warner Books, New York, 1975.
　A Civil Tongue, Warner Books, New York, 1976.
Onions, C. T., *Modern English Syntax*, seventh edition (prepared by B. D. H. Miller), Routledge and Kegan Paul, London, 1971.
Oxford Dictionary for Writers and Editors, Oxford University Press, Oxford, 1981.
Oxford Dictionary of English Etymology, Oxford University Press, Oxford, 1982.
Palmer, Frank, *Grammar*, Penguin, Harmondsworth, 1982.
Partridge, Eric, *Usage and Abusage*, fifth edition, Penguin, Harmondsworth, 1981.
Phythian, B. A., *A Concise Dictionary of Correct English*, Hodder and Stoughton, London, 1979.
Quirk, Randolph, *The Use of English*, Longmans, London, 1969.
Safire, William, *On Language*, Avon, New York, 1980.
　What's the Good Word?, Times Books, New York, 1982.
Simon, John, *Paradigms Lost: Reflections on Literacy and Its Decline*, Clarkson N. Potter, New York, 1980.
Strunk Jr, William, and White, E. B., *The Elements of Style*, third edition, Macmillan, New York, 1979.
Wood, Frederick T., *Current English Usage*, Papermac, London, second edition, (revised by R. H. and L. M. Flavell), 1981.

Glossary

Grammatical terms are, to quote Frank Palmer, 'largely notional and often extremely vague'. In 'I went swimming', for instance, *swimming* is a present participle; but in 'Swimming is good for you', it is a gerund. Because such distinctions are for many of us a source of continuing perplexity, I have tried to use most such terms sparingly throughout the book. Inevitably, however, they do sometimes appear, and the following is offered as a simple guide for those who are confused or need refreshing. For a fuller discussion, I recommend *A Dictionary of Contemporary American Usage* by Bergen and Cornelia Evans and *A Concise Dictionary of Correct English* by B. A. Phythian.

adjective. A word that qualifies a noun or pronoun: 'a *brick* house', 'a *small* boy', 'a *blue* dress'. Most adjectives have three forms: the positive (*big*), the comparative (*bigger*) and the superlative (*biggest*). Although adjectives are usually easy to recognize when they stand before a noun, they are not always so easily discerned when they appear elsewhere in a sentence, as here: 'He was *deaf*', 'I'm glad to be *alive*', 'She's *awake* now'. Adjectives sometimes function as nouns (the *old*, the *poor*, the *sick*, the *insane*) and sometimes as adverbs (a *bitter*-cold night, a *quick*-witted man). The distinction between an adjective and adverb is often very fine. In 'a great book', *great* is an adjective; but in 'a great many books', it is an adverb.

adverb. A word that qualifies (or describes) any word other than a noun. That may seem a loose definition, but, as Palmer says, the classification is 'quite clearly a "ragbag" or "dustbin", the category into which words that do not seem to belong elsewhere are placed'. In general, adverbs qualify verbs (*badly* played), adjectives (*too* loud) or other adverbs (*very* quickly). As with adjectives, they have the three forms of positive, comparative and superlative (seen respectively in *long*, *longer*, *longest*). A common misconception is the belief that words that end in *-ly* are always adverbs. *Kindly*, *sickly*, *masterly* and *deadly*, for example, are usually adjectives.

case. The term describes relationships or syntactic functions between parts of speech. A pronoun is in the nominative case (sometimes called the subjective) when it is the subject of a verb ('*He* is here') and in the accusative (sometimes called the objective) when it is the object of a verb or preposition ('Give it to *him*'). Except for six pairs of pronouns (*I*/*me*, *he*/*him*, *she*/*her*, *they*/*them*, *we*/*us* and *who*/*whom*) and the genitive (which see), English has shed all its case forms.

clause. A group of words that contains a true verb (i.e., a verb functioning as such) and subject. In the sentence 'The house, which was built in 1920, was white' there are two clauses: 'The house was white' and 'which was built in 1920'. The first, which would stand on its own, is called a main or principal or independent clause. The second, which would not stand on its own, is called a dependent or subordinate clause. Sometimes the subject is suppressed in main clauses, as here: 'He got up and went downstairs'. Although 'and went downstairs' would not stand on its own, it is a main clause because the subject has been suppressed. In effect the sentence is saying: 'He got up and he went downstairs'. (See also PHRASE.)

complement. A word or group of words that completes a predicate construction – that is, that provides full sense to the meaning of the verb. In 'He is a rascal', *rascal* is the complement of the verb *is*.

conjunction. A word that links grammatical equivalents, as in 'The President and Prime Minister conferred for two hours' (the conjunction *and* links two nouns) and 'He came yesterday, but he didn't stay long' (the conjunction *but* links two clauses).

genitive. A noun or pronoun is in the genitive case when it expresses possession (*my* house, *his* car, *John's* job). Although some authorities make very small distinctions between genitives and possessives, many others do not. In this book, I have used the term *possessives* throughout.

gerund. A verb made to function as a noun, as with the italicized words here: '*Seeing* is *believing*'; '*Cooking* is an art'; '*Walking* is good exercise'. Gerunds always end in *-ing*.

infinitive. The term describes verbs that are in the infinite mood (that is, that do not have a subject). Put another way, it is a verb form that indicates the action of the verb without inflection to indicate person, number or tense. There are two forms of infinitive: the full (*to go*, *to see*) and bare (*go*, *see*), often called simply 'an infinitive without *to*'.

mood. Verbs have four moods:

1. The indicative, which is used to state facts or ask questions (I *am* going; What time *is* it?);

2. The imperative, which indicates commands (*Come* here; *Leave* me alone);

3. The infinite, which makes general statements and has no subject (*To know* her is *to love* her);

4. The subjunctive, which is principally used to indicate hypotheses or suppositions (If I *were* you ...). The uses of the subjunctive are discussed more fully in the body of the book.

noun is usually defined as a word that describes a person, place, thing or quality. Such a definition, as many authorities have noted, is technically inadequate. Most of us would not think of *hope*, *despair* and *exultation* as things, yet they are nouns. And most of the words that describe qualities – *good*, *bad*, *happy* and the like – are not nouns but adjectives. Palmer notes that there is no difference whatever in sense between 'He suffered terribly' and 'His suffering was terrible', yet *suffered* is a verb and *suffering* a noun. There is, in short, no definition for *noun* that isn't circular, though happily for most of us it is one part of speech that is almost always instantly recognizable.

object. Whereas the subject of a sentence tells you who or what is performing an action, the object tells you on whom or on what the action is being performed. In 'I like you', *you* is the object of the verb *like*. In 'They have now built most of the house', *most of the house* is the object of the verb *built*. Sometimes sentences have direct and indirect objects, as here: 'Please send me four tickets'; 'I'll give the dog a bath' (cited by Phythian). The direct objects are *four tickets* and *a bath*. The indirect objects are *me* and *the dog*. Prepositions also have objects. In the sentence 'Give it to him', *him* is the object of the preposition to.

participle. The participle is a verbal adjective. There are two kinds:

present participles, which end in *-ing* (*walking*, *looking*), and past participles, which end in *-d* (*heard*), *-ed* (*learned*), *-n* (*broken*) or *-t* (*bent*). The terms present and past participle can be misleading because present participles are often used in past-tense senses ('They were looking for the money') and past participles are often used when the sense is of the present or future ('He has broken it'; 'Things have never looked better'). When present-tense participles are used to function as nouns, they are called gerunds.

phrase. A group of words that does not have a subject and verb. 'I will come sometime soon' consists of a clause (*I will come*) and phrase (*sometime soon*). Phrases always express incomplete thoughts.

predicate. Everything in a sentence that is not part of the subject (i.e., the verbs, its qualifiers and complements) is called the predicate. In 'The man went to town after work', *The man* is the subject and the rest of the sentence is the predicate. The verb alone is sometimes called the simple predicate.

preposition. A word that connects and specifies the relationship between a noun or noun equivalent and a verb, adjective or other noun or noun equivalent. In 'We climbed over the fence', the preposition *over* connects the verb *climbed* with the noun *fence*. Whether a word is a preposition or conjunction is often a matter of function. In 'The army attacked before the enemy was awake', *before* is a conjunction. But in 'The army attacked before dawn', *before* is a preposition. The distinction is that in the first sentence *before* is followed by a verb. In the second it is not.

pronoun. A word used in place of a noun or nouns. In 'I like walking and reading; such are my pleasures', *such* is a pronoun standing for *reading* and *walking*. Pronouns have been variously grouped by different authorities. Among the more common groupings are personal pronouns (*I*, *me*, *his*, etc.), relative pronouns (*who*, *whom*, *that*, *which*), demonstrative pronouns (*this*, *that*, *these*, *those*) and indefinite pronouns (*some*, *several*, *either*, *neither*, etc.).

subject. The word or phrase in a sentence or clause that indicates who or what is performing the action. In 'I see you', the subject is *I*. In 'Climbing steep hills tires me', *Climbing steep hills* is the subject.

substantive. A word or group of words that performs the function of a noun. In 'Swimming is good for you', *Swimming* is a substantive, as well as a gerund.

verb. Verbs can be defined generally (if a bit loosely) as words that have tense and that denote what someone or something is or does. Verbs that have an object are called transitive verbs – that is, the verb transmits the action from a subject to an object, as in 'He put the book on the table'. Verbs that do not have an object are called intransitive verbs, as in 'He slept all night'; in these the action is confined to the subject.

When it is necessary to indicate more than simple past or present tense, two or more verbs are combined, as in 'I *have thought* about this all week'. Although there is no widely agreed term for such a combination of verbs, I have for convenience followed Fowler in this book and referred to them as compound verbs. The additional or 'helping' verb in such constructions (e.g., *have* in the example above) is called an auxiliary.

Practical Research Methods
for
Media and Cultural Studies

Practical Research Methods
for
Media and Cultural Studies

Making People Count

Máire Messenger Davies and Nick Mosdell

RAWAT PUBLICATIONS

Jaipur • New Delhi • Bangalore • Mumbai • Hyderabad • Guwahati

ISBN 81-316-0100-5

Indian Reprint, 2007

Published by
Prem Rawat for **Rawat Publications**
Satyam Apts., Sector 3, Jawahar Nagar, Jaipur - 302 004 (India)
Phone: 0141 265 1748 / 7006 Fax: 0141 265 1748
E-mail : info@rawatbooks.com
Website: rawatbooks.com

New Delhi Office
4858/24, Ansari Road, Daryaganj, New Delhi 110 002
Phone: 011-23263290

Also at Bangalore, Mumbai, Hyderabad and Guwahati

Printed at Chaman Enterprises, New Delhi

Contents

Acknowledgements

We would like to thank the following people for their contributions to this book: Sarah Edwards, Dr Claire Wardle and Dr Ema Sofia Leitao.

Everyone involved with the 'Consenting Children?' project – the staff at the BSC, the research team, and the children and families who participated.

Everyone involved with the West Yorkshire Playhouse project, especially Professor Roberta Pearson. Special thanks are due to Patrick Stewart for help with access.

All the students who have kindly allowed us to use examples of their work.

Finally, this book is dedicated to all the students, past, present and future, who have motivated us to develop our teaching courses and materials and who, unlikely though it may sound, have made the experience of teaching quantitative research methods rewarding and fun.

PART ONE

DESIGN: 'PLANNING IT'

CHAPTER 1

Introduction

'I am happy to teach them about research with
people and audiences, but I can't do numbers.'

This remark, from a professor in Media Studies who had received a
number of grants from the British Economic and Social Research
Council to conduct research on questions of media representation, is
typical of many scholars and students in the Humanities. You could
throw a book in any number of Humanities departments in well-
regarded universities and the chances of hitting somebody who 'can't
do numbers' would be extremely high.

This book is for people who think they can't do numbers and
moreover don't want to do them, perhaps because 'doing numbers',
in the form of studying mathematics at school, has been associated
with feelings of struggle, bewilderment and incompetence. For many
such people, even if numbers eventually were mastered, numerical
formulae still seem less adequate at explaining the complexity of the
world, or of personal experiences, than language or artistic forms.
This sense of inadequacy and boredom with numbers can be uncomfortable for bright, imaginative young people, used to succeeding
intellectually in other areas of the curriculum based on linguistic and
creative skills, such as English, history and the arts. Such feelings can
lead to rejection and suspicion of any kind of knowledge which is
based on the systematic acquisition of data analysed in numerical
form; we have found this to be the case with many students and colleagues throughout our careers. Yet much of the everyday knowledge
we all have about the world does come in numerical form, or can be
translated into that form for easier manipulation and prediction.
Often we do not realise that when we 'calculate the odds', we are
dealing in mathematical probabilities, or that when we make value
judgements about what is 'best', 'better' or 'worse', we are manipu-
lating 'ordinal data'.

One example of a very common way in which we organise our
knowledge about the world is through graded preferences or 'rankings' – an example drawn from popular culture is 'Top Tens'. Every

student is familiar with such phenomena. 'Top Tens' can be based on your personal likes and dislikes, which may vary over time: your top ten favourite albums or movies today may be different this time next year. But they are still ranked from 1 (the best) to 10 (the 10th best – or worst), with 5 being in the middle (or is it? . . .). Rankings may also be based on more systematic and large-scale number-crunching, as with the commercial industry Top Tens, which are derived from the number of sales of a recording, or, in the case of movies, from the number of people paying to go to see a film in the first weekend of its release. These numbers are *precisely measurable* and are based on *accurate counting* at sales points of the numbers of tickets sold.

Unlike your personal tastes, this way of counting *won't* vary (as such, it is called 'interval data'), but the figures amassed in this way can affect your personal preferences just the same. Collecting precise records of what kind of product does well at the box office will affect what becomes available to you as a cultural consumer next year. If the current fashion in cinema production is for fantasy (*Harry Potter*, *Lord of the Rings*), the chances of next year's cinematic offerings including fantasy films are going to be greater. These 'chances' are not in fact 'chance' (we'll say more about 'chance' in Chapter 10); the odds of repeating the success of a *Harry Potter* will be very precisely calculated by the financial and marketing advisers to the Hollywood production companies.

Getting a degree and getting a job

If you are a Humanities student, it is likely that at some stage you will be required to study a research methods module or course. This is particularly the case for postgraduate students, and increasingly so for undergraduates. We have found that some colleagues in Humanities departments are a bit sceptical about 'methodology' and the possibility of teaching 'how to do research'. Research is just something you do. We have found that our practical approach to teaching quantitative methods – which can also be applied to other methods – has helped to bridge this perceptual gap. This book is a basic introduction to the principles of empirical quantitative research, many of which, we believe, underpin *any* effective approach to methodology teaching. These principles state that research should be rigorous, systematic, replicable, valid, derived from clear research questions and properly operationalised, whatever your subject area. The book describes pedagogic procedures which, in our experience, have been effective with students who are highly resistant to the idea of 'statistics', 'scientific methods' or 'measuring' abstract concepts.

As a Humanities student it is also likely that you will be seeking employment in the cultural or service (whether public or private) industries when you graduate. If you want to work in the cultural industries at any level – whether in production, or administration or management, or marketing, or training, or government policy (as in the Department of Culture, Media and Sport in Britain, or the Federal Communications Commission in the United States) – you will need to understand something about the kinds of calculations made from box office and sales figures and – more controversially – the assumptions about audiences and their feelings, which are sometimes inferred from these calculations. You will need to understand how to interpret figures and how to be sceptical of some of the claims you will hear based on them. The best way to understand a procedure, we believe, is to learn to *do it yourself*. Hence this book.

This book is primarily a practical guide to the uses of quantitative (numerical) research methods in the Humanities, with particular reference to different kinds of media and cultural research. Before we get down to the specific details of designing and carrying out such a research project, we want to say something about the historical and intellectual background to the systematic study of human beings and their tastes, feelings, attitudes and behaviour – the disciplines of social science, from which quantitative research methods are mainly drawn.

'How can you study human beings as if they were specimens?' The case for social science

A common difficulty for Humanities students in studying social science research methods is the word 'science'. As with mathematics, science may be associated with difficulty and failure at school; also with dehumanising formulae, experiments, laboratories, abstractions, 'men in white coats', and various moral, social and political ills – nuclear weapons, environmental degradation, cruelty to animals, 'playing God' by cloning embryos, colonial exploitation of developing countries, and so on. Many of people's notions about science come from popular media: from dystopic movies of the future in which current problems brought about by human scientific and technological overkill create terrifying threats to humanity: *Blade Runner*, *Soylent Green*, *Logan's Run*, *The Day after Tomorrow*, and so on. The fact that science provides major solutions in helping to solve these problems may sometimes be forgotten because such solutions are cumulative and incremental, and have much less narrative and spectacular potential as stories.

Conversely, the human impact of scientific development may sometimes be overlooked by 'pure' scientists (those who study the 'natural' sciences such as physics, chemistry, biology). Fantasy stories express these human anxieties in ways that scientists and policy-makers would do well to address. Also, science can only work well within human social institutions which are rationally and compassionately organised and which allow scope for human imagination, creativity and instincts for ethical behaviour. A laboratory is a human social institution too, and as such can be studied using **social scientific methods**.

What are workable social systems? The uses of social science

Social science raises, and helps to answer, questions that the natural sciences tend to take as given and that people in the Humanities may argue can be answered purely by critical analysis and interpretation: the question of how we bring about workable social arrangements in which both science and the arts can flourish in the first place. How do we understand the human organisations, whether family groups, schools, nation-states or workplaces, that appear to work effectively, and how can we learn and apply lessons from them in order to ensure that new social arrangements will also work well? Similarly, where human social organisations do not appear to be working well – where there is conflict, relationship breakdown, extreme poverty, inequality, abuse or crime – how do we understand these phenomena, and how can we put them right?

In the field of media, culture and communications – the study of the myriad ways in which human beings acquire and convey meaning about themselves and to others – social science may seem even less relevant. In fact, it can raise, and help to answer, many useful questions:

- How does language develop in the first place, and how can we devise reliable methods of evaluating the way that babies communicate, given that they don't yet use words?[1]
- What forms of communication do different kinds of people use, and how might this differently affect their perceptions of meanings?
- What difference do culture, ethnicity and genetic inheritance make to people's communication behaviours, creativity and tastes?
- What factors determine the industrial production and distribution of commercial media products?
- What is the degree of public support for public service media?
- How do media institutions change over time?
- What is the relationship between art, culture, media and government?
- How do you evaluate, compare and predict different people's tastes, comprehension, influence or susceptibility to persuasion?
- What makes people change their attitudes?
- What makes people want to buy things? Or not buy them?
- How do different people set a value on media products – whether economic, political, cultural or moral?
- How do people *learn* to make sense of different forms of communication? How do they adapt to 'new' media?
- Where do 'new' media come from?
- Do we learn more from images or from words?
- What stops people understanding and learning effectively?
- How do we distinguish between propaganda and 'truth'?
- When people have learned something, what makes them forget it again?
- Does watching violent films make children violent?
- What is violence anyway?

---

[1] M. M. Davies, E. Lloyd and A. Scheffler (1987) *Baby Language*, London: Unwin Hyman.

And so on, and on.

These are questions which the social sciences: psychology, sociology, anthropology – the study of human beings and their behaviour – can help to answer. Indeed, they are the kinds of questions that are much more likely to be *asked* by social scientists than by other scholars. An art critic may value and write about 'creativity' or 'originality' in a work of art. The social scientist asks:

> 'What does the term creativity *mean* to the people who use it? Who does use it? And how might they apply it in their everyday lives and jobs?'·

Scientific method

A major usefulness of science as applied to the study of human beings, we want to argue, is its *method*. There are many ways of studying human beings, but the quantitative research methods we write about in this book are based on rigorous and systematic procedures drawn from science, and these research design procedures are very useful tools, not only for research, but for logical thinking generally. Learning these procedures provides 'transferable skills' which can be used in all walks of life. This book is a simple introduction to such methodologies. It does not pretend to be a guide to carrying out complex professional research projects, such as social policy surveys or criminological or educational experiments. It is a guide for the classroom; a way of learning (and teaching) social scientific procedures, specifically quantitative research methods, which can be practically and (we hope) relatively painlessly applied within an academic teaching programme. This could be:

- a research methods course for postgraduate training; or
- an undergraduate research methods dissertation module; or
- a short, intensive research methods workshop for professional short courses; or
- a short workshop within a larger research methods training programme, like those we have conducted at Cardiff University.

As such, this book may seem to some fully-fledged social scientists, whether in universities or outside them, shockingly simple and basic, and sadly lacking in the more sophisticated, complex, mathematical research techniques employed, for instance, in advanced experimental psychology or in major social policy surveys. As former psychology postgraduates and researchers, we have done a bit of advanced experimental psychology ourselves; we have even helped out on some social policy surveys and know what the possibilities are for answering complex questions in these research areas, especially with the exciting new software packages for designing and conducting statistical and other kinds of research which have been produced since we began our own studies. All we can say in defence of our simplistic approach is that most of the many students to whom we have taught research methods over the years don't want to be experimental psychologists or social policy researchers: they want to be film-makers, or journalists, or PR executives, or teachers, or just want to get a good degree and go travelling. But they do need to carry out research as part of their educational training, and – heretical thought – they do have some expectations that carrying out a practical project, including doing research with numbers, ought to be enjoyable and enlightening, even fun. We think so too.

Introducing social science research on the media: background reading

This is primarily a 'how to' book, but it is also important for students to understand some of the intellectual background of the social sciences as well as some of the history of empirical research into the media. Therefore, we recommend some basic reading before embarking on detailed methods training. Every teacher and student may have their pet textbooks or theorists who are useful to them, but two key texts in media research which we have found valuable and which flesh out in more detail some of the procedures we talk about in this book are Wimmer and Dominick's *Mass Media Research*, now in its eighth edition (2006), and Bauer and Gaskell's edited collection, *Qualitative Research with Image Text and Sound* (2000). Williams' *Science and Social Science: An Introduction* (London and New York: Routledge, 2000) is also a useful account of the conceptual and methodological commonalities and distinctions between pure science and its application to human activities. Williams makes a helpful distinction between scientific method and the social constructionism and relativism of cultural studies:

> An important task of science and one in which it is (I think) partially successful, is to distinguish between the 'real' and what is socially constructed as 'real' . . . gravity for example does not differentially affect cultures in time or space. (p. 85)

It is also useful for students to be aware of general theoretical debates surrounding the operation of human institutions such as the media, and their political, economic and social roles, as well as their historical origins. Jürgen Habermas's work on 'the public sphere' underpins much of the thinking about the social role of media institutions and he has articulated the value of empirical evidence and systematic and rigorous ways of gathering it:

> we consider methods and procedures of gathering and presenting evidence as essential for social scientific research . . . they place research squarely within the public sphere and subject it to the demands of accountability. Methods and procedures are the scientific way of being publicly accountable for evidence. However, we have to assume a public sphere that is free to allow the uncensored pursuit of evidence, which is not to be taken for granted. (Habermas, 1989; quoted in Bauer and Gaskell 2000, p. 12)

The claim here is that social scientific methods make research publicly 'accountable' – that is, they provide a guarantee of a minimum level of reliability, consistency, validity and replicability because these are universally accepted procedures which are in the public domain and can be used and checked by other scholars and by other people generally; this is necessary in a democracy. Habermas makes a warning point that 'the uncensored pursuit of evidence' is 'not to be taken for granted'. Under some forms of government 'uncensored pursuit of evidence' could be seen as a challenge to the ruling powers. Although learning how to design a standardised questionnaire and to analyse the results using proven statistical techniques may not seem like a particularly heroic enterprise in the advancement of human enlightenment, there is a sense in which it does have this heroic aspect: these methods are an attempt to make knowledge independent, and not reliant on human subjectivity, 'instinct', emotional reactions, common sense, mere habit or authority. There is a long history of totalitarian regimes threatening scientific enquiry; young people who challenge received wisdom – who ask 'why?' or 'how?' or 'why not?' – may get into trouble if they live in communities where challenging traditional modes of thought is discouraged.

Scientific method not only does not *dis*courage challenges to received wisdom; it positively *en*courages them.

The scientific method

Scientific method – the empirical testing of hypotheses – can be distinguished from other sources of knowledge, such as:

a) **Tenacity**, or tradition: 'We've always done it this way. What's good enough for the people who came before us is good enough for us.'
b) **Intuition**: the 'gut feeling' that can't be put into words, which many creative people talk about when asked why or how they did something.
c) **Authority**: religious texts; parents; famous authors: 'I believe it because a particular authority, or guru, says so.'

In contrast, the scientific community and the discoveries produced within it have different characteristics: scientific knowledge is often **anonymous**. Although discoveries may be associated with particular individuals, the process of acquiring scientific information depends on many people and teams working over time. Hence scientific knowledge is **cumulative** and **reactive** (research is done in response to other people's research). It is a kind of jigsaw in which no one individual can be dominant – unlike in the arts, where (despite French theorists announcing 'the death of the author') the study of individual artists and authors historically, economically and critically, is still central to scholarship.

Scientific characteristics

Science is:

1. **Public**: known and available for testing and especially for *replication* (see Chapters 2 and 3).
2. **Objective**: scientific method attempts to rule out, or control for, subjective judgements; for example, behaviour is seen as a more

reliable indicator of someone's state of mind than an observer's interpretation. If you want to demonstrate that someone's attention is not held by a TV programme, seeing them switching the TV off is a more reliable measure (because directly observable and not subject to interpretation) than trying to analyse the facial expression of the viewer.

3. **Empirical**: knowable, measurable, based on evidence. Abstract concepts, such as 'boredom', as above, have to be *operationally defined* (see Chapter 2).
4. **Systematic and cumulative**, based on methods which can be known and shared by all scholars everywhere, and hence built on, adapted, revised, extended, changed by other scholars.

Quality versus quantity?

In their book about qualitative research (that is, research which is not based on numerical analysis or scientific procedures such as experiments, but is based on individual observation and critical analysis), Bauer and Gaskell argue that such research can learn a lot from scientific methods. Among the advantages they claim for science are:

- procedural clarity – a set of steps and activities which are generally universally agreed on by quantitative researchers;
- 'a developed discourse on quality in the research process which establishes a basis for self-criticism'. Such an emphasis on quality in the research process:
- serves to demarcate good from bad practice,
- helps to establish credibility in the context of publicly accountable research, and, as we have argued,
- these procedures are a valuable didactic tool in the training of students.

The purpose of science is to make valid predictions, based on 'empirically supported universal laws', which, under certain conditions (which may vary), can be predicted with some certainty to operate in the same way more than once.

Bauer and Gaskell also scrutinise what they call the 'stronger claim often made for qualitative research that it is intrinsically a more critical and potentially emancipatory form of research' (2000, p. 14). Qualitative research aims to see through the eyes of those being studied. It is seen as necessary to understand the interpretations that social actors (people themselves) have of the world, because it is these interpretations that motivate the behaviour that creates the social world itself. However, as these authors point out, it does not necessarily follow that the outcome is a critical piece of work. Understanding may also 'serve as a basis for the establishment of mechanisms of social control'. Quantitative and qualitative methodologies need to be compared in terms not only of how reliable and replicable they are, but also how sensitive they are to the needs, rights and points of view of the people, or groups, being studied. Both kinds of method need techniques which respect these needs and rights and do not assert or privilege the personal points of view of the people doing the research.

Falsifying hypotheses

One further important characteristic of scientific method is that it is often 'counter-intuitive' – that is, it seems to fly in the face of common sense. One of the most difficult things for beginners in research methodology to grasp is the notion of falsification (more is said about this and about the 'null hypothesis' in Chapter 2). As we've said, science – no matter how objective, rigorous and replicable its procedures may be – still operates within fallible human institutions, and one of the most enlightening books on how science itself changes historically and culturally is Thomas Kuhn's *The Structure of Scientific Revolutions* (1970). Kuhn states:

> Few philosophers of science still seek absolute criteria for the verification of scientific theories. Noting that no theory can ever be exposed to all possible relevant tests, they ask not whether a theory has been verified but rather about its probability in the light of the evidence that actually exists. (p. 145)

Kuhn refers to the work of the philosopher Karl Popper,[2] who, says Kuhn, 'denies the existence of any verification procedures at all'. Popper emphasises the importance of 'falsification': a test that,

---

[2] K. R. Popper (1959) *The Logic of Scientific Discovery*, New York: Basic Books.

'because its outcome is negative, necessitates the rejection of an established theory'. This approach – that you can't prove anything, you can only disprove it – may sound somewhat negative to the beginning researcher. It is also counter-intuitive. By trying to falsify your hypotheses rather than to support them, it would seem that all you're doing with your research is knocking down ideas, rather than building them up. Where can new knowledge come from in this case?

In fact, 'falsification' is not only important intellectually, it is also a practical way of keeping your project manageable, especially important for amateur and student researchers with limited resources. As Kuhn says, 'no theory can ever be exposed to all possible relevant tests', not even by full-time professional scientists or social scientists, never mind a student on a one-year MA course. A useful way of showing how sensible 'falsification' is as a way of limiting and making research design manageable comes from Jean Aitchison in her book on language, *The Articulate Mammal* (1983):

> The point is, science proceeds by *disproving* hypotheses. Suppose you were interested in flowers. You might formulate a hypothesis, 'All roses are white, red, pink, orange or yellow.' There would be absolutely no point at all in collecting hundreds, thousands, or even millions of white, red, pink, orange and yellow roses. You would merely be collecting additional evidence consistent with your hypothesis. If you were genuinely interested in making a botanical advance, you would send people in all directions hunting for black, blue, mauve or green roses. Your hypothesis would stand until somebody found a blue rose. Then in theory you should be delighted that botany had made progress and found out about blue roses. Naturally when you formulate a hypothesis it has to be one which is capable of disproof. A hypothesis such as 'Henry VIII would have disliked spaceships' cannot be disproved and consequently is useless. (pp. 187–8)

The social scientific study of the media

Social science methods began to be applied to the media as the result of a number of political and historical developments. During the twentieth century, particularly arising from the First World War, and even more during and after the Second World War, a concern with propaganda and its effects led to the academic study of mass media institutions and politics, particularly broadcast media – first radio, then television. This was also linked with the development of behaviourist psychology in the 1930s and 1940s, leading to what has been popularly called 'the magic bullet', or 'hypodermic needle', theory of media effects: the view that people will be influenced directly by examples of behaviour they see in film and television, and will therefore imitate them. Further developments leading to systematic research into the relationship of the media with society included the growth of advertising and the consumer society, particularly in the United States. There was also public concern especially about children and other vulnerable groups in their susceptibility to harmful media effects.[3]

As media institutions became more powerful economically and politically, with increased competition for advertising income and hence for the attention of the public, the question of how to attract and mould public attitudes became more pressing for media institutions themselves. The television ratings (audience measurement) are a major example of how systematic audience research, based on large-scale quantitative surveys, is absolutely central to the operation and economic survival of broadcasting. Within educational establishments, and also within many media and cultural institutions, other kinds of questions about how effective particular creative techniques could be in helping people learn and understand also stimulated research. An example is the formative and evaluative research for the preschool programme *Sesame Street* (see Lesser, 1974),[4] which continues to this day, and guides production decisions.

This book and what it will do

So, this book can be summarised as a 'Rough Guide' to social science research methods, aimed at empowering Humanities students and helping them in a sympathetic way to master complex research skills. It aims to show how different disciplinary research approaches can be integrated. It particularly demonstrates how quantitative research

---

[3] See e.g. A. Bandura et al. (1963) 'Imitation of film-mediated aggressive models', Journal of Abnormal and Social Psychology, vol.66, No.1, 3–11, and the many similar experiments 'replicating' his findings

[4] G. Lesser (1974) *Children and Television: Lessons from Sesame Street*, New York: Random House.

methods, including statistical surveys and content analysis, can be used to answer qualitative questions about, for instance, audience tastes, interpretation of texts and the relationship of demographic factors, such as social class and gender, to cultural consumption and behaviour. All of this is illustrated with examples drawn from our teaching and student work.

The book aims particularly to show how students' *own* choices of 'themes, concepts and ideas' can be refined to produce manageable research questions, and how – depending on the choice of theme – an appropriate research method and design can be formulated. The book will focus on quantitative approaches, such as surveys and content analysis; however, qualitative approaches, such as focus groups, discourse analysis and case studies, although technically 'left out', will be touched on, since multiple methods – or 'triangulation' – are necessary for humanities-type research questions. We will leave out dense theoretical discussions, since the book is meant to be a practical and accessible work of reference and advice. There will also be no complicated mathematical formulae. We will base our explanations on the standard SPSS tabulated printouts, as we do in class, with our own 'glosses' written in clear language to help students understand what they are doing.

What will readers gain from it?

Readers will gain:

a) mastery of something they may have found difficult and inaccessible, and therefore a real sense of achievement;

b) mastery of computer technology, and familiarity with a powerful and complex analytical computer program;

c) transferable intellectual skills, such as a critical approach to numbers and statistical claims; an ability to interpret research reports and surveys; problem-solving; precise formulation of research questions, methods and goals;

d) real-world applications of research skills, based on students' own ideas and interests;

e) for teachers, useful tools and teaching approaches – as well as knowledge and skills for themselves.

CHAPTER 2

What is Your Research Question?

This chapter deals with one of the most difficult issues for students, and it comes right at the start of the project, which can lead to a feeling of 'why bother?' This is the task of formulating a precise research question. How, for instance, can a feeling that:

'the press is biased', or that
'advertising exploits women', or that
'children are corrupted by violence on television'

– topics proposed by many students for their dissertation projects, reflecting popularly held beliefs – be translated into a practicable research question and project?

Students often choose a dissertation or research project topic because they have a strong 'gut feeling' about a particular issue – and this can be a good way to start. It's very hard to investigate something for several months (or for PhD students, years) when you have no particular emotional investment in it. However, emotional investment can be a drawback, because it creates – yes – 'bias'. Many students are convinced that something is already the case ('I know that advertising really does exploit women'). But why bother to carry out research, if you already know the answer? The first step in the art of producing a good and do-able research topic for a student project or dissertation consists in coming up with a question *which needs an answer*, in other words, which requires some research. Second, it has to be a practicable question which can be answered during the time-scale and the research resources of the course you are studying.

In this chapter we will address the following key preliminary issues in choosing and setting up a design for a research project:

- practicability;
- formulating the question;
- formulating a hypothesis;
- the concept of the 'null hypothesis';
- validity;

- generalisability;
- the 'wh' questions: what, why, where, when, how and with whom?
- Group versus individual projects

Practicability

It is essential to point out from the beginning that student projects are limited in terms of what they can do: limited in time, in financial resources and in access to specialised research resources such as visits to overseas archives or to eminent interviewees. A good student project should thus not be too ambitious in its scope. If you are writing a master's or undergraduate dissertation, it is likely that you will have at the most six months in which to carry out the project and write it up. Even if you are a PhD student with three years to complete your project, your time needs to be carefully managed: good forward design and planning are essential if you are intending to carry out empirical work, particularly fieldwork with human subjects. Fieldwork will always require a *pilot study* (see Chapter 8), and this increases the amount of time needed to collect and analyse data.

It is wise for people teaching dissertation modules to ensure that students' topics are chosen and their methods decided on fairly early in the academic year during which the project must be carried out (see Chapter 12 for more advice for teachers on this). As mentioned, planning, piloting, carrying out and analysing fieldwork takes time and you are unlikely to have large amounts of external research funding for a student project. Hence, if you wish to study the alleged bias in the press in your own country (assuming you are an international student from, say, Africa, Asia or Europe, as many of our students are), it is not practicable to finance a special trip to do this. However, with the kind of good forward planning we are recommending in this book, it may be possible to combine a holiday visit home with fieldwork or archive work. Many of our students have done this.

Formulating the question

The key issue is: *what do you want to know?*

Let us take the question of 'bias in the press', using a real example from the country in which one of us is working, Northern Ireland. An MA student in an introductory research class said he was interested in studying 'press coverage of the North'.

How might we refine this topic and turn it into a practicable research question and project? For a start we need to define terms – we need to provide what are called **'operational definitions'** of this topic.

First, 'the North'. Does he mean Northern Ireland or the North of some other place? He means Northern Ireland, and the use of the term 'North' immediately implies the existence of an alternative – 'South'. In the case of Ireland, the term 'South' connotes both a political and a geographic entity: the 'opposite' of Northern Ireland is the Republic of Ireland, often called 'the South of Ireland', even though the most northerly county of the island of Ireland, Donegal, is in the Republic, whereas Northern Ireland is part of the United Kingdom. Hence, our student's research question has a number of hidden complexities; he might want to include an element of contrast between 'North' and 'South' and between the two different political situations in the two parts of Ireland. This student is studying journalism and it turns out he is interested in the political situation in Northern Ireland. So his topic is not 'the North' in general, but needs to be redefined as 'politics in Northern Ireland'.

Next 'the press': Does this mean newspapers? Printed or online? British newspapers? Irish newspapers? International newspapers? Local or national newspapers? *All* newspapers from the time they were first printed or just some of them, and if only some of them, on what basis would his selection (or **sample** – see more about this in Chapter 4) be made? This student did mean newspapers, but was not sure at this stage if he wanted to look at both British and Irish newspapers, or why this might be a relevant decision to his project, since he did not yet know what his research question was in any detail. Hence the importance of deciding precisely what the research question will be: only then can appropriate decisions be taken about **method**.

Finally 'coverage': does this mean the sheer *amount* of 'coverage' – the number of stories, or column inches, devoted to the North of Ireland – or does it mean the way in which these stories are written and presented (something more intangible and difficult to define)? (We will come to this in our chapter on **content analysis**; see Chapter 7.) Again, the answer to this will vary depending on the precise research question.

Given that it transpires that this student is worried about possible 'bias' in the reporting of Northern Irish politics, before we go any further, it is important to find an **operational definition** of what he means by bias. Bias towards? Bias against? Bias on the part of individual reporters? Or bias on the part of the editorial line of the paper generally?

What does bias look like?

Answering questions like this is one of the hardest things for Humanities students to do: to produce an **operational definition** of an abstract concept. Those of us trained in the social sciences – in our case, psychology – had to learn how to do this, sometimes with difficulty, in setting up experiments to measure human reactions and emotions. For instance, one measure of bias in a psychology experiment could be *reaction time* in carrying out a task: if asked to press a button to say whether they agreed or disagreed that a particular Irish politician was 'trustworthy', a person biased in favour of the politician would find it easier to press the button marked 'agree' and is likely to react more quickly than someone who disagreed. (Negative judgements take longer to process mentally.)

The operational definition of bias here is thus:

'Speed of reaction to a statement about the politician's character.'

Another operational definition of bias – this time in the case of written text – could be:

The use of negative language in reporting.

Bias in press coverage could be recognised by the consistent use of negative terms about a politician, such as 'ANGER AT' or 'LACK OF TRUST CLAIM' in headlines about him. You will note that terms like these include a further operational definition of possible bias in that they are:

reported reactions, not actual factual evidence

of the man's untrustworthiness.

Formulating a hypothesis

Question or hypothesis? Do it both ways

So is our student any nearer to formulating a research question? Before we come up with some possible questions arising out of the preliminary refining and defining processes described above, we need to alert the novice researcher to one more important approach: the need to have a **hypothesis**. A hypothesis is an assumption, or hunch, that something is likely to be the case; your research will test whether your assumption is right or not. For instance, in the case of bias in the press, your hypothesis, or hunch, might be that 'the press is biased against Northern Irish politicians'. In such a case, we can see that the *method* question about which particular newspapers we are going to study is very important. We might expect that newspapers published in England (such as the national dailies, originating in London) are more likely to be biased against Northern Irish politicians than Irish newspapers, whether in the North or South. This bias might express itself in sheer lack of coverage (as measured by number of stories, or column inches) in English newspapers, compared with Irish newspapers. Or our researcher might want to compare newspapers in the Republic of Ireland with newspapers in the North of Ireland in terms of the emotive language they use. Or he might want to compare newspapers in the North only, and look at publications with differing political constituencies among their readers and study how they report on the 'others'. *It all depends on what the research question is.* Thus, we see that no decisions about research methods (which newspapers, how many, where we should look for them, how we analyse them) can be taken until the research question/hypothesis is properly formulated.

Preliminary research question about press bias and Northern Irish politics

We do have the beginnings of a research question which can also be expressed as a hypothesis. It may well be that this question will be further refined once the student embarks on the research, but it is better to be clear from the outset what you want to know before you get going on time-consuming and possibly expensive data-gathering. Phrased as a question, the student's inquiry could be:

> To what extent do newspapers originating in England differ from newspapers published in Northern Ireland in a) the amount and b) the emotional tone of their coverage of Northern Irish politicians?

Preliminary hypothesis based on this question

This can also be expressed as a hypothesis:

> It is predicted that newspapers originating in England will be a) less likely to give lengthy coverage and b) more likely to give negative coverage of Northern Irish politicians than newspapers originating in Northern Ireland.

You can see that turning the question into a hypothesis gives the researcher something to go on. You have a working assumption to guide your search for evidence and your analysis. Of course your hypothesis may be wrong – it may turn out that you cannot find evidence of this kind of bias in your study. But that is the purpose of research: to test hypotheses and – quite often – to show that, at least from the evidence you have gathered, these assumptions cannot be supported after all. (We will say more about the **null hypothesis** and other hypothesis-testing procedures later.) The purpose of empirical research is never to reinforce or prove what you think you know already; it is to put this knowledge to the test and to question how reliable it is by seeking evidence.

The source of hypotheses: reviewing the literature

The final point to emphasise in this early stage of formulating your topic is to stress the importance of acquiring solid background knowledge of the topic you are interested in through appropriate reading; a review of this reading material (**literature review**) will be the first chapter of a thesis. Our student who wanted to study the press coverage of Northern Irish politics had some preliminary knowledge of Irish politics, but before finally deciding on his research question, it will be important for him to read some existing studies, first, of media coverage of Northern Ireland (such as Bill Rolston and David Miller (eds.) (1996) *War and Words: The Northern Ireland Media Reader*), and second, some more general studies to help with methodology: how to evaluate media 'bias' (for instance, the work of the Glasgow Media Group on television news coverage, or the major study of the British press by James Curran and Jean Seaton (1997) *Power without Responsibility*). From this background reading he will be able to develop a research question arising from these earlier studies, perhaps applying lessons learned by researchers in Glasgow to the Northern Irish situation.

The null hypothesis

Before we leave the topic of hypotheses, we must briefly mention another concept that can be quite difficult for many Humanities (and other) students to grasp: the concept of the 'null hypothesis'. The null hypothesis states that 'there is *no difference* between any particular sets of observations' – whether these observations suggest that the British press is more hostile to Irish politicians than the Irish press, or vice versa. The null hypothesis assumes that any observed differences are likely to be due to *chance*, not to 'bias' or to any other deliberate or intentional process. It is this assumption – that observed differences in your data are due only to chance – that is tested in statistical tests. We will say more about these tests later; at this stage all we will say is that it is likely that you, as a keen researcher, will be hoping that the null hypothesis will *not* be supported by your research; in other words, you hope that the evidence that you have collected about bias in the press (or whatever topic you are studying) is so repeated and systematic, that it must be due to deliberate intention, not to chance. You may be wrong though, and you must not allow your *own* desires and intentions to distort the research process. Hence the importance of proper design and method in research.

The null hypothesis is a technical way of expressing what we discussed in the introductory chapter – Popper's concept of the *falsification* of hypotheses. Assumptions must be challenged, not just supported, by the research process.

Validity

The next key term to take account of in designing a good empirical study is **validity**, or making your study *reliable*. It is important to note that in social science we do not use the term 'truth' about the findings of a study. We call our findings 'valid' – that is, they are as reliable as they can be at the present moment (but times and circumstances may change, which could lead to different findings being produced in a future study). Our findings are valid because we have made every effort to ensure that there were no avoidable mistakes in the way we designed and carried out the study. We also do not use the term 'prove' because absolute proof is impossible in an area of study – the social sciences – where human judgements, emotions and cultural variability are so diverse and complex.

We don't use the term 'true' because for every categorical statement you might make about human beings and their behaviour –

'men like fighting',
'women care a lot about what they look like',
'children are innocent'

– you can always find counter-examples: men who don't like fighting, women who don't care about fashion, children who appear to be evil incarnate. The most we can ever do is 'provide convincing evidence' that, given certain circumstances, and given the selected sample, in most of the examples we've gathered something appears to be the case; but we can never conclusively 'prove' it.

In seeking evidence, in order to make our study 'valid', we have to design our study so that mistakes don't creep into the findings. Because of human variability and human fallibility, there will always be some margin of error in any scientific or social scientific study. This 'error' value is factored into statistical tests looking at whether the results of a study are significant or not; all numerical analysis recognises that there will be some sources of error. Error can never be eliminated, only minimised and factored into the final statistical analysis.

Again, the importance of choosing a precise and specific research question helps to minimise error in the final analysis. For instance, in the case of Northern Ireland, it is much easier to demonstrate that some newspapers devote less *space* to Irish politics, or use more *negative language* in headlines, than it is to 'prove' that:

'Most English journalists are historically prejudiced against Ireland because the Brits can't be trusted when it comes to Ireland'

as some populist views might have it. Space and words are measurable; they can be counted (whether through column inches, or through the number of negative words as a proportion of all words) and, more importantly, they can be *checked by another researcher* to make sure that they have been counted accurately. (This is called '**intercoder reliability**'; we say more about it in Chapter 7.) If your unit of measurement has been chosen carefully (that is, if it is reliably measurable, as inches or emotive words are), then people who are able to count, regardless of their cultural or demographic background, will come up with the same answers as you do. With such an exercise, you may not prove much about the origins of supposed historical prejudices, but you may be able to demonstrate what you set out to do: that there is a persistent negative bias in two key attributes of the British press in its coverage of Ireland, these key attributes being space and language.

So, the most important thing we have to do in designing our research project to ensure validity is to minimise the chances of error.

There are two key aspects to validity: *external* and *internal*.

External validity

External validity has been defined by Wimmer and Dominick (1994, p. 35) as 'how well the results of a study can be generalized across populations, settings and time'. When a study is externally valid it means that we can apply its findings to other similar people, or similar texts, in similar situations, which didn't take part in our study. To make the study externally valid, the sample of people, or material, that we choose to study (and remember, as we said above, you can never study everything – you always have to make a selection) must be **representative** of the people or material you are interested in.

For instance, we can take an example from a student project carried out at Cardiff comparing the drinking habits of postgraduate and undergraduate students, including males and females. In this case, it was essential that whoever the researchers asked to take part in their project, these people a) needed to be students, b) should include roughly equal numbers of postgraduates and undergraduates, c) should include roughly equal numbers of males and females, and d) should include people who liked a drink sometimes. In other words, the sample had to be *representative* of the student drinker population of

Introduction - the effects of drinking

- Each of us drinks equivalent of 28 bottles of vodka a year

- 70% of hospital admissions at weekend are alcohol-related.

- Binge drinking causes rapid damage to the brain.

- Medical bill for binge drinking is £3 billion which is 12% of total amount NHS spends on its hospitals

Figure 2.1 From 'Binge Britain: Drinking Trends in University Students', Cardiff University MA research project by Sara Glynn, Miniushka Mujtaba, Andrea Doungas, Catherine Cunningham, Karl Tufuoh, 2005

Cardiff. The sample was of 100 students randomly chosen – that is, the researchers made no special effort to select particular kinds of people, they simply asked whoever walked by. But they made sure that their final 100 had the necessary equal proportions of postgrads, undergrads, males and females. (More will be said about random sampling and other forms of sampling in Chapter 4.)

In a real-life study, with more resources, the researchers would have wanted to have a bigger sample, including students from universities across the country, and students with different social, geographical or ethnic backgrounds. But for the purposes of a student research project, 100 students, fifty in each category, was a reasonably representative group to answer the questions about alcohol consumption that our researchers were interested in. By making sure their sample was reasonably representative of the group they were interested in, they ensured that their project had external validity.

Internal validity

Internal validity means making sure that your findings are as reliable as they can be because you have eliminated all possible sources of error in the way you have designed your study. Problems of design that could invalidate your study's findings include the following.

1. Problems with subjects

People change over time; in the case of a long-term (*longitudinal*) study, people change in ways that are nothing to do with what's happening in the project and that could affect their responses to your questions. In the case of a long-term study of bias among journalists on a newspaper with a particular political agenda, the staff on the paper might change their jobs, or the journalists in question might change their views, or simply get better at their job. Their opinions can't just be attributed to the paper's editorial line, or the diktats of its proprietor, or whatever you think the reasons for 'bias' might be.

In the case of children in particular, *maturation* is a factor – children grow up and change very quickly, and the younger they are, the more rapid and profound are these changes. There are solutions to these problems, the most common being a '*control group*' of people who are similar to the people in your study, but not taking part in it. Let us say, in a study of primary school children, that they were being observed to evaluate their responses to an educational TV programme over the period of a broadcast season: six months. The researchers might be interested in children's understanding of gender roles and the programme could be showing non-stereotypical activities for boys and girls. Your control group would be a similar group of children who were *not* being shown this educational programme. Each group would be evaluated on its attitude to gender roles at the beginning and at the end of the six months. Changes might come about in both groups as a result of maturation. But the research expectation would be that that those who saw the non-stereotypical gender programme would have changed *more* in their attitudes towards gender than those who did not see the programme.

2. Demand characteristics

The other main problem threatening internal validity is 'demand characteristics' – the problem we've already mentioned of your bias and your perhaps unconscious desire to point the people in your study towards particular answers or particular responses. There are ways round this too, including using people who do not have a stake in the study as interviewers, or using the more anonymous technique of the questionnaire. We say more about this extremely valuable research tool in later chapters.

Other problems that can lead to invalid results include problems with equipment such as faulty computer programs or out-of-date test procedures, and a phenomenon known as *statistical regression*. This means that in any accumulation of statistical information, there will be a 'regression towards the mean', a numerical drift towards the average score, which is a mathematical artefact. In layperson's language, 'things even out by themselves', not because of anything anybody has consciously done.

3. The risk of only doing it once: replication

Ideally, all studies should first be *piloted* to iron out snags of procedure, such as not having reliable computer programs or not having comprehensible questions in your questionnaire. Students can certainly manage to carry out pilots; even just trying out your research instrument (your questionnaire, your interview schedule or content coding sheet) on a few friends enables you to make useful practical decisions, such as whether your procedures take too long, or whether the questions you ask make sense to people whose first language isn't English. But even more ideal is to carry out the main study more than once – to *replicate* it. If, using the same procedures and similar groups of people (or similar material in the case of content analysis), you get broadly the same results each time, then you have a reliable, solid, valid set of findings, which can be published and be useful to other scholars. It isn't usually possible for student projects to be replicated because of lack of time and resources, but sometimes, if you have done a good undergraduate project, you can do it again, in more depth and with more resources, at postgraduate level. This can be a form of replication and again, can lead to good, publishable results.

Generalisability

We have already mentioned the importance of having a representative sample, whether of people or material in your study. As we said, if your sample is representative of the population you are interested in (student drinkers, or the British or Irish press, or whatever), then your findings can be *generalised* to other similar student drinkers, or other examples of the press. Again, we say more about sampling and how to do it effectively in Chapter 4.

The 'wh' questions: what, why, where, when, how and with whom?

In the box below, we give an example of an exercise which we have carried out with every group of students we have worked with in teaching research methods. Students are required to answer these questions at the beginning of the course, and they can find them quite tough. This can be done in collaboration with other students or individually. Discussing with others can be a help in formulating ideas and tightening up definitions.

STEPS FOR DRAWING UP A DISSERTATION OR RESEARCH PROJECT PROPOSAL: THE 'WH' QUESTIONS

TOPIC

1. WHAT?
Is the topic you would like to study?

2. WHAT
Do you want to know about it?

OUTCOME 1:

RESEARCH QUESTION
AND
RESEARCH HYPOTHESIS
Formulate your topic of inquiry in BOTH ways.

2. WHY?
Are you interested in it?
Does it matter?

3. WHO?

Else has done similar research? (mention some readings, at least three citations at this stage, of prior literature in the field)

Would be interested in knowing about it?

Will you do it with? (if you want to do empirical fieldwork, interviews or surveys).

METHOD

4. HOW

Will you do it? (The method question)

5. WHERE

Will you do it?

6. WHO

Will you do it with?

OUTCOME 2: Description of at least TWO appropriate methods for your research question and why you think they are appropriate

5. WHAT (AGAIN)

Do you hope your study will add to the existing knowledge in your chosen field of inquiry?

OVERALL OUTCOME:

A two-page, 750–1,000 word dissertation proposal which includes:

- answers to all the above questions;
- a brief account of the process by which you arrived at them;
- an account of any remaining areas of uncertainty and how you might address these.

Group versus individual projects

Our final section in this introduction to formulating a research question and beginning to design a way of answering it concerns whether you work as an individual or in a group. We have worked with students under both conditions: on individual dissertation projects with BA, MA and PhD students and with groups of students in research methods classes. Sometimes, but perhaps not often enough, students carry out a dissertation project either in pairs or in a group, but generally because students have to be given an individual mark for a dissertation, and because dissertations carry quite a high proportion of marks on many courses, individual projects are more encouraged in educational courses than group ones. Nevertheless, in the real world, social science research is carried out in teams, with groups of people working together, and it is valuable experience for students to learn how to design and carry out a project in conjunction with other people.

Steps in carrying out group projects

In the kinds of research described in this book – questionnaire surveys and content analysis – it is quite difficult for students to conduct all the work required to collect large numbers of samples and to analyse them individually. When only a short time is available – as in the postgraduate workshops we taught, where we had only four weeks for each workshop – it was essential that students divided the labour and worked in groups. In this case, students had to carry out the following steps:

1. They had to get themselves into groups of four or five people who were interested in pursuing broadly similar research questions. Sometimes lecturing staff prefer to put people into groups and not allow students to choose their team-mates, but, while this is usually necessary with children, this is less ideal for adults. Autonomy of judgement is to be encouraged in research, as are good working relationships within a group.
2. They had to decide on a research question collectively, using the above 'wh questions' exercise.
3. They had to divide the labour of the project, e.g. one person was responsible for typing and printing questionnaires; another was responsible for entering data into the computer program; a third was responsible for designing a PowerPoint (or other) presentation of the findings; all were responsible for collecting data – for example, each person had to find twenty respondents for their questionnaire, or each person had to code and analyse a quarter of the sample material in a content analysis.
4. In formal presentations to the rest of the class, which were marked and assessed, each student had to make a contribution of some kind. We have also used procedures where students contributed

a proportion of the marking by carrying out a self-assessment of the project in their final report.

5. Each student had to write up their own version of the project in the final research report, which was given an individual mark. Thus the introduction/literature review and the final discussion of the results in each report had to be the work of each individual. This way, less hardworking individuals could not benefit from the extra work of others, and conversely, good and conscientious students were not 'carrying' those who were less conscientious.

In our next chapter we leave the practicalities of devising and setting up a research project and turn in more detail to the all-important question of *method*.

CHAPTER 3

Choosing a Method

This chapter deals with the **'how'** question: the methodology of your research project and some basic elements and terms of quantitative research design. As we pointed out in the last chapter, the research question you formulate will largely determine the methods you choose, so it's important to be clear and precise about what your question is. A further key ingredient for validity in research design is to have *more than one method* to answer your research question; questionnaires using number coding should also include space for qualitative information in the person's own words, such as a question at the end asking:

'Do you have any other comments?'

and some space for people to write these comments. These comments have a dual function: to act as a further reliability check on the numerical information in the questionnaire answers; and to provide extra, more nuanced and personalised details to augment or explain this information more clearly. Approaching a conclusion from two different points in this way is sometimes called **triangulation.** An example from our own research is described below.

In some research on children and television drama carried out by Máire Messenger Davies and colleagues at the London College of Printing for the BBC (*Dear BBC*, 2001, pp. 175–6), 1,332 children in different parts of the UK, aged between six and thirteen, were asked in their questionnaires to say whether they agreed, disagreed or weren't sure about the following statement:

'I want more programmes for children my age.'

The proportion agreeing to this statement – 70 per cent – was the highest level of agreement of anything we asked in the questionnaire. In the case of 9–12-year-olds, the pre-teens, the proportion agreeing was even higher: 74 per cent. Clearly, 'my age' was an important concept for children in determining how they saw themselves and other children, and how they formed their tastes, and we wanted to know more about the reasons behind this. The research team got more insight into this finding from some of the free comments on the questionnaire, for example this eleven-year-old boy from Cardiff:

> I would like to see a lot of drama on telly. I hate to see too much children's cartoons because they're on every day of the week, even on the weekend. There should be more interesting programmes for children that have grown out of cartoons. (quoted in *Dear BBC*, p. 39)

This comment drew attention to two key features of children's attitudes to 'age', which we could not have obtained from the purely quantitative data in the rest of the questionnaire: first, it appears that, for children, there are specific genres associated with different age groups. Cartoons for this boy are clearly 'children's' and he does not include himself in this category. One of the questions on the questionnaire was:

'Cartoons are only for little children'

and there was a range of responses to this, with the oldest group (11–13-year-olds) disagreeing most strongly. The research team interpreted this to mean that these pre-teens were dissociating themselves from 'little children', rather than that they didn't like cartoons as a genre. This boy's comment supports our interpretation.

The second revealing comment made by this boy was his use of the term 'grown out of'. It implied that, for him, one reason why children's tastes change is not that they are cultural and imposed by society, but developmental, an unavoidable part of growing up. This view was an example of the way in which children show awareness of academic debates, such as the relative importance of genetics versus social conditioning in shaping people's behaviour and tastes. Children themselves are going through the process of 'growing up' and are in a particularly favourable position to comment on it.

In the qualitative discussion tasks carried out afterwards with small groups, even more insight into this answer emerged when the children were asked to create a schedule of programmes for other children. 'Age' came up repeatedly as a reason for including, or excluding, programme titles, for example:

> 'We tried to think of the age of the children [in our schedule]. *Live and Kicking* was for our age and *999* and *The X Files* was for older people and older children.' (Girl, 9, Inner London primary school)

So the qualitative information supported and enhanced the quantitative information; it allowed the children to expand on what they meant by 'age' and what they thought was suitable entertainment for different age groups. Having this information in the children's own words also meant that there was some lively and readable material to give to our clients, the BBC, and to the general readers of Máire Messenger Davies's book, *Dear BBC*. But the qualitative information would not have been enough on its own, because it came only from small groups of articulate children, not from the whole sample of over 1,300 children. It was not **generalisable**.

Focus groups

Another way of providing back-up information for a questionnaire is to carry out a **focus group** – a small group discussion with some of the questionnaire respondents. We did this in conjunction with a questionnaire given to visitors to the West Yorkshire Playhouse in September 2001, in which we were investigating the relationship between popular culture, such as cult TV series (*Star Trek* in this case), and 'high' culture, such as live theatre. The theatre was running a J. B. Priestley (local author) festival and had revived his play, not performed since 1960, *Johnson over Jordan*, starring Patrick Stewart. Stewart was the star of *Star Trek: The Next Generation*, as well as being a distinguished stage actor.[1] We asked the theatre-goers to respond to the following statements:

I go to the theatre	6–12 times a year	2–5 times a year	Once a year	Less than once a year	Never
I go to the West Yorkshire Playhouse	First time visit	Rarely	Sometimes	Often	Very often

---

[1] M. M. Davies and R. E. Pearson (2003) 'Stardom and Distinction: Patrick Stewart as an Agent of Cultural Mobility: A study of Theatre and Film Audiences in New York City', in M. Barker and T. Austin (eds.), *Contemporary Hollywood Stardom*, London: Arnold, pp. 167–86; M. M. Davies and R. E. Pearson 'To boldly bestride the narrow world like a colossus: Shakespeare, *Star Trek* and the European TV Market', in I. Bondebjerg and P. Golding (eds.), *European Culture and the Media: Changing Media Changing Europe*, Vol. 1, Bristol: Intellect Books, pp. 65–90; R. E. Pearson and M. M. Davies (2005) 'Class Acts? Public and Private Values and the Cultural Habits of Theatre-goers', in S. Livingstone (ed.), *Audiences and Publics*, Bristol: Intellect Books.

When we analysed the answers we found a surprisingly high number of infrequent theatre-goers. The questionnaire responses didn't give us any insight into *why* these infrequent theatre-goers came to this particular play, although we had a hunch (hypothesis) that they were there because they liked the leading actor, Patrick Stewart, and that they might have been fans of *Star Trek: the Next Generation*. Our focus group discussions gave us support for this hypothesis – for instance, these comments from 41-year-old Steven, a postman driver: 'The main reason I came is that I heard such good reviews and I wanted to see Patrick Stewart . . . I'm not a regular theatre-goer.'

The qualitative discussions, as qualitative discussions often do, also gave us some information that we hadn't asked for, but were valuable for our research all the same: an extra insight into the powerful impact that live theatre can have on someone who isn't used to it. This is Steven again:

> I was tired, because I'd just come off nights and I'd had just about four hours' sleep in the previous two weeks and every scene I thought was fascinating, you know. Every one was an eye-opener to me. I didn't get bored at all and didn't fall asleep or anything.

This was valuable information for the theatre marketing team, and also for us in terms of our interest in people's cultural tastes generally, and how and why they change – information that we could not have obtained just from the questionnaire answers.

The building blocks of survey research: a 'baby questionnaire'

We are now going to backtrack a little from the more complex, real-world examples of questionnaire research which we have carried out, to a much simpler example: a training exercise on how to design, code, administer and analyse a short questionnaire, using SPSS (Statistical Package for the Social Sciences). We call this our 'baby questionnaire' in that it is extremely simple, basic and minimal in the questions it asks. To pursue the baby analogy, it enables students to learn to walk before they try to run.

Questionnaires are one of the most powerful research tools; they are the most economical way of collecting a lot of information from a large number of people in a relatively short time. This brief exercise is an introduction to basic questionnaire design and analysis using SPSS. Note that this little 'baby questionnaire', even though it has only five questions in it, has the two essential ingredients of all good questionnaires:

1. A 'demographic' section: information about the person filling it in.
2. An information section: the questions you are interested in for your project, in this case a hypothetical survey on political attitudes.

QUANTITATIVE RESEARCH WITH SPSS: 'BABY QUESTIONNAIRE' EXERCISE

* *

ATTITUDES TO THE EUROPEAN UNION QUESTIONNAIRE

Please circle or tick the answer that applies to you:

ABOUT YOU (*using multiple-choice*)

1. I am	Male/Female
2. My status is:	Undergraduate
	Postgraduate
3. I am enrolled on:	BA
	MA
	PhD
	Other (please specify) (*using post-coding*)

YOUR VIEWS ON THE EU (*using the Likert scale*)

4. Britain's membership of the European Union is a good thing.

1. Strongly disagree   2. Disagree   3. Not sure   4. Agree   5. Strongly agree

5. The UK Government is doing a good job.

1. Strongly disagree   2. Disagree   3. Not sure   4. Agree   5. Strongly agree

Any other comments? (*using qualitative data*)

Thank you for your help.

Questionnaire sections

1. Demographics

All questionnaires require a section in which respondents give information about themselves. These characteristics are called **demographics**. People's demographic characteristics can make an important difference to how they answer your questions. What exactly you want to know about them will – again, as always – depend on your specific research question. In our 'baby' example we've used just two: age and sex (gender).

Age and sex

Whatever your research question, it is always wise to have information about the two basic human characteristics of age and sex/gender. This is because they apply to everybody, whereas the other characteristics on the list may not (e.g. children may not have an income; not everybody is educated; even place of origin may not be relevant or known). Also, past research with human beings, as well as your personal experience, indicate that these two characteristics are highly likely to *make a difference* to the ways in which people answer: the different responses people give, as well as their different demographic characteristics, are called **variables**; we will say more about the more technical meanings of this term later. For the time being it's sufficient to note that the common-sense meaning of 'vary' is relevant to defining this term; research asking about people's characteristics is based on the assumption that people vary.[2]

Other demographic characteristics include:

* **income;**
* **occupation;**
* **nationality;**
* **ethnicity/race;**
* **education;**
* **place of origin;**
* **religion.**

---

[2] Or, strictly speaking, using the null hypothesis, we can make the assumption that people *don't* vary and that any differences we observe between people are due to chance, until the differences become so marked that they would appear to show a genuinely *significant* distinction, as measured by statistical tests.

Depending on your research question you may want to know about any or all of the above characteristics. For instance, you may well think that 'religion' will affect the way people answer questions about news from Northern Ireland or from Saudi Arabia, because Ireland and the Middle East are areas of religious conflict. If we take the student example we used in the last chapter, a researcher carrying out research into supposed journalistic bias in the reporting of Northern Ireland would be justified in thinking that the journalists' religion could be relevant to their reporting. A question about religion therefore needs to be included in a questionnaire given to journalists. Any of these categories can be potentially controversial, but if people do not wish to answer questions about themselves, they do not have to. You can include the category 'do not wish to respond' as part of your list of potential responses, and then these people can be distinguished from those who couldn't be bothered to respond or forgot the question.

If you think that religion isn't relevant to the questions you are asking, then don't include it. The same goes for income or occupation: if you are surveying students, these questions are unlikely to be relevant, so leave them out. However, in the case of our theatre-goers at the West Yorkshire Playhouse, questions about income and education were relevant to our interest in people's cultural tastes and how they might vary and change, so they were included.

2. An information/attitude section

In this section people answer the questions you are especially interested in for your research project. For the purposes of our exercise, we have included just two: a question about people's attitudes to the European Union and one about their attitudes to the UK domestic situation. In a student study about alcohol consumption which we are using as an example of a student project, there were fourteen questions about students' attitudes to drinking. In the BBC study about children's views on television drama, the research team included fourteen questions asking their views about various aspects of TV storytelling. We will say more about the optimum number of questions, how they should be worded and how they should be laid out in our chapter on questionnaire design (Chapter 6). But no matter how long and diverse the questions in a questionnaire are, it will still consist of the same two basic sections: demographics about the people answering, and information about their responses to your particular research question. Your assumption will be that the answers given in the first section (age, sex, income level or whatever) will *make a difference* to the answers given in the second section. This assumption can be tested, very straightforwardly, through the SPSS analysis, as we shall see.

3. Cultural consumption/tastes

In the case of media research, a sub-section to your demographic section may be desirable, asking about people's media consumption and tastes. For instance, in the West Yorkshire study, we asked people how often they watched particular television programmes and how often they went to the theatre. In the case of our student project about journalistic bias, the student might want to know how often people watched television news or how regularly they read a daily newspaper, and which news programmes and newspapers they used. The assumption is that being a regular theatre-goer or newspaper reader is likely *to make a difference* to how you answer questions about particular theatrical experiences or particular items in the news (see footnote 2).

Questionnaire instruments

In the 'baby questionnaire', you will see that we have attached the following labels to the questions:

*   **multiple-choice;**
*   **post-coding;**
*   **Likert scale;**
*   **qualitative data.**

These are labels for the kinds of questions that most often occur in questionnaires; below we give a brief explanation of them. All, with the exception of qualitative data, are designed to make it easier for you to give the answers numerical *codings* and thus to analyse them statistically with SPSS.

Multiple-choice

Rather than ask people to say whether they are male and female (or to say how old they are, or how much they earn), it is simpler to give them some options and ask them to choose one: in the case of age, you may use age categories, as we did in the West Yorkshire project:

Please **circle** the appropriate category, e.g. if you are 28-years-old, circle 26–35:

Age (Years)	0–10	11–16	17–25	26–35	36–45	46–55	56–65	65+

You can do this with other kinds of questions, for instance questions about media tastes: rather than ask people what newspapers they read, give them a list of newspapers and ask them to circle the ones they usually read, or the one they read most often. The preference for multiple-choice questions in research is based on the long-established finding in psychological studies of memory that 'cued recall' (when people are given prompts to answer a question) is a better way of finding out what they remember than 'free recall' (when they are asked to describe what they saw or what they read).

Post-coding

Having said that, sometimes you *do* want people to give their own answers, especially when you cannot be sure what those answers might be. For example, in our West Yorkshire Playhouse study, we had a hunch that many people came to the theatre to see Patrick Stewart, but we were not sure that we were right and we did not know what other reasons people might have had for coming. So we could not have constructed an accurate multiple-choice list for this question. We also did not want to prompt them with a 'demand characteristic' by suggesting that 'Patrick Stewart' might be a 'right' answer. Instead, we gave them an open-ended question:

> **What was the main reason that you came to see this play today?**

Table 3.1 below shows the numbers of people who gave particular answers and these were all given 'value labels' under the variable label 'reason for coming'. So 'Patrick Stewart' was coded 1, J. B. Priestley coded 2, and so on. This table has been arranged in 'descending counts' so that you can see the most frequently mentioned reason at the top. It could also have been counted simply according to the order in which the values had been coded. This is shown in Table 3.2.

Table 3.1 Reasons for coming to the West Yorkshire Playhouse to see *Johnson over Jordan*, September 2001: 'Descending counts' (in order of 'votes cast')

Main Reason For Coming*

		Frequency	Per cent	Valid per cent	Cumulative per cent
Valid	Patrick Stewart	264	27.5	30.3	30.3
	J.B. Priestley	136	14.2	15.6	45.9
	Friends/family/ partner	76	7.9	8.7	54.6
	Stewart + Priestley	68	7.1	7.8	62.4
	Interest in this production	37	3.9	4.2	66.6
	Curiosity/general interest	36	3.7	4.1	70.8
	Opportunity – tickets	31	3.2	3.6	74.3
	Recommendation	30	3.1	3.4	77.8
	Subscription/regular at WYP	22	2.3	2.5	80.3
	Publicity	20	2.1	2.3	82.6
	Interest in theatre	16	1.7	1.8	84.4
	Opportunity – holiday/ in the area	12	1.2	1.4	85.8
	Educational/study	11	1.1	1.3	87.0
	Opportunity – group travel	8	0.8	0.9	88.0
	Member of Priestley Society	8	0.8	0.9	88.9

Entertainment/ pleasure	7	0.7	0.8	89.7
Interested in this production + Stewart	5	0.5	0.6	90.3
Spur of the moment	5	0.5	0.6	90.8
Birthday present/ special occasion	5	0.5	0.6	91.4
Patrick Stewart + recommendation	4	0.4	0.5	91.9
Forced	4	0.4	0.5	92.3
Avril Clark	4	0.4	0.5	92.8
Shakespeare	3	0.3	0.3	93.1
Priestley + interest in this production	3	0.3	0.3	93.5
Free tickets + Patrick Stewart	3	0.3	0.3	93.8
Subscription + Priestley	3	0.3	0.3	94.2
Opportunity – production not often shown	2	0.2	0.2	94.4
Because of the actors	2	0.2	0.2	94.6
Good show	2	0.2	0.2	94.8
Jude Kelly + Stewart	2	0.2	0.2	95.1
Priestley + Stewart + theatre generally	2	0.2	0.2	95.3
Priestley Theatre +	2	0.2	0.2	95.5
Patrick Stewart + birthday present	2	0.2	0.2	95.8

* Table does not show all data.

Table 3.2 'Reason for coming' presented according to post-coding order
Main Reason For Coming*

		Frequency	Per cent	Valid Per cent	Cumulative Per cent
Valid	Patrick Stewart	264	27.5	30.3	30.3
	J.B. Priestley	136	14.2	15.6	45.9
	Stewart + Priestley	68	7.1	7.8	53.7
	Interest in theatre	16	1.7	1.8	55.5
	publicity	20	2.1	2.3	57.8
	Curiosity/general interest	36	3.7	4.1	61.9
	Opportunity – tickets	31	3.2	3.6	65.5
	Opportunity – group travel	8	0.8	0.9	66.4
	Friends/family/ partner	76	7.9	8.7	75.1
	Subscription/ regular at WYP	22	2.3	2.5	77.6
	Member of Priestley Society	8	0.8	0.9	78.6
	Opportunity – production not often shown	2	0.2	0.2	78.8
	Interested in performing art	1	0.1	0.1	78.9
	Recommendation	30	3.1	3.4	82.3

Interest in this production	37	3.9	4.2	86.6
Interest in theatre and interest in production	1	0.1	0.1	86.7
Because of the actors	2	0.2	0.2	86.9
Patrick Stewart + recommen- dation	4	0.4	0.5	87.4
Good show	2	0.2	0.2	87.6
Member of Kendall Theatre Club	1	0.1	0.1	87.7
To get a life	1	0.1	0.1	87.8
Educational/study	11	1.1	1.3	89.1
Interested in this production + Stewart	5	0.5	0.6	89.7
Shakespeare	3	0.3	0.3	90.0
Interest + Stewart	1	0.1	0.1	90.1
Jude Kelly + Stewart	2	0.2	0.2	90.4
Opportunity – holiday/in the area	12	1.2	1.4	91.7
Read the book	1	0.1	0.1	91.9
Priestley + stewart + theatre generally	2	0.2	0.2	92.1
Theatre + Priestley	2	0.2	0.2	92.3

* Table does not show all data.

From the answers we were able to construct a list of 'reasons', to each of which we gave a numerical coding. This list is shown in the tables 3.1 and 3.2 and is called 'post-coding' because you don't allocate the numbers until after you have the answers. We also gave people the option of giving their own answer in one of the questions in our 'baby questionnaire'. If they weren't enrolled on a BA, MA or PhD programme, we asked them to say what kind of course they were taking – Diploma, Foundation, or whatever, which could then be given a numerical 'post'- (or 'after') coding. We will say more about this when we get to the general question of coding below. Suffice to say here that it is possible to turn people's own words into numerical form when you have given them a 'free recall' question in a questionnaire, so you should not be afraid to give the occasional free-choice question.

Likert scale

This is probably the most widely used tool for assessing people's opinions in survey research: the five-point scale, stating a range of positions from strong disagreement to strong agreement with three points between. An example is given below:

'People should have to pay subscriptions for all television channels'

1	2	3	4	5
Strongly disagree	Disagree	Neutral	Agree	Strongly agree

The five-point scale is a robust way of allowing people to express variations in opinion or behaviour which provide meaningful answers to researchers about these variations. In the case of the question above, people who agree, or strongly agree, might be those with specialised interests, like sport, and we might also suppose that they earn more than other people because subscription isn't a problem for them. These assumptions can be checked with reference to their demographic information (their income) and to their media consumption (as in the question below). Those who disagree we might expect to be older and less familiar with multi-channel television – again, we can check this against the demographics. (And of course, our assumptions may be wrong, which is why we must test them.)

An alternative format for the Likert scale is to ask people how often they do something – for example, we might want to ask people who'd answered the question above about their viewing habits:

'I watch sports on television'

1	2	3	4	5
Never	Hardly ever	Sometimes	Often	Very often

We might expect there to be a relationship (*correlation*) between people who were in favour of subscription channels and people who watch sports often; thus, we could predict that those who circled 4 or 5 on the first question are more likely to circle 4 or 5 on the second. This can be checked with SPSS.

Statements not questions

There are two important points to note about the Likert scale. The first is the wording. These types of questions are never, in fact, questions; they are always statements. Rather than ask people 'Do you agree with subscription?' in which case the only possible answer is 'yes', or 'no', you give them options which enable them to express a range of agreement or disagreement. The same is true of people's behaviour or habits, which very rarely fall neatly into the 'always' or 'never' categories. The five-point scale provides a subtler and more nuanced way of evaluating people's habits and attitudes than simply asking 'yes' or 'no' questions; it allows people a range of choices rather than forcing them to give an answer which may not correspond exactly to what they really think, so in effect, they end up lying. It acknowledges the ambiguity and complexity of most people's attitudes and it has proved surprisingly revealing in the many studies in which it has been used.

The second point to note about the Likert scale is the numerical order. In both cases we give above, the scale represents a range, with one end of the scale being very negative and the other being very positive, with a range of feeling/experience going up the gradient in between: the numbers 1–5 have some relationship to what they are measuring in that they go from low to high, but it is a rough-and-ready relationship, rather than a very precisely accurate one. This is called '**ordinal**' measurement and we say more about it below.

So in our 'baby questionnaire', you can see that we have given two Likert scales in which people are asked to rate their attitudes to political issues on a scale of 1–5. In a proper research project, of course, we would give a lot more Likert statements.

Qualitative data

We have already talked about qualitative and quantitative information. The 'any further comments' space on the questionnaire allows people to say something in their own words, such as, 'I think the domestic situation is OK, but this doesn't mean I approve of everything the Government does.' This can be used to support, or further enhance or explain, the information you get from the other questionnaire answers. At this point, we should also say something about the term 'data', which we have been using and will use a lot more. 'Data' comes from the Latin verb 'dare' (pronounced dah-ray), meaning 'to give'; 'datum' means 'given' and 'data' is the plural of this, meaning a number of things that have been given, in other words, all the information derived from your research procedures. Data (always a plural word) can be qualitative or quantitative, as we have said.

Coding

- **Variable labels**
- **Value labels**
- **Nominal data**
- **Ordinal data**
- **Interval data**

We now need to turn our 'baby questionnaire' into a form of information that the computer program can understand: we need to code each piece of information and give it a numerical value. We do this using the terminology (language) of the SPSS program.

Each question is called a '**variable**' and, in the first column of the SPSS table, it has to be given a short **variable label**, no longer than six letters.

Nominal data

Within each variable, there are, as we've said, a number of options, or *values*, and each option/value also has to be given a numerical coding. In the case of 'variable 1', 'gender', there are two options/values, male and female: we can use the terms 'male' and 'female' as **'value labels'**.

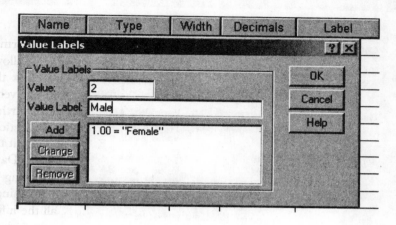

We can code male as 1 and female as 2, or vice versa; it makes no difference. This kind of number coding is called **nominal data**. From the Latin for 'name', nomen, 'nominal data' means that the numbers in this case are simply names, like Fred and Alice. Switching them round and making female 1 and male 2, has no significance: 1 is not superior to 2, nor is 2 twice as good as 1. Other sorts of nominal data could be, for example, occupations: your questionnaire might have a list of six different professions: medicine, law, teaching, business, social work, architect. They would be coded 1–6 but it wouldn't matter in which order; calling social work 5 or 3 has no numerical significance at all. It is simply a label.

Ordinal data
In the case of variable 2 in our sample questionnaire, 'status', there are also two options: 'undergrad' and 'postgrad'. These too can be coded 1 and 2, but in this case, although the data could be seen as nominal, we might argue that 2 is higher than 1 because a postgrad is at a more advanced stage of education than an undergrad. In the case of this little questionnaire it doesn't really matter very much. But if we were conducting a study in which people's level of education is relevant to our main research questions, it *would* matter.

ATTITUDES TO THE EUROPEAN UNION QUESTIONNAIRE

Please circle or tick the answer that applies to you:

ABOUT YOU (*using multiple-choice*)

1. I am	Male / Female:	**Variable 1: Label: 'gender'** **value label: 'male' – 1** **value label: 'female' – 2**
2. My status is:	Undergraduate: Postgraduate	**Variable 2: Label: 'status'** **Value label: 'undergrad' – 1** **Value label: 'postgrad' – 2**
. 3. I am enrolled on:	BA MA PhD	**Variable 3: Label: 'degree'** **Value label: 'BA' – 1** **Value label: 'MA' – 2** **Value label: 'PhD' – 3**
	Other (please specify) (*using post-coding*)	

YOUR VIEWS ON THE EU (*using the Likert scale*)

4. Britain's membership of the European   **Variable 4: Label: 'eumemb'**
   Union is a good thing: **Value labels: as in the scale**

1. Strongly disagree   2. Disagree   3. Not sure   4. Agree   5. Strongly agree

5. The UK Government is doing a good job.**Variable 5: Label: 'ukgov'**
     Value labels: as in the scale

1. Strongly disagree   2. Disagree   3. Not sure   4. Agree   5. Strongly agree

Any other comments? (*using qualitative data*)

Let's say we were interested in people's attitudes to politics generally; we might have a Likert scale question stating:

'It's important for everybody to vote in national elections.'

People who 'strongly agree', we might assume, are more likely to be highly educated. (Again, we might be wrong.) So we would arrange our options in the 'status' question in *order* of educational level to see whether the higher up the order a person is, the more strongly they feel about voting. In coding the variable 'status', we could do this:

1. 'secondary education to age sixteen';
2. 'sixth form/further education';
3. 'BA degree';

4   'MA degree';
5. 'PhD'.

In this case the numbers *do* represent a range from low to high and are not just names; in this case we would call the numbers **ordinal data** because they constitute an order, or rank, which represents real differences in level and length of educational experience. People coded 5 are at a more advanced stage in their education than people coded 1, so we might expect there to be a numerical relationship between higher codings (4 and 5) on 'educational status' and higher levels of agreement (4 and 5) about the importance of political issues.

Ordinal data, that is, rankings from low to high, require different sorts of statistical analysis from nominal data, and the computer program needs to know this, hence the column at the end of the SPSS table asking for information about the kind of data you are using for each question, or variable.

The final two questions on our 'baby questionnaire' are Likert scales, asking people's opinions on the European Union and the UK Government. Likert scales, too, are ordinal data – they represent a range of opinion from one extreme to the other. This is not the same as saying 'from low to high' so there is a sense in which a five-point Likert measure of disagreement/agreement doesn't rise straight-forwardly from 1 to 5. Strong disagreement is a strong measure, so coding it as 1 might be seen as misleading. Nevertheless, for the purpose of most attitude questions, which are only rough estimates of people's feelings, the 1–5 scale can be assumed to correspond broadly to a range of feeling from negative to positive.

Interval data
The final kind of data that is identified in an SPSS data file is called **'scale'** or **'interval'** data. In our sample questionnaire (above) we don't have any examples of interval data, and they don't turn up that often in survey research of the kind we are describing. (They are more likely to turn up in content analysis; see Chapter 7.) However, we could have included an example of interval data under the label (variable) 'age'. Rather than give people a range of options (values) for 'age', as we did in West Yorkshire, we could have asked them simply to give their age in years: 12; 15, 33, 41, 65 or whatever. This kind of numbering is called **interval data**. Sorting out the difference

between interval and ordinal data has proved to be one of the most difficult problems for students that we have encountered in our experience of teaching quantitative methods. *But it is absolutely essential that these distinctions are understood.*

Is the difference 'one'?

The clearest way of identifying interval, as distinct from ordinal, data is to ask: *What is the difference between each point on the scale?* In the case of age, what is the difference between one year and two years; between two years and three years; between 22 and 23 years? If the answer is *always 'one'*, then you are dealing with interval data. In other words, you are dealing with the kinds of numbers you are most used to for counting in everyday life; the difference between £1 and £2, between five oranges and six oranges, and so on: the difference is always 'one'.

In the case of the ordinal codes 1–5 which we allocated to different levels of education in the example above, we can see that asking about the difference between each point on the scale is not such a meaningful question: the difference between point 1 on the scale, 'secondary education to age sixteen', and point 2, 'sixth form/further education', is not an exact numerical difference. The two points simply represent a higher and lower level of education. However, if we had asked people to say how many *years* they had spent in full-time education, *then* we would have had an interval scale: the difference between six years and seven years, or nine years and ten years, is always one. Such a question however, would not be particularly meaningful if we want to know – as we do in this case – how well qualified these people are. We need to know what 'level' they have reached, not just how long they spent sitting at a desk. Here, an ordinal scale is more useful.

Test question

And, in this hypothetical case, if we needed to code which school they went to, as Davies et al. did with the nineteen schools in the BBC study discussed above, with School A being coded 1, School B being coded 2, School H being coded 3, School Y being coded 4, and so on, what sort of data would that be?

See if you can work it out.

Postscript: post-coding

In question/variable 3 in our 'baby questionnaire', labelled 'degree', we had three options/values: 1, BA, 2, MA, 3 PhD and an 'other' option. In this case we need to use numbers from 4 onwards to post-code any answers that people put in the 'other' section. Let us say that the first person answering the 'other' option put 'Postgrad diploma'; we would include 'diploma' as another option/value, and code it 4. If the next person put 'Foundation' we would code it 5. And so on, in this free comment section, we would go on allocating numbers for each new course mentioned.

Another test question: post-coding

If a second person, in addition to the first person, put 'Foundation' in the 'other' section, how would you code this answer?

If the next person after this one put 'exchange student, Erasmus programme' how would you code it?

In our West Yorkshire study, there were a number of free-choice questions, such as the one we mentioned above:

'What was the main reason you came to the theatre today?'

With each new answer we received–

    'regular subscriber',
    'free tickets',
    'birthday treat'

– we gave it a numerical coding. The first reason in the first questionnaire we looked at was:

    'I came to see Patrick Stewart'

so we coded 'Patrick Stewart' 1 in our 'reason' variable. Each time one of our questionnaires showed that the main reason this person came to the play was 'Patrick Stewart', their answer to this question was coded 1. There were sixty-seven reasons altogether, including combined reasons coded, 1–67. As you can see, with post-coding there can be a lot of options/values and you go on adding numbers until you have no more new reasons being added. This is fine; the program will handle them with no problem. For instance, one of our questions was:

'What is your favourite television programme?'

and people came up with 206 different titles. They were coded 1–206. By asking the SPSS program to count how many of the values under variable/question 29 'favourite TV' were labelled '1' or '201' or whatever, we could then check to see how many people had 'voted' for each title.

Missing values
What happens if someone does not answer one of the questions? You can't leave the coding sheet blank, nor can you put '0', because zero is a real numerical value which you may need; you need to tell the computer program that the answer to the question is 'missing' and this is usually done by putting in an 'impossible' number, such as 99, or 999. This is a number that won't be used in your coding because you don't have that many questions or values.

What do the answers look like?
The spreadsheets (pp. 55–6). show two versions of some answers to our 'baby questionnaire' – data from twenty imaginary people who 'filled it in'. The first version shows the verbal version of this information; the second version shows the number coding. In modern versions of SPSS, in which you can see the verbal versions, it is much easier for students to understand what they are dealing with. In earlier versions, there were no words, only number codings: you can imagine how baffling these columns and grids of 1's, 5's, 3's, and 99's were. However, we managed!

In our classroom exercises, we give these data to our students and get them to answer some simple questions using the program. We will not be asking you to do this at this stage. In Chapters 10 and 11, we will discuss in more detail how to analyse and interpret the data you have collected and coded with your questionnaires. Meanwhile, we continue with the next important stage of setting up a research project: selecting a **sample** to work with. This can be either a human sample – people you want to answer your questionnaire – or, in the case of content analysis, it will be a sample of media material. Appropriate sampling is absolutely essential in ensuring external validity for a research project, and as always, the sample you select will depend on your research question.

Spreadsheet 1

	sex	status	degree	eumemb	domsit
1	Female	Postgraduate	MA	Strongly Agree	Good
2	Female	Undergraduate	BA	Strongly Agree	Very Good
3	Female	Undergraduate	BA	Strongly Agree	Very Good
4	Female	Undergraduate	BA	Strongly Agree	Good
5	Male	Undergraduate	Other	Somewhat Agree	Very Good
6	Female	Postgraduate	PhD	Strongly Agree	Good
7	Male	Undergraduate	BA	Somewhat Agree	Neither Good nor Bad
8	Male	Undergraduate	BA	Somewhat Agree	Very Bad
9	Male	99.00	MA	Somewhat Disagree	Very Bad
10	Male	Postgraduate	Other	Strongly Agree	Good
11	Female	Postgraduate	Other	Somewhat Agree	Good
12	Male	Undergraduate	BA	Somewhat Agree	Neither Good nor Bad
13	Male	Postgraduate	PhD	Strongly Agree	Good
14	Female	Postgraduate	PhD	Somewhat Disagree	Bad
15	Male	Undergraduate	BA	Strongly Agree	Good
16	Male	Postgraduate	PhD	Somewhat Disagree	Good
17	Female	Undergraduate	BA	Somewhat Agree	Good
18	Male	Undergraduate	Other	Neutral	Neither Good nor Bad
19	Female	Postgraduate	MA	Strongly Agree	Very Good
20	Male	Postgraduate	PhD	Strongly Agree	Good

Spreadsheet 2

	sex	status	degree	eumemb	domsit
1	1.00	2.00	2.00	1.00	2.00
2	1.00	1.00	1.00	1.00	1.00
3	1.00	1.00	1.00	1.00	1.00
4	1.00	1.00	1.00	1.00	2.00
5	2.00	1.00	4.00	2.00	1.00
6	1.00	2.00	3.00	1.00	2.00
7	2.00	1.00	1.00	2.00	3.00
8	2.00	1.00	1.00	2.00	5.00
9	2.00	99.00	2.00	4.00	5.00
10	2.00	2.00	4.00	1.00	2.00
11	1.00	2.00	4.00	2.00	2.00
12	2.00	1.00	1.00	2.00	3.00
13	2.00	2.00	3.00	1.00	2.00
14	1.00	2.00	3.00	4.00	4.00
15	2.00	1.00	1.00	1.00	2.00
16	2.00	2.00	3.00	4.00	2.00
17	1.00	1.00	1.00	2.00	2.00
18	2.00	1.00	4.00	3.00	3.00
19	1.00	2.00	2.00	1.00	1.00
20	2.00	2.00	3.00	1.00	2.00

PART TWO

EXECUTION: 'DOING IT'

CHAPTER 4

Sampling

The question of sampling is absolutely central in making sure that your project is **externally valid** (see p. 25) External validity means that the findings of your study can be applied more widely than just to your particular project – that is, they can be generalised. This is possible because you have taken every precaution to make sure that the people you have surveyed, or the media material you have selected to analyse, are *representative* of the group of people, or of the media material, you are primarily interested in.

For example, if you are doing a study about young girls' attitudes to body shape and the possible influence of advertising on their attitudes, you need to be sure that the young girls you include in your study are *typical* of the young girls as a whole at whom the advertising campaign is aimed. (Think about how you might find out what the *demographics* of this market might be.) Similarly, if you want to study the advertising material itself as well as the people it is aimed at, you need to make sure that the examples of advertising you select are generally typical of advertising aimed at young girls.

Having said this, with student projects, it is not always possible in the short time available, and with limited resources, to ensure that you have a truly representative sample of the whole population you are interested in. There are two basic ways round this, which we will say more about later:

1. Choose a topic – as with the example of student drinking habits mentioned on page 25 – where the people you want to study will be easily available, as in a university environment. 'Student drinkers' are obviously easier to sample than a huge, vague category like 'young people'.
2. Choose a sampling method where full representativeness is less of a crucial requirement. More details of these different sampling methods are given below.

Principles of sampling: key terms

The following are some key terms to understand the principles of sampling.

1. Population

This is the group from which the sample is drawn and which it represents. This need not be people, although we usually use the term to apply to people; it could be, for example, all TV sitcoms or a time period (e.g. Davies and Corbett's [1997] analysis of children's broadcasting output in the UK between 1991 and 1996)[1] or, as above, all advertising aimed at young females.

In the case of a survey of people, a population is everyone you are concerned with, e.g.:

• all the citizens in a country;
• all the PR professionals working in health care;
• all the people who read a certain newspaper;
• all students in your department;
• all MA students in your department.

Once again, you can see that the nature of the 'population' that you select for your study is derived from specific research questions. For the purpose of the national census, which needs to find out what everybody in the country is and does, the 'population' has to be 'all citizens'. For the purpose of looking at people's attitudes to the redesigned *Guardian*, the population has to be 'all *Guardian* readers'. If you are doing a survey of MA students' satisfaction with the technical resources available to them in the school (as one group of our MA students managed to do in a four-week workshop), 'all MA students in the department' is the population from which you will draw your sample. Even when you've reduced your 'population' to a specific group, unless you are doing a census, you still will not be able to question everybody in that population. You will need to select a **sample** from these populations.

---

[1] M. M. Davies and B. Corbett (1997) *Children's Television in Britain: An Enquiry for the Broadcasting Standards Commission.* London: Broadcasting Standards Commission.

2. Census

A census is a counting exercise which involves *everybody* (or every item) in the population. The national census is carried out in the UK every ten years, and every single person in the country, including children, is included in this survey; hence no sampling is involved.

3. Sample

For most research it is not practicable (or necessary) to count every single person. For most research, a sample is chosen from the population of interest to the project. A sample is a subgroup which is typical of the population as a whole. As we've said, sampling is necessary first, because it is not possible to ask everyone, for reasons of both cost and time; and second, for statistical reasons which we will not go into here, surveying everyone is not necessary: in a well-designed study, once you have a sufficiently large sample to cover all the ground of your research question (e.g. enough of each demographic subgroup), you will not get more reliable results statistically if you go on adding to the numbers in your sample.

It is possible to get a good idea of the population as a whole from a well-constructed sample. For example, the television ratings in the UK are based on a sample of only around 4,000 households in the whole country. Making the sample larger would not make the analysis of viewing figures any more reliable for reasons to do with statistical margins of error. (If you are interested in the precise reasons for this, and the mathematical analysis of it, see Chapter 14 of Wimmer and Dominick.)

4. Ways of sampling

(i) Random or probability sampling

With this most rigorous form of sampling every member of the population has an equal chance of being sampled. This is mainly used in large-scale quantitative surveys where having a representative sample is essential to provide results which can be generalised to a population at large. This is particularly necessary for governmental and policy research, where the findings of the survey could determine, for instance, the distribution of health care resources, or new housing. In random sampling the units (or people) are selected by chance and every unit has an equal likelihood of being selected. This may seem counterintuitive but in fact, this way of doing things (like putting a lot of numbers into a giant drum, rotating it and pulling out a number without looking at it, as in a lottery) is much the fairest way of selecting truly representative samples.

Types of random sampling
Random sampling can be done in a number of ways.

Systematic
- Number the entire population for example, 150 MA students.
- Depending on your research question (e.g. how many demographic subgroups you want to include), decide your sample size, for example, fifty.
- Work out an interval for picking your fifty out of the 150, for example every third student in the list.
- Start at random (e.g. by closing your eyes and pointing to a name) then use every third name until you have fifty.

Stratified
This is similar to the method described above, but the population is divided into particular groups (gender, age, nationality). Thus your population list may be divided into two lists of seventy-five males and seventy-five females and you sample each list randomly until you have twenty-five of each. You then subdivide the two lists into age groups to ensure you have sufficient numbers of, say under- and over-thirties (assuming age is relevant to your research question). As you can see, if you are going to subdivide your sample into particular demographic subgroups, your subgroups will become smaller and smaller the more categories you include, until the sample size for these subgroups cannot be seen as reliably representative. For instance twenty-five females, split equally into under- and over-thirties will give you only twelve or thirteen people in each group. If you want to look at four age categories, you will get only six or so people in each age and gender subgroup. The more demographic subgroups you divide your sample into, the larger your sample needs to be: another argument for keeping your research question and research design simple – for example, looking in detail only at the

differences between *two* groups (males and females; or action adventure films versus romantic comedies).

Students sometimes want to make more complex comparisons between more than two or three groups of variables and this is possible using different forms of **multivariate analysis**, including a form of **multiple correlation** (see Chapter 10) called **multiple regression**. This analyses all demographic (and other) variables together, and works out which of them, and which combinations of them, make the biggest, or smallest, contribution to the overall results. However, we are not going to talk about multivariate analysis in this book, because, for the purpose of teaching research techniques and setting assessment exercises for Humanities students, such techniques have not been necessary for the kinds of questions they want to ask. Again, we recommend an SPSS handbook if you want to know more about these techniques. The SPSS 'help' facility within the program may also assist you, although in our experience students usually need to have access to flesh-and-blood teachers or fellow students when trying to navigate software help programs.

Quota

In this case, you decide what characteristics you want (how many males/females; how many of different age groups). Again, this decision depends on your research question. If gender differences are important, you need to make sure of having sufficiently balanced numbers of males and females in your sample, so you need to go on sampling names from the list, or add to the list, until you have this balance. When you split your population into males and females, you may find that you have very few females. If gender is important to your research question, you may need to recruit more females to your sample. Or you can carry out a statistical procedure known as '**weighting**' when you get to your data analysis stage. We advise you not to attempt advanced statistical procedures when carrying out simple student projects on a research methods course. For a MA or PhD dissertation, more advanced statistics may be necessary and feasible. In this case a good statistical chapter like the one in Wimmer and Dominick, or a text explaining the workings of SPSS, such as Andy Field (2005) *Discovering Statistics Using SPSS* (London, Thousand Oaks and Delhi: Sage), can be referred to. It would also be a good idea to enrol in a statistical research methods workshop offered by your university or college, although in our experience statistical training offered as a generic course or module, for instance in a multidisciplinary Graduate School, often does not take into account the particular needs, questions and interests of Humanities, Media and Cultural Studies students.

Quota sampling is typical of pollsters who may stop you on the street and ask if you belong to a particular group (journalism, advertising and so on) so that they can get the necessary representative percentage of different professional groups into their sample.

Student projects cannot usually use large, randomised, scientifically representative samples, because getting these involves gaining access to official records of households and then approaching these households, which is not possible for students conducting short-term projects. However, there are a number of other forms of sampling which students can adapt for their purposes. We list these ways below.

(ii) Non-probability (non-random) sampling

There are several kinds of non-random sampling, which is more often used in qualitative methods and in small-scale student projects which lack the time and resources to construct a full-scale, socially representative sample. These are:

- **Volunteer samples**: This is the kind of sample produced, for example, by magazine polls in which readers are invited to fill in a questionnaire in the magazine and send it in. The people who volunteer may be quite untypical of the readership as a whole or the population at large. Thus, even though quite large numbers may be involved, with thousands of respondents, this method is unscientific and unreliable. Pilot studies often use volunteers (friends and relatives who are willing to help) and this is fine so long as you don't try to generalise from them.
- **Purposive samples**: these are selected for a purpose, for example, TV soap viewers or student drinkers. However, even here, if your primary interest is only in soap viewing or student drinking, you can still construct a reliable sample from these groups, provided that you don't generalise from your findings

about them to make other claims about all TV viewing or general student attitudes.

- **Quota samples**: If – to take the example of our student project on student drinkers – you know from your preliminary background research that the population of student drinkers as a whole includes 70 per cent who drink primarily beer, and 30 per cent who primarily drink other kinds of alcohol, then you need to make sure that these proportions are reflected in your sample – assuming that this question is of interest to your project.

- **Haphazard samples**: e.g. every tenth person, as when you stand in a shopping mall and decide to ask every tenth person who comes along to fill in your questionnaire. This may, or may not, be 'representative' of shoppers generally, so cannot be seen as a strictly scientifically chosen sample.

- **Cluster sampling**: as in the TV ratings, which select samples of households according to 'clusters', first of regions, then of towns, then of neighbourhoods, in order to ensure that the whole country is included. (See Wimmer and Dominick, Chapter 14, for a full explanation of how this is done.)

- **Convenience sample**: again a common choice for student projects. You simply ask the people who are handiest to you (such as all the people living in your hall of residence or dorm) to fill in your questionnaire. This is acceptable for an academic exercise, so long as you don't attempt to generalise to a larger population. That said, it can be possible to construct a representative sample from people who are 'convenient', if you know exactly what you want (research question again!). For example, when Davies et al. constructed their sample of 1,332 6–13-year-olds in schools in England and Wales for their BBC study (*Dear BBC*), they had to rely on 'convenience' in the sense that they approached schools through people who were known to them and who they thought were likely to be receptive. The sample of schools was also designed to be reasonably (although not totally) representative of different types of state school: urban/rural; primary/secondary; inner-city/outer-city; London/ non-London. When we compared our demographic breakdown (gender; age; socio-economic status as measured by special needs status in the schools; media consumption and ownership) we found that our breakdown very closely matched a similar breakdown of a similar sized sample in a study that *had* been scientifically selected: this was a study carried out by Sonia Livingstone and Moira Bovill at the LSE and published in 1999: *Children, Young People and the Changing Media Environment.* Comparing our sample to theirs was a helpful validity check.

- **Case study:** This is where you focus on just one or two examples of your focus of interest. For instance, if you were studying advertising aimed at young girls, you might choose just one product – shampoo or skin-care cream – and carry out an analysis only on advertising for that product. In the case of research with people, you could choose just one household and study its use of cosmetics and toiletries. An undergraduate student of Máire Messenger Davies at Ulster did a case study of the ads for the Diesel fashion group for her BA dissertation project. She constructed her sample from a time period of two years and chose three different campaigns to look at in detail. She also got some consumer response through a questionnaire with a convenience sample of young people (male and female) in their twenties. This single-case approach allows you to be much more detailed in what you find out. If you are going to focus on particular households, or small groups, this has similarities to ethnographic research carried out by anthropologists in that you may become closely involved in the household yourself while you conduct your survey. We are not giving detailed information about ethnographic methods in this book, although the general principles we recommend about having a proper research question and about general research design and practice apply to all studies with human subjects. We do recommend that if you are conducting qualitative research with human beings, a good ethnographic methods handbook, such as David Machin's *Ethnographic Research for Media Studies* (2002) is useful to consult.

Sampling errors

No sample will be perfect. If the errors (imperfections) are random, then it's not a problem (statistical tests allow for this). The problem arises when you get non-random errors, when there is a pattern of bias in your sample – for instance, you deliberately only talk to young women who wear a particular kind of outfit, when your focus is on young women's attitudes to fashion generally; or young men who support a particular football team, when your focus is on young men's attitudes to football generally.

How do you select a sample?

At the risk of tediously repeating ourselves, we must emphasise again that your choice of sample initially depends on your research question. So once again, it is really important to be clear about **what** you want to know and **why**, and to bear in mind the following **practical** point:

> **Choose a question that can be relatively easily answered** *with the resources to hand*, **i.e. with a student population, or (in the case of media material) with media archives that can be found in your university or local library, or online**.

If, to take our example above, you want to look at an advertising campaign aimed at young girls, bear in mind the possible difficulty of getting people under eighteen to answer a questionnaire. Ethical issues arise when you are carrying out research with children and teenagers, so you may want to confine your sample to, say, first year undergraduate females. These will be legal adults, but still teenagers (aged 18–19) and likely to be representative of some of the demographics of advertising aimed at young women.

In terms of getting access to advertising material, remember you may not be able to get hold of all the components of the campaign, especially if it's been running for years. Print material is a lot easier to find and study (e.g. it's possible to photocopy it) than television material, so you may decide to stick to ads in magazines and again, just one magazine is easier to sample than several.

Sampling film and television

Because of the relative ease of access, media students often end up doing research on newspapers and magazines rather than film and television. This is a pity, and if you think that you would like to study film and television as part of your research project, start thinking very early on about where you are going to find the material, and tailor your research question accordingly. For instance, getting hold of copies of recent film releases will be difficult because they have not yet been released on DVD or video for the domestic market. Looking at all of 'Hollywood cinema' as one undergraduate announced he was going to do as his dissertation project is completely impossible. It is easier to do an analysis of, say, all adventure film releases in a single week two years ago (which are likely to be available on DVD), or a close comparison of two contrasting single films, or an analysis of one or two evenings' TV output on *one* channel, than to try to survey the whole output of a particular director, or all of 'television advertising'.

Being this selective about your material means, in turn, that your research question has to be very specific (and all the better for it), for instance:

> **'What is the incidence and type of product placements in one week's movie releases, (*in a year from which these releases are available on DVD*); and is there a significant difference in product placements between genres (e.g. action adventure versus romantic comedy)?'[2]**

Sampling television

With television, you can do what we did with a study we conducted for the Broadcasting Standards Commission about the use of children in adult programmes, and whether children were able to consent to the ways in which they were shown on TV (Davies and Mosdell, *Consenting Children?* 2001). We wanted to get a sense of:

> **how often children are used in adult programming on television, in what genres and for what purposes**.

We chose two days in October 2000 and arranged to videotape four terrestrial channels from 6 am until 6 pm on both days. This was still a lot of material to review, but because our question was very specific – the incidence of children in different types of programming – it was

---

[2] For an interesting analysis of product placement in movies, see Toby Miller, Nitin Govil, John McMurria and Richard Maxwell and Ting Wang *Global Hollywood 2* (London: BFI Publishing, 2005), especially Chapter 5, 'Getting the Audience'.

relatively easy to answer. The results, with a brief interpretation of them, are shown below:

Analysis of children in adult TV programming (from Davies and Mosdell, 2001)

- In an analysis of 32 hours of daytime programming on BBC1, ITV, Channel 4 and Channel 5, nearly 13 per cent of material was either aimed at or featured children.
- Most images of children were in adult material: 60 per cent in advertisements; 20 per cent in news broadcasting; 15 per cent in children's programming; and 5 per cent in all other kinds of shows.
- Children's representation had three main characteristics:
    - (i)   Passivity – children did not speak, and were not interviewed.
    - (ii) Entertainment value – children were 'cute' or 'funny'.
    - (iii) Appeals to emotionalism – children were used to evoke sympathy.

Because our sample included both public service (BBC) and commercial channels; because it included all time-periods throughout the day; because it included every type of daytime genre; and because it included both a weekday and a weekend day, we felt confident that this was a *representative sample* of terrestrial daytime programming in general and that the above conclusions were likely to apply to another similar sample of daytime programming.

Sample size

The most frequent question is. 'How many do I need?'

With a large-scale, socially representative sample, where you want to draw conclusions about the population generally, there needs to be at least 100 people in every demographic group. For students, finding such a large group may be difficult if not impossible. As we've said, depending on your research question, your sample should not have to be subdivided into so many groups that any particular subgroup is smaller than five. Statistical tests such as the **chi-square** (see Chapter 10, page 150) become unreliable when numbers in each subgroup are less than this. So again, make your original research question relevant to at the most two or three subgroups (male/ female; UK/non-UK students; older/younger) and don't try to analyse more than this.

Beware percentages

The other point to bear in mind is that you will want to translate your numbers into percentages. Percentages become extremely misleading when they are based on small numbers: 10 per cent of a sample of ten people is only one person. You cannot generalise from this. Ten per cent of 100 people is ten people and this is a slightly more reliable number to draw conclusions from, But 10 per cent of 200 people is even better.

Figure 4.1 shows an example of a cross-tabulation in which suchsubdivisions have occurred. This comes from our study of theatre-goers at the West Yorkshire Playhouse in 2001 and shows the proportions of males and females who came from different loca-

Home Base * Sex Crosstabulation

			Male	Female	Total
Home Base	Leeds/Bradford	Count	130	214	344
		% within Home Base	37.8%	62.2%	100.0%
		% within Sex	37.0%	36.4%	36.6%
		% of Total	13.8%	22.8%	36.6%
	Yorkshire Other	Count	120	241	361
		% within Home Base	33.2%	66.8%	100.0%
		% within Sex	34.2%	41.0%	38.4%
		% of Total	12.8%	25.7%	38.4%
	UK Other	Count	98	126	224
		% within Home Base	43.8%	56.3%	100.0%
		% within Sex	27.9%	21.4%	23.9%
		% of Total	10.4%	13.4%	23.9%
	Outside UK	Count	3	7	10
		% within Home Base	30.0%	70.0%	100.0%
		% within Sex	.9%	1.2%	1.1%
		% of Total	.3%	.7%	1.1%
Total		Count	351	588	939
		% within Home Base	37.4%	62.6%	100.0%
		% within Sex	100.0%	100.0%	100.0%
		% of Total	37.4%	62.6%	100.0%

tions: the **variables** entered in the crosstab analysis were 'sex' (in the columns going down) crossed with 'home base' (in the rows going across). As you can see, with such a large sample (939 people) only one of the cells had fewer than five in it. (Can you find it and identify what kind of people these were?) Most of the cells had at least 100 people in each. This made the statistical analysis of the data very reliable.

So the answer to 'How many'? is 'As many as possible within the parameters of your research question'. For instance, adding more people overall to the crosstab above wouldn't have made much difference to the final statistical analysis. However, if we could have found a few more people in the 'outside UK' category, that would have given us more useful comparisons between British and non-British theatre-goers.

For a small-scale student project we suggest you need at least sixty in your questionnaire sample to get anything significant. If you are working in groups of five and you manage to get twenty each, this makes the task for each individual less arduous and will give you a sample of 100. The more data you have, the better chance you have of getting significant results.

CHAPTER 5

The Practicalities

This chapter aims to identify and anticipate some of the possible – and sometimes very real – problems that you may encounter 'in the field'.

Even the most well-funded research will have practical limitations – budget, time, personnel, etc. – and planning the most efficient use of these resources is essential in getting the most from the data that you eventually collect.

Most of this may seem like common sense but it's surprising how many 'Doh' moments we've had as researchers, and how many others have been related to us by students.

Personnel

Your human resources are just as important as any other. When working in groups, in real-world research teams as in student groups, each individual needs to have a clear understanding of the aims of the project and where the work is going at any given time.

We have always found it useful for each group to have a 'minute-taker' – someone who records the group's thoughts from the first brain-storming session through to the end of the project, and who can circulate these to the other members. These notes serve to keep everyone on track and can also be valuable in developing, refining and eventually writing the project report.

Other specific roles can be allocated to other members. Perhaps someone is particularly adept at phrasing questions for the research instrument; someone else may have a flair for designing a questionnaire layout; someone else may relish the task of inputting data (a mind-numbing distraction or a Zen-like state of meditation, depending on your point of view). How you allocate these roles depends on the individuals that make up your particular team; there will inevitably be disagreements and sometimes heated discussion but, as the saying goes, that's life. It can also be constructive for the project as a whole for everyone to feel able to make a contribution to any of the various stages and to debate these ideas with colleagues. In real-world research you will often have to work with people with whom you may not personally agree or even like very much, but it is an important skill to be able to work professionally within a group, whatever the task. Functioning effectively as a team dramatically reduces workload and tension, and increases everyone's involvement in and satisfaction with the project.

Advance planning

Know your audience

Having selected a sample, you need to know where and when they will be available to complete your questionnaire. One of the (many) criticisms about conducting questionnaire-based research is the use of convenience sampling, even though the sample may have been perfectly designed back in the office or classroom. If you intend to sample members of the public, think about the bias that you will introduce if you hand out questionnaires only in a town centre on a weekday lunchtime.

One of the examples that we use in teaching this module comes from the West Yorkshire Playhouse data. We gave out questionnaires over three days, and over different performance times during those days. One simple finding was that the vast majority of the Friday matinee performance was aged over sixty-five. Why might that be? Because other age groups were at work? Because there was a particular, age-related discount on those days? Because that particular age demographic felt less comfortable about going out in the evenings?

A neat example comes from (yet another) student project about alcohol consumption in student union bars. Think about how time of day might affect this, not just in terms of who might be actually capable of filling in a questionnaire, but who the clientele of the bars are at different times of the day. Are people who are questioned at midday likely to give different answers about their weekly alcohol consumption from those questioned at midnight? Are those questioned at midnight on a Friday likely to give different answers from those questioned at midnight on a Monday? Are those questioned at midnight on a Friday likely to give different answers than those questioned at 9 pm on a Friday?

Are those questioned at 2.00 a.m. likely to give any answer at all? (The group in question dealt with this by sampling at different times on different days, and had a lot of fun doing so.)

On a more serious note, if you intend to conduct research any-where other than a public area, those who are 'hosting' your target sample will want to know exactly what you are doing as well. We have had several students conducting research into various airlines that have run into all sorts of difficulties from airport authorities in the current security climate, although they were very supportive in the end. This can be useful – if you gain the permission and approach the 'hosts' with honesty, they may well come up with suggestions that can aid your project. The project with the West Yorkshire Playhouse was conducted in close partnership with their marketing department, which made a number of suggestions for questions based on their own expertise and experience, which were invaluable to the final work.

Special care has to be taken when working with vulnerable groups – in particular children. These themes are addressed in Chapter 9. See also the section on ethics below, pp. 75–6.

Know your venue
We decided, and were given permission, to hand out questionnaires at the West Yorkshire Playhouse.

Where is the West Yorkshire Playhouse?

Traffic will be late, roads will be jammed, offices will be down a tiny side street that is invisible to all but those who work there and that are, in reality, in a completely different area/city/continent from the main reception building.

Make sure you know where you are going; how to get there; how long it will take (plus additional times for unexpected 'adventures').

Thinking about these things in advance will significantly reduce stress.

Check your instruments
Make sure you have a sufficient number of questionnaires printed or photocopied and bring more than you think you might need.

If you are planning to photocopy questionnaires at the venue, make sure you know where these facilities are (and that they are working).

Bring pencils. Lots and lots of pencils. Far more than you think you will need. Unless you are administering the questionnaire face-to-face, pencils will get lost behind chairs or wander off on their own.

Remember to number the questionnaires when they have been completed. This will not only make data entry easier (ensuring that you don't enter the same data set twice) but will also allow you to separate out which questionnaires were given out and where. This can also be useful when you come to analyse the data. Mistakes may be made during data entry, but if the questionnaire is numbered, it's easy to go back and check.

Ethical considerations

Whenever you are doing research with people you need to consider the ethics of the project. This involves being polite and courteous, but also not deliberately misleading people in any way, and keeping their responses confidential.

As we have suggested in Chapter 6, it's always useful to have some sort of introduction at the beginning of your questionnaire that sets out the ground rules. This should include a statement about the nature of the project both as a way of getting your respondents into the right frame of mind to think about the topic, and also as reassurance that the research is for academic purposes and not market research or collection of personal information. Try not to give too much away here though – it's equally important that you don't introduce bias by detailing your hypotheses, and perhaps thereby subconsciously influencing possible responses.

It is also very important to state that it is an academic project. There are no right or wrong answers and you want people to respond honestly, but the information will not be used for any other purpose (e.g. marketing information). All information is also confidential. You will not usually ask people their names or contact details, but if you do – perhaps as a way of recruiting people for follow-up focus groups – it's important to reassure them that this information will not be given to a third party.

Finally, many universities have standards of ethics that apply to all kinds of research. These are more obvious if you are thinking about a project that involves vulnerable groups such as children; some of these concerns are set out in Chapter 9. However, collecting personal information from members of the public may also raise ethical and practical issues. It's worth discussing these with a lecturer but, since the primary focus of this book is to illustrate these methods as an exercise, it may be safer to stick with conducting your research on classmates and other students.

The seven P's

We have found the following checklist very useful in preparing and conducting field research.

Personnel

Make sure everyone in the team has a role but also has a clear understanding of everyone else's role, and of the project direction as a whole.

Piloting

Make sure you test your questionnaire for presentation, administration and wording. Run a simple **pilot** on a few classmates and check the results. Chapter 8 discusses the value of piloting in more detail.

Pencils

You can never have too many.

Photocopying

Make sure you have sufficient copies of the questionnaire, and then add some more. If you intend to get the instrument copied at the location where you intend to do the research, make sure you have confirmed access and financial details for copying.

Plan B

Be prepared for things to go wrong. It's always worth trying to anticipate any potential hiccups in the entire research process and thinking of alternative solutions. Again, the process of piloting will inform your thinking here.

Planning

Thinking carefully about the practical administration of the questionnaire will reduce stress considerably.

Pholders

OK, so we cheated a bit there. Maintaining good records and care-fully storing completed data are crucial though, and having a filing and storage system that all group members understand will avoid problems when you come to look at the data.

The following chapters discuss instrument design in more detail but bear these practicalities in mind all the way through the project.

CHAPTER 6

Instrument Design: The Questionnaire

In this chapter, we discuss the main research instrument used in quantitative research methods: **the questionnaire**, used for surveys with members of the public. We address this topic from a number of points of view, bearing in mind: the practicalities of administration (in the case of questionnaires, often in a public place); the diversity of the sample, especially if you are dealing with a representative sample of people with different interest, intelligence and education levels; the internal validity (does the instrument address the questions you are interested in?); and the clarity of subsequent analysis, whether quantitative or qualitative.

Questionnaire design

A questionnaire is one of the simplest and quickest ways of getting information from large numbers of people and, with modern versions of statistical software, it can be a very easy instrument both to design and analyse. However, the people you ask to answer it may not find it easy at all – so careful design is very important in order to get the clearest answers to your questions.

In general, simple questionnaires of the kind used in student projects (and, we believe, simplicity is also a virtue of professional questionnaire design) is likely to have just two main sections (as we said in Chapter 3):

1. **A demographic section** – in which respondents give information about themselves relevant to your project, including the standard demographic information about age and gender.
2. **An information/attitude section** – in this section people answer the questions you are interested in as part of your research project.

In the case of media research, a third section may be desirable, asking about people's media consumption, habits and tastes. For instance, you may have a hunch (hypothesis) that people who read the tabloid press might be more inclined to be sympathetic to the royal family than people who read broadsheet newspapers. So you may want to include a section on what newspapers people read and how often, and then check whether tabloid readers have more positive answers to questions about royalty – a project that an undergraduate group of students in a BA module we taught wanted to carry out. People's tastes in film, television, books and music may also be **correlated** (see Chapter 10) with social class or other demographic characteristics or social attitudes. So, again, *depending on your research question*, information about people's general media consumption may be useful.

Relating the research question to question design

Once again, to emphasise the importance of having a clear research question and how this will helpfully influence your instrument design, we draw on an example from our own research. In our West Yorkshire Playhouse study, in which we were interested in the relationship between people's attitudes to popular culture (such as television watching) and 'high' culture (such as theatre-going) we asked for information about both, as follows:

Every day I watch TV for	5 or more hours	3–4 hours	1–2 hours	1 hour or less	Never

and

I go to the theatre	6–12 times a year	2–5 times a year	Once a year	Less than once a year	Never

Among the 903 theatre-goers who answered these questions, we found a **significant correlation** (see Chapter 10) between amount of television watching and regular theatre-going, with the highest concentrations of answers coming in the 1–2 hours TV group (188 people, 48.5 per cent of the television viewers) who also went to the theatre 6–12 times a year. There was also a high concentration of people in the 3–4 hours a day TV group who went to the theatre 2–5 times a year (102 people, 46.2 per cent of this group of TV viewers). There was no relationship at all between heavy TV viewing and *never* going to the theatre, which was what some people might expect if they believe that watching TV is lowbrow and going to the theatre is more intellectually highbrow. Our focus group discussions supported these questionnaire findings: the people who volunteered for the groups, some very passionate theatre-goers, were also very knowledgeable and enthusiastic about television. Not surprisingly, considering the star of the play (Patrick Stewart), some of these people were also passionate *Star Trek* fans – and again, very far from the geeky, 'Trekkie' stereotype. This kind of research is valuable in **'falsifying'** (see Chapter 1) popular, and academic, assumptions about class-related cultural habits.

Designing your questions

Questionnaires are a very quick way of gathering a lot of data, but the quality of those data depends a great deal on:

- the clarity with which you have formulated your research question;
- the extent to which the questions in your questionnaire are related to the research question;
- the wording of the questions and their comprehensibility to the people answering;
- the extent to which you don't prompt desired answers in your respondents by asking leading questions.

Avoiding leading questions

Questions should not lead your respondents in the direction you hope they will go. For instance, if we had asked our West Yorkshire respondents: 'Television watching is more lower-class than going to the theatre', we would have pointed them towards one of the possible desired answers underlying our research question; some people might have been tempted to circle the 'agree' or 'strongly agree' boxes, because they know that many academic researchers disapprove of television, and might have thought that this was the answer we wanted. Asking a behavioural question about what people *did*, whether going to the theatre or watching television, was more revealing. Even though their answers were only *estimates* of their habits and perhaps not entirely accurate, there was still a positive relationship between both sets of estimates: they *saw themselves* as both regular TV viewers and regular theatre-goers without any apparent inconsistency.

Closed and open-ended questions

As we've said, questions can be *closed* or *open-ended*. For ease of coding, the most common form is closed-ended, in which a question is posed and a list of possible answers is provided (**multiple-choice**). Open-ended questions allow the respondents to answer in as much detail as they wish, and good questionnaires, as we've pointed out, include opportunities for people to do both.

If your target audience is likely to be very multicultural, it can be problematic to provide an exhaustive list of possible responses, particularly in the cases of nationality or religion. In such cases, it may be better to allow respondents to write in their answers and then postcode these once the data have been collected.

Questionnaire structure

The demographics section – information about the people themselves and their characteristics – usually appears first on the questionnaire. These are straightforward questions to answer and may put your respondents at ease. However, again, don't put too many of these types of questions in – only use those relevant to your research question. You don't want the questionnaire to appear pointless or boring (or indeed, impertinent, if you ask too many personal questions). If you do feel it is necessary to include several demographic questions, you can always have some at the beginning (as a 'warm-up' to the questionnaire) and the rest at the end.

Giving 'grouped' options for variables such as age (e.g. age 25–30; 31–35; 36–40) and income (e.g. under £10,000; £11,000–15,000, and so on) is standard practice. Here's an example from our West Yorkshire Playhouse questionnaire:

A. ABOUT YOU

Please **circle** the appropriate category, e.g. if you are 28 years old, circle 26–35:

Age (years)	0–10	11–16	17–25	26–35	36–45	46–55	56–65	65+

Annual household income	Below £10,000	£10,000– £20,000	£21,000– £35,000	£36,000– £50,000	£51,000– £70,000	£71,000– £90,000	Above £91,000

We also give an example from a student questionnaire about attitudes to alcohol, which – again as determined by the research question – does not include age-groups under eighteen because the question is about drinking habits. Asking under-eighteens (who quite clearly do drink alcohol sometimes) would not be advisable for ethical and practical reasons in a student project:

2. What is your age group?

☐ 18–25   ☐ 26–35   ☐ 36–45   ☐ 46+

Getting to the point of your research

The most important section will be where you directly address the research topic that you are investigating. Here you are more likely to use a mixture of closed-ended, multiple-choice questions and those that try to tap into the respondents' feelings and attitudes towards the topic.

Below, we use an example from a student project on drinking habits and attitudes to illustrate the basic principles of questionnaire design. We will also use data from student projects to illustrate our later chapters about data analysis and interpretation. We stress that these are examples for teaching and exercise purposes: they are a *how to* illustration, not a model to follow in real-world research (although in fact, this project on drinking is not a bad piece of research, even from a professional point of view). The students' original questionnaire is printed in bold type; our comments are in normal type.

Questionnaire on drinking habits

In the case used here, the students have not headlined their questionnaire 'drinking habits'. Sometimes such a headline can be off-putting to respondents, especially if it's a sensitive topic. However, as must be done with all questionnaires, the students do identify themselves as being from Cardiff University and explain why they are doing the research (for a student project); they also promise confidentiality. You will note that there is no space on the questionnaire for the name of the person answering. If you *do* ask for the person's name, you *must* keep it confidential. All questionnaires, once completed, must be numbered. When you enter the data into the SPSS program, the number on the questionnaire MUST correspond to the number in the data set, i.e. the person who filled in questionnaire No. 1 should be the first person whose data you enter in SPSS 'data view' (see Chapter 10). The reason for this should be obvious: if you need to check the accuracy of your SPSS data, or if there are qualitative comments on the questionnaire of person No. 1 (or 51, or 151) which need to be matched to the quantitative responses, we need to be able to put our hands quickly on questionnaire No. 1 (or 51, or 151). Accurate numbering of all completed questionnaires is one of the most essential jobs in carrying out surveys. We give an example below from our West Yorkshire data set of the first two people who answered our questionnaire.

S	Performance attended	Age	Sex	Ethnicity	Income	Education	Homebase
1.	Thursday Matinee (13/09/01)	65+	Female	White	99.00	Postgraduate	UK Other
2.	Thursday Matinee (13/09/01)	65+	Female	White	£10–20k	HE	Leeds/ Bradford

As we can see, S (Subject) No. 1 attended the Thursday matinee performance, was in the 65+ age group, was female, white, didn't give her income, was educated to postgraduate level and came from the UK outside Yorkshire. The topics in bold across the top of the columns are the first seven **variables** in our West Yorkshire survey, and the answers that these women gave are the **values** (levels) associated with these variables. All had been numerically coded. 'Female' had been coded 2, with 'male' 1; Postgrad had been coded '6' out of six levels of education; 'UK other' had been coded 3 (one of four different categories for where people lived). If we wanted to know more about subject No. 1, and what her comments were in the 'other' section, or if she'd volunteered for a focus group, we would go to the hard copy of the questionnaire labelled '1'. This seems so eminently common sense that it would seem not worth saying; however, we have bitter experience of coming across unnumbered questionnaires and not being able to identify the data associated with them in our data sets. Sitting down with a cup of tea and one of your pencils (see Chapter 5) and numbering your questionnaires as soon as you've collected them, then putting them in a folder labelled 'Thursday Matinee, Nos. 1–150' can save hours of grief.

Cardiff student questionnaire example:

***Disclaimer*: We are students at Cardiff University and are undertaking a study for our MA programme and would be very grateful for your comments. Your responses are confidential and strictly for research purposes only.**

1. What is your gender?

☐ **Male**   ☐ **Female**

2. What is your age group?

☐ **18–25**   ☐ **26–35**   ☐ **36–45**   ☐ **46+**

3. What is your employment status? (Please select more than one if necessary)

☐ **Unemployed**

☐ **Self-employed**

☐ **Full-time employment**

☐ **Part-time employment**

☐ **Student**

☐ **Other .... (please specify)**

☐ **Retired**

The demographic section ends here, and the next section – getting to the point of the research, with fourteen questions about drinking habits and attitudes to them – starts very helpfully with some explanations of what 'a unit' means when applied to alcoholic drinks:

If a pint of lager is 2 units; a glass of wine is 1 unit; a single measure of a spirit is 1 unit and the average cocktail is 3 units:

4. **On average how many units of alcohol do you consume in the average week?**

   ☐ **None**   ☐ **1–10**   ☐ **11–20**   ☐ **21–30**   ☐ **31–40**
   ☐ **40+**

5. **How many times on average would you say you consumed alcohol?**

   ☐ **None**

   ☐ **Once/twice a week**

   ☐ **Three/four times a week**

   ☐ **Every other day**

   ☐ **Everyday**

6. **Where do you usually consume alcohol? (Please choose up to three answers and rank answers 1–3, with 1 being most often and 3 being the third most likely)**

   ☐ **At home**   ☐ **Pub**   ☐ **Restaurant**
   ☐ **Bar**   ☐ **Club** ☐ **Other (please specify)**

This is an example of 'multiple responses' – in other words, people are being given the option of ticking more than one box. There is a way of dealing with this when it comes to analysing the data which we explain in Appendix 2 ('Multiple-responses').

7. **Do you drink in order to get drunk?**

   ☐ **Yes**   ☐ **Occasionally**   ☐ **Don't know**

8. **Do you have concerns for your health if you drink regularly?**

   ☐ **Yes**   ☐ **Sometimes**   ☐ **No**   ☐ **Don't know**

9. **For the purposes of this questionnaire we are using** *Alcohol Concern*'s **definition of binge drinking: 'Drinking sufficient alcohol to reach a state of intoxication in the course of one drinking session.' To what extent do you agree?**

☐ Strongly agree

☐ Agree

☐ Somewhat agree

☐ Neither agree nor disagree

☐ Somewhat disagree

☐ Disagree

☐ Strongly disagree

Again, these students have helpfully found an official definition of the term 'binge drinking' – a term widely used but not often defined – in order to help their respondents answer the question.

You will notice that they are using a seven-point scale for this first question – sometimes used, but less often than the five-point scale for reasons which you may spot yourself. For instance, if you have to decide between 'agree' and 'somewhat agree' how do you do this? It's simpler for people (especially those in a hurry) to distinguish between 'strong feeling' and just 'feeling'. If you subdivide your answers by seven rather than five, you will also get fewer subjects in each category and, as we pointed out in Chapter 4, the smaller the subgroups in your sample, the less reliable your findings will be.

From now on, the students are using a five-point scale, and they are also varying the wording of their questions, as with questions 11, 14 and 17. This is a good idea to stop people answering routinely; if the format of the question is always the same, the temptation to make the format of the answer the same is greater.

10. **'I need to consume alcohol on a regular basis just to have a good time.' To what extent do you agree?**

☐ Strongly agree

☐ Agree

☐ Neither agree nor disagree

☐ Disagree

☐ Strongly disagree

11. **When drinking in groups, would you say that you were more likely drink in 'rounds' or buy your own drinks individually?**

☐ Drink in rounds   ☐ Buy drinks individually

☐ It varies   ☐ Don't know

12. **'It has been suggested that drinking in rounds leads to binge drinking.' To what extent do you agree?**

☐ Strongly agree

☐ Agree

☐ Neither agree nor disagree

☐ Disagree

☐ Strongly disagree

13. **'When I see an advertisement for an alcoholic product, I feel driven to purchase it.' To what extent do you agree?**

☐ Strongly agree

☐ Agree

☐ Neither agree nor disagree

☐ Disagree

☐ Strongly disagree

14. **Do you think that the Government is right to introduce legislation where drinking establishments have 24-hour licences?**

☐ Yes   ☐ To an extent   ☐ No   ☐ Don't know

15. **'The 24-hour licensing for the sale of alcohol will cut down on anti-social behaviour.' To what extent do you agree?**

☐ Strongly agree
☐ Agree
☐ Neither agree nor disagree
☐ Disagree
☐ Strongly disagree

16. **'The Government is going to introduce a policy to ban the selling of alcohol on public transport, i.e. aeroplanes and trains.' To what extent do you believe this will be successful in restraining binge drinking culture?**

☐ Strongly agree
☐ Agree
☐ Neither agree nor disagree
☐ Disagree
☐ Strongly disagree

The wording of this question is a little complicated. People are being asked to what extent they believe 'this', but it's not clear at first glance what 'this' refers to. Is it aeroplanes and trains? The Government? Or is it in fact the policy? It is in fact the policy, so simplifying the question might have been wiser, e.g.:

'Banning the sale of alcohol on public transport will reduce binge drinking.'

17. **Do you think that the consumption of alcohol can be connected to antisocial behaviour?**

☐ Yes   ☐ Indirectly linked   ☐ No   ☐ Don't know

This could be seen as an example of a 'leading question'. Obviously, it's an example of the good practice of varying wording, but it might have been better to make it a Likert scale statement:

'The consumption of alcohol is directly connected to antisocial behaviour.'

Or it could have been worded even more precisely to avoid what are sometimes called 'hidden contingencies'. That is, a person answering the questionnaire might have different definitions of 'antisocial' than the researchers. Again, being specific is the better way:

'Drinking alcohol makes people aggressive.'

Or

'Drinking alcohol contributes to rowdy behaviour in the street.'

18. Do you have any other comments?

. . . .

. . . .

. . . .

~ THANK YOU FOR COMPLETING THIS QUESTIONNAIRE ~

Presentation

Even if you are administering the questionnaire in person, the design and layout reflect your status as a researcher. Spelling mistakes and sloppy layout will not make your respondents feel confident in your abilities, so do your best to make the presentation as professional as possible. It's also very important to be as simple as possible. Even if you are giving a questionnaire to a group of people who pride themselves on being intellectuals, clarity and an absence of ambiguity are essential in good questionnaire design: the simpler and clearer the language, the better.

Introduction

It is a good idea to have some sort of brief introduction at the top of the first page. This should include the name of the institution you are working for and a brief outline of the project. It is very important that you do not give too much information away here though. As we've said, telling respondents all about your hypotheses before they answer the questions will inevitably influence their answers and bias your data. You can also use this space to state the purposes of the data (e.g. research for your undergraduate project) and to emphasise the facts that:

- Respondents do not have to answer any questions that they feel uncomfortable with (some people do not like stating their age or salary, for example).
- The data will not be used for any other purpose. This is especially relevant if you have asked them to give contact details (for example, for follow-up focus groups or telephone interviews). If this is the case, you should also stress that they will remain anonymous in any reports that you prepare.
- It is also worth stating that there are no right or wrong answers – this is particularly the case with younger children. Respondents should be encouraged to be as honest and open as possible in their answers.

How long?

The most frequent question we have from our students is 'How long should the questionnaire be?' Unfortunately, there is no simple answer. Whether singly or as a research team, you should consider some of the following issues that will have a bearing on the number of questions that you can reasonably ask:

- What are the most important demographic questions?
  There is no point in including questions simply because they pad out the questionnaire or because they might have some vague bearing on your research question.

- What are the most important research questions?
  Remember you are likely to get only one shot at collecting your data so try to ensure that you cover all of the areas you are interested in. The ways in which these questions are structured is vital, so try to think creatively and bear in mind the comments we made

about the student questionnaire and its wording, above. Remember the value of piloting the first draft (see Chapter 8).

- Who will be answering your questionnaire?
  Someone who is approached in their lunch-break or during a shopping trip will not be very likely to answer a questionnaire that looks as thick as a telephone directory and that takes more than a couple of minutes to complete. Someone who is sent the questionnaire via e-mail or post, or who deliberately visits a website to answer it, is likely to have a bit more time. The length of the questionnaire is crucial in determining your *response rate* (the number of people who complete the instrument) and a common cause of a low response rate is an over-long questionnaire that looks time-consuming or that becomes so tedious that people don't finish it. This will undermine **internal validity**. It will also distort your sample, which will end up consisting only of very patient or under-employed people, and this undermines **external validity**. Again, piloting will help here.

- How will you administer the questionnaire?
  Questionnaires that you hand out or leave for respondents to complete themselves must not look intimidating. If you are administering the questionnaire yourselves (face to face with the respondent or via the telephone), it is common courtesy to give the respondent some indication of how long it will take. You will know this, of course, from having piloted your questionnaire first.

Question structure

The way in which you ask your questions will have great bearing on the quality and validity of the data that you collect. It is important to spend time considering the detail of the wording and again, this is where **piloting**, even if only on one other person, is essential. In our class workshops, we always have some form of exercise in which students either work in pairs, first answering and then critiquing each other's research instruments, or in groups, and the groups swap their draft instruments with each other. This way, a group can get at least five responses to their questionnaire, and also some useful criticisms of it from their peers.

Standard demographics

These will include some or all of the following: age; gender; income; nationality; ethnicity; education; religion; number of children (and ages); home base. Other demographic information (for instance, in the case of the drinking project above) could include employment or student status.

Considerations of coding

These, and your intended analyses based on coding, will influence the design of the responses to demographic questions, for example, as we've said, using grouped categories such as a span of a few years for age (e.g. Under 15; 16–20; 21–25, etc.). Multiple-choice questions also facilitate ease of coding, as does the standard five-point Likert scale.

Research questions

Most questionnaires include questions which relate to attitudes (approval/disapproval; likes/dislikes; agree/disagree, and so on) or frequencies of behaviour (for example, of television viewing or of consumption of a particular product). Social science and humanities students and researchers are particularly interested in people's opinions and tastes. As we explained in Chapter 3, the most common way to get at people's attitudes is through the Likert five-point scale, asking people to express levels of agreement or disagreement with a statement.

Some do's and don'ts

The wording of the statement is often crucial here.

- Don't make statements that appear to have a very obvious answer.
- Don't make statements requiring extremely complicated judgements.
- Do make statements that are thought-provoking to try to elicit a range of responses.
- Do try to avoid offending your respondents' sensitivities.
- Do think carefully about who will be answering your questions and the amount of knowledge that they are likely to have about

particular topics. This will avoid eliciting the 'don't know/neutral' response too often.

- Do provide enough space for the respondents to elaborate or specify. Such responses can later be post-coded.

Neutral/don't know/undecided

The mid-point on a Likert scale may attract people who like to 'sit on the fence'. This can be avoided by using a four-point scale in which the respondent is 'forced' to express some degree of, for example, agreement or disagreement. However, a high number of neutral responses may actually be revealing; they may reflect a problem with the wording of your question (which you will pick up and amend at the piloting stage) or the fact that your sample, or a particular subgroup of your sample, really do feel neutral about that issue. This is a finding. Hence, we recommend that you play safe with the five-point scale and are very precise about your wording.

Checking internal validity

If you are concerned about the possibility of respondents answering in a haphazard way, then it is sometimes useful to have another question aimed at the same topic but that is phrased differently, perhaps even with the scales reversed. This will allow you to check respondents' consistency. For example, in the drinking questionnaire: 'I need to drink alcohol in order to have a good time' you could include another question later in the questionnaire: 'You can have a really successful party without alcohol', plus the 'agree/disagree' scale. A person who strongly agreed with the first question is likely to strongly disagree with the second. There will be a **negative correlation** between the two answers.

Response set

Reversing the scales of questions will also help to prevent respondents developing a pattern of responses, for example, always ticking 'strongly agree', known as 'response set'. The above example about drinking shows how you get round this: a social drinker will have to tick 'disagree' on the second question.

Qualitative data

Although much of the data from a questionnaire will be considered as quantitative, as we've said, you can often benefit from adding space at the end of the questionnaire to allow respondents to add their own comments. Many of these will not relate directly to your topic; some may be downright insulting (for instance, there will always be a few members of the public who know much better than you do how to design a questionnaire). But there may well be some valuable nuggets that draw attention to aspects of the topic that you may not have considered before.

A brief revision of key terms

We described how to code a very simple 'baby questionnaire', with only five questions, in Chapter 3. Here we revisit these terms to remind you that, now you've designed a more extensive and professional-looking questionnaire, these are the tasks that await you.

Coding
Before you can begin the task of analysing your data you need to put it in a form that the computer software can deal with. Coding is assigning numbers to your answers. REMEMBER THE DATA TYPES THAT YOU HAVE SEEN BEFORE: nominal; ordinal; interval/ scale (see Chapter 3). Also, have another look at the example of the first two lines from the West Yorkshire data set and see how you could adapt them for coding your own project (p. 83).

Variables
Each aspect that you want to look at is called a **variable**. For example, one variable is likely to be gender and you may decide that a person's gender will have an effect on one of your other variables, such as their attitude to television news or, in the case of the West Yorkshire study, their visits to the theatre. The variables in this study were chosen when we designed our questionnaire because we thought they'd be relevant to our basic question about the cultural habits of theatre-goers. Variable 7, 'home base', for instance, was useful to us in revealing just how far some people were prepared to travel to go to the theatre and

see a favourite actor. Usually, each of the questions on your questionnaire can be considered as a separate variable and so each needs to be coded before you can do any analysis using SPSS.

Demographic factors are often described as **independent variables**. That is, they are assumed to function 'independently' in such a way that they *influence* the other factors that you are interested in, such as people's attitudes to Irish politics, or binge drinking, or theatre-going. The factors that *are influenced* by these independent demographic characteristics (age, sex, nationality, etc.) are called **dependent variables**, because the influence doesn't work (at least in research design) the other way round: your attitude to Irish politics isn't going to influence which sex you are, for example, but your sex may influence your views on politics.

Independent variables may not always be demographic factors; in an experimental study, the factor exerting an influence on how people behave, or perform, can also be something created by the experimenter.[1] For instance, one dissertation student we worked with was interested in the difference between tabloid layout and broadsheet layout of the front pages of newspapers and the possible different effects this would have on the ways in which readers remembered the content. She was also interested in online versions of these front pages. Did the online version influence people's understanding and recall more than, or differently from, the print version? Did the tabloid version produce different responses from the broadsheet version? In this case, the **independent variables** were the experimental conditions that she manipulated: in one condition students saw a broadsheet version, in the other, a tabloid version. The name of this variable could be 'page design' or 'layout type'.

Values

The numbers that you assign to each possible answer of the question are known as the **values** of that variable. If we look at gender, the

---

[1] We have not talked much about experiments here, as experiments are rarely chosen as a research tool by media and humanities students, and they are not often appropriate for the kinds of questions these students want to ask. But both of us, as trained psychology graduates, believe strongly in the value of experiments as research tools for certain kinds of specific research questions, for instance, questions to do with variations in media format.

values of that variable could be 1 to stand for males and 2 to stand for females – it makes no difference which, as these are 'nominal' data. You can use 1, 2, 3, etc. as values for the next variable (for example, age). In the West Yorkshire study, there were eight values for age. When coding, you need to give a value to ALL of the possible answers for EACH question. This will help you enter your data later.

Post-coding

In some circumstances it will not be possible to assign codes before you have looked at the data. This is quite legitimate. For example, if you ask people what their favourite television programme is, it would be impossible to anticipate all of the possible answers in advance. Similarly, sometimes you may want to analyse some of the qualitative data that you get from comment sections – those labelled 'Other' or 'Do you have any further comments?'

Post-coding is the same as pre-coding, but you do it as you go along. Start with your first completed questionnaire and assign '1' to the first instance on the specific question. Each time you come to a new answer simply assign a value to it. For example, if the answer to 'What is your favourite television programme' in the first questionnaire you analyse is 'EastEnders', you code 'EastEnders' as 1; every time you come across this answer, you code it as '1'. If the next questionnaire has 'Blind Date' in answer to this question, this is coded as 2, and every time someone says 'Blind Date', you code it '2'. It's worth noting that the range of favourites in answers to such questions can be very wide, with codings going up to 300 or so – there can be hundreds of different responses in a large sample. This gives an indication of the diversity of people's tastes and is another important, but sometimes neglected, measure of media influence. With this kind of survey, not only do we find out what the most frequently mentioned programmes are (usually the top-rated shows, like 'EastEnders') we also find out the range, variety and distribution of people's tastes – something not mentioned so much in standard competitive league tables, like 'Top Tens'.

Piloting

We can do nothing at all with our design instruments without piloting them first. It is absolutely vital that, before you do any research with members of the public, or with material for a content analysis, you try it out first with a few volunteers in the case of questionnaires, or with some sample texts in the case of content analysis. Piloting enables you to identify any problems with your instruments and procedures (for instance, questions that are hard for people to understand, or coding categories that don't make sense to other coders) in advance of carrying out the investigation proper. Piloting is discussed in Chapter 8, but before we talk about this essential ingredient of all good empirical research, we turn to the question which many media students want to answer: How do you apply quantitative research methods to the analysis of media texts, whether word or image: the technique of **content analysis**?

Test questions: Chapter 6: questionnaire design

1. In the student questionnaire on pages 84–9, can you think of any further information you would have added to the introduction of this questionnaire?

2 You are conducting a project on young people's attitudes to 'celebrity culture'. Construct two Likert-scale statements evaluating these attitudes.

3. Show them to a colleague and amend them, if necessary, according to the following guidelines:

   • Don't give statements that appear to have a very obvious answer.
   • Don't give statements that require extremely complicated judgements.
   • Do make statements that are thought-provoking to try to elicit a range of responses.
   • Do try to avoid offending your respondents' sensitivities.

4. How would you code the following three subjects' characteristics, giving both **variable labels** and their number codings and **value labels** with their number codings?

   S. No. 1: 25-year-old male student, studying BA history, originating from France, parents' occupations doctor and university lecturer.

   S. No. 2: 40-year-old female, occupation transport worker, originating from North London, parents' occupations not given.

CHAPTER 7

Content Analysis

Content analysis is a very common method in media studies. There are many texts that deal with the weightier concepts behind this popular technique, but the aim of this chapter is to give some ideas about how to actually go about conducting a quantitative content analysis.

What is it?

Quantitative content analysis does pretty much what it says – it is a *systematic* and *objective* analysis of any particular text, whether a newspaper article, a book, a television clip or an advert. The quantitative aspect distinguishes this method from other more qualitative techniques. What we are doing here is essentially counting things – how many articles in a given time period; how many instances of a particular word, and so on.

As with other quantitative techniques, objectivity and rigour are vital, but especially so in content analysis to avoid accusations of deliberately creating a technique that will find what you are looking for. The ways in which your sample and your measurements are defined are very important in your methodology section and we aim to deal with these below.

Strictly speaking, content analysis is a quantitative method but it is often confused with other ways of looking at texts. Other ways of analysing texts include more qualitative methods such as visual and discourse analysis. These techniques aim to investigate less systematic (perhaps more subjective) concepts of meaning and association and involve a great deal of attention being paid to each individual text. Quantitative content analysis will allow you to analyse a greater number of examples of a particular type of text by applying the same criteria to each instance.

What it is not

It is very important to realise that content analysis is simply a quantitative description of what the text contains. You cannot make any other inferences from this, and the technique has often been abused in this way. For example, just because 57 per cent of television adverts during a (carefully selected) sample period of children's television programming were for this year's must-have children's toy does not mean that they created a desire in children to purchase it or to pester adults into doing so.

There is absolutely no guarantee that the viewers even watched the advert, never mind suddenly had a desire for the product. Likewise, a comprehensive analysis of the linguistic elements of a newspaper article or book assumes that the piece was actually read in detail, not simply skimmed or ignored completely.

An example we use in teaching this idea is that of television advertising. In the UK there was a visually stunning advert for a particular brand of automobile. The advert clearly cost a great deal of money to produce and the majority of the class could recall having seen it and could describe it in detail. However, not a single person could name the car manufacturer, let alone the specific model that was being advertised.

Technical terms

Before continuing, it is important to become familiar with two key terms.

Unit of analysis

This is your text – where you will find the information you are interested in – and what specific part of the text you will be analysing. For example, if you are interested in looking at newspaper coverage of a particular topic you will need to think about the following:

a) Which newspapers will I look at?
b) How will I create a sample of these newspapers (if a sample is needed)?
c) What specifically will I analyse?
   • Just the articles on the front page or all articles in the newspaper that relate to the topic?
   • Just the headline?
   • Just the images that accompany the text?

- Do I treat the whole article as a single entity or should I break it down into paragraphs or sentences?

Considerations that are specific to different media are dealt with in more detail below.

Units of measurement
These are the things that you are looking for within your unit of analysis and will depend very much on your research questions/ hypotheses. If, for example, you are looking at newspaper coverage and consider the whole article to be your unit of analysis, some simple things to look for might be date of the article, word length and how many times a particular theme is mentioned. More details are provided later in this chapter.

Where to start?

As with questionnaire design, the first place to start is with your hypotheses. These will help you work out your *sample, units of analysis* and *units of measurement* so that you can construct a coding sheet that allows you to gather data to support (or refute) your ideas. Think carefully about what it is you want to investigate and where and how you will find the evidence to help you do this.

Another way of looking at this is to think backwards from your 'findings and conclusions' section in a report. What is it *exactly* that you want to say, and what elements of a text will help you investigate and provide evidence for this?

It is especially important to give *operational definitions* of all of the elements of your research questions/hypotheses. This means being very specific about what it is that you are looking for and will guide you in the selection of your sample, and the design of your coding sheet. For example, if your hypothesis is that 'media coverage of topic X is biased', you must be able to give very precise definitions of:

- Media coverage – Newspapers? Television? Magazines? From when?
- Topic X – What particular aspect of the topic?
- Biased – One-sided? Ill-informed? Compared with what?

Sampling

Sampling techniques for content analysis throw up a set of specific issues in addition to those found in other quantitative methods (for example, surveys). These are influenced by two factors:

1. your topic;
2. your unit of analysis (the material).

Census

If you are studying an event or a topic that has a discrete time period and a manageable amount of material, it may be possible to take a *census* – that is, to look at *all* of the occurrences of this material. One example might be a particular billboard advertising campaign that might have just a few different examples.

Event-driven

You may be studying the coverage of a particular event that occurs over a specific time period, for example, a political election. You will need to consider the time-frame of the event in order to decide your sample. Clearly, there will be more coverage as the election approaches and at certain 'peak' times (when the candidates are announced or when a major speech is given). You will need to think carefully about your hypotheses in order to construct a sample that addresses the relevant aspects of this.

To continue with this example, if you are looking at the coverage of a particular political organisation over a year, you will need to take any such 'peaks' into account. You might need to think about how you would analyse the coverage of the key issues and then construct a sample period in which relatively little is happening as a comparison.

Sampling considerations – print

If your topic involves the analysis of newspapers or magazines there are certain features that you will need to be aware of in order to construct a good sample.

1. Editorial stance – Many publications will have a particular political or social stance that may affect the way that they portray certain issues.
2. Target audience – The intended readership will also affect this coverage, not just in terms of appealing to particular beliefs or attitudes, but also in the type of coverage that an issue may receive. For example, if you are studying the reputation of a particular multinational company, there will be publications that feature that company in terms of 'headline-grabbing' stories or events and there will be others that place more emphasis on financial performance.
3. Publication dates – The regularity with which the text is published will also affect content. You could reasonably expect a daily newspaper to be slightly different from one that is published at weekends only, perhaps in terms of the depth of coverage.
   Daily newspapers will have their own considerations. If you are looking at sporting coverage for example, you may need to consider the differences daily (given that a lot of sporting events take place on weekends). There may well be differences in the amount and type of coverage during the build-up to the event compared to the post-event reaction and analysis.
4. Circulation – The reach of the publication will also be important, and this will include the three factors above. You could reasonably expect a regional publication to vary in editorial stance, target audience, frequency of publication and depth of coverage of particular issues from those of a national or international publication.

Analysis considerations – print

As we've mentioned, deciding on your unit of analysis (the text that you will analyse) will depend very much on your hypotheses. If you are looking at newspapers, some of the things you may want to consider are whether you treat an entire article as a unit or whether you break this down. For example, you may consider only the headline and the first leader paragraph to be of interest, or you may break the article down into separate paragraphs.

You may also consider whether you are simply interested in articles that appear on the front page or whether the whole newspaper is of interest, bearing in mind that this will also contain in-depth articles, opinion pieces, editorials and letters.

You may also want to give some thought to the use of images that accompany a piece of text, particularly in a newspaper article.

If you are looking at the representation of a phenomenon in a fictional genre, will you need to consider all of the relevant texts or can you break this down to make a representative sample – for example, by only using the top ten best-sellers (although this may introduce some bias in itself)?

Sample considerations – television

Broadcasting also has a set of considerations when considering sampling issues, some of which are broadly analogous to those for print media.

1. Editorial stance – Some television networks have particular idiosyncrasies in their programming and editorial style. The nature and depth of news coverage may depend on the ethos of the editors (authoritative and austere, or more populist); but another consideration may be whether the station is publicly funded or commercial.

2. Target audience – Particular networks or particular programmes will appeal to a particular audience. News coverage in particular will vary according to time of day (see below) and length of programme (bulletin or in-depth analysis). Programming and content will also vary according to the nature of the network (some are subscription-only while others may be far more widely available).

3. Broadcast time – Time of day will clearly have implications for programming. Particular times may be assumed mainly to be aimed at a specific audience demographic – people who are working from home, children, insomniacs – and this will affect not only the types of programme broadcast (for instance, if you are looking at commercial channels and their advertising), but also the content of programmes that appear regularly throughout any given day, particularly news broadcasts. For example, in the UK

there is a regulation that deals with what is known as the *watershed*. This is a cut-off point (currently 9.00 p.m.) after which it is assumed that fewer children will be watching. This has implications for the types of programming acceptable by the regulators, as well as the types of adverts (and products/services) and, to some extent at least, the nature and imagery of news broadcasts.

4. Reach – Again, related to target audience and broadly analogous to circulation, some networks or specific channels are available regionally, while others are available nationally or internationally. This will also be influenced by whether they are transmitted terrestrially or via satellite or cable.

Analysis considerations – broadcast

Analysing broadcast material can be very complex given the interplay of script and visual material. If you are looking at a news broadcast for example, you will need to think about how to break this into units of analysis. Where does one segment end and another begin? In a recent project looking at the coverage of the 2003 war in Iraq, the coders spent many merry hours agonising over the differences between a one-minute piece to camera by a journalist and a ten-second introduction by the studio anchor.

The imagery in a piece of television obviously provides a great deal of the context and careful thought is needed to take this into account.

Yeah Ok, but how do I DO it?

The process of conducting a content analysis essentially involves designing a questionnaire, except that, instead of people answering the questions (about how old they are, for example), you will get the answers from the text that you are analysing (for example, which newspaper the article comes from). This is known as a *coding sheet* and the answers can be very simple or very complicated, depending on your research questions or hypotheses.

Each unit of analysis (news story, television broadcast, etc.) will need a separate coding sheet. You can either spend time in a darkened room surrounded by piles of paper ticking off each attribute of the text, or you can construct an electronic version of your coding sheet and enter data straight to the computer for subsequent analysis.

Constructing a coding sheet

As in a questionnaire, you can divide a coding sheet into discrete sections.

The first is analogous to the *demographics* section. This will analyse elements of the medium itself that you feel will make a difference to the ways in which the issue is covered. Some things you might want to look at are:

1. When and where – Year; date or day of the week; time of broadcast. Does coverage change over time? What publication or television outlet the piece appeared in.
2. Prominence – Word length or timing. Position in the publication (lead story, editorial, letter) or in the broadcast (lead story or further down the running order).
3. Context – What other material surrounds the piece you are interested in? For example, what are the themes in the other stories on a front page, or what are the preceding and following items in a news broadcast?

The second major section will directly concern your research questions/hypotheses. This will need extremely careful planning (and good justification in your methodology section).

Again, some things will be simple counts, but others may involve the identification of themes and language that will need to be operationally defined to avoid straying into the realms of more qualitative analysis.

1. Simple counts:

    Speakers – who gets to speak directly?
    Sources – who is quoted (and how are they identified)?
    Themes – what are the key themes or messages running through the text?

2. Linguistic modifiers

    Labels – are there recurring labels used for a particular group or issue?

Language of the headline – are there any recurring words (for example, those that are particularly emotive)?

3. Imagery

What are the most common images that accompany the issue?

Piloting

Content analysis can be very time-consuming so it is important that you get it right. It's worth taking a small sample of texts and testing your coding sheet before you begin the entire analysis.

Check that your coding sheet works and that you haven't missed anything important. As a tip, it can be useful to have an 'other' section so that you can fill in details of occurrences that were unexpected and then add this to the final version of the coding sheet.

Remember that all categories must be mutually exclusive, i.e. something that is coded can only be coded in one way. Often there will be a blurring of the categories so you should take the time to decide which category an example might fit into now.

It is worth experimenting at this stage *to some extent*.

The final version of the coding sheet is one that you must stick to. You must follow the rules of quantitative methods – this is not an exploratory method, and you cannot change the coding sheet as you go through the final analysis.

Inter-coder reliability

A final, and essential, check on your coding sheet is that another person would code a text in the same way that you have. This will avoid accusations of subjectivity, but will also help you construct the final version so that categories are clear and mutually exclusive.

Many pieces of published content analysis work will include a mathematical check on inter-coder reliability that quantifies the amount of agreement between different coders (see, for example, Wimmer and Dominick, 2006). As part of an introduction to this technique it's not strictly necessary, but it really is worth taking a selection of examples of your text and get at least one other person to code them.

Get together with your other coders and compare notes.

Analysis

Since this is a purely descriptive method, the good news is that the analysis you will use will be descriptive statistics.

Frequencies and cross-tabulation will be sufficient to describe your findings and can prove very powerful.

Chapter 10 shows you how to run these simple tests and interpret the results.

CHAPTER 8

Piloting

Now that you have a research question and have the most cunning, comprehensive, cute questionnaire ever created, you may feel that you're ready to get out there and begin collecting vast amounts of data.

Don't.

Not yet.

A *vital* stage to go through now is the process of piloting – testing the questionnaire. This chapter aims to explain why this process is important, what you might look out for and how you might go about it.

There are several reasons for going through this testing process, but the most crucial is that you do not waste all your time and effort distributing this first version, collecting the data, entering the results and completing the analyses, only to find out that the questionnaire doesn't measure what you intended it to, or that respondents have misunderstood the questions, or that you wish you had asked different questions altogether.

Although this process may seem laborious it is designed to save you time and effort in the long run. Often you will only get one shot at collecting your data so it's important to get it right.

Piloting the pilot questionnaire

There are several parts of the questionnaire that you can check as a group even before the piloting process begins.

Question wording

- Is the wording of each question clear and unambiguous?
- Is each question asking exactly what you want it to?
- Can each question be answered simply and easily by the respondent?
- Do all closed-ended questions have the complete range of possible answers? (Remember *Other*.)

Instructions

- Is it clear to the respondent how they should answer questions (circling the answer, ticking a box, etc.)?
- Is there any ambiguity about how the respondent can answer the question? (Should they give only one answer or can they make multiple responses? Do they have to rank responses in order of preference or frequency?)
- If the questionnaire is to be printed double-sided, are there clear instructions to turn over? (Trust us – it can be disastrous if they only complete one side of the page.)
- If the questionnaire is designed to be split into relevant sections, is this clear? (For example: *If Yes, go to Question 7. If No, go to Question 10.*)

Presentation

- Does the questionnaire look professional?
- Is it clear which answers relate to which questions?
- Are there typographical errors?
- Does it look scary/baffling/time-consuming?

Always check for typographical errors/spelling mistakes/poor grammar. If the questionnaire is in English but this is not your first language, make sure you get a classmate to check it over.

If the questionnaire is in your first language, get someone else who speaks the same language to check it (and perhaps even translate it).

Courtesy

- Have you explained who you are and the purpose of the questionnaire (without giving too much away, of course)?
- Have you guaranteed anonymity?
- Have you made it clear that respondents should not feel obliged to answer anything they do not wish to?
- Have you thanked your respondents for taking part?
- How long does it take to complete?

Piloting the questionnaire for real

Checking the instrument

If you are working in groups within a class, hand out copies of your questionnaire to the other groups and offer to complete their questionnaire in return. If you are working individually or in a group outside the class situation, use friends or flatmates.

It's worth giving out at least twenty questionnaires; this will give you a wider range of respondents and will also provide you with some data to test. If you're in a class, get everyone to do it (and return the favour). This is a useful exercise for all concerned, not just to check the questionnaires themselves, but also to look at how other groups may have designed their layout and phrased their questions.

Ask them to make notes on your draft version about anything they were unclear about or any other comments they might have. Explain that their comments are welcome. Take them seriously, but you don't have to adhere to all of them.

Go through the checklists above and see if the pilot sample has raised any issues that you might not have thought of as a group.

You may well be surprised at people's responses. Often a question that seems the epitome of simplicity to you and your team can be completely unintelligible to others. Often people will respond in an unexpected (or bizarre) fashion. One of the most common problems we have found is that people will give more than one answer unless explicitly told not to. This can cause all sorts of complications at the coding and data entry stage and so it's best avoided or anticipated now.

Checking the coding

Now that you have some pilot data you can begin to create the SPSS coding frame. This is where the fun begins. Work as a group to do this so that everyone knows how the data are entered (and therefore how to interpret the results).

- Does everyone agree on how to code each question? This is known as 'intercoder reliability' and is a good check on the validity of your questionnaire. Remember that the best research aims to be easily replicated – that is, someone else, in another classroom, country or continent, would come up with the same way of processing the data from your questionnaire as you have (or at least see how and why you did what you did).

- Are there any problematic questions? For example, has any respondent given more than one answer to a particular question? If so, think about how you might deal with this. Have any respondents given unusual or unanticipated answers? If so, you may want to include these answers in your list for closed-ended questions.
- Does a particular question remain unanswered more than once? This may be a result of poor or ambiguous wording, or it could reflect the fact that your pilot sample lacked the knowledge or experience to provide an answer. Decide if this will be a problem for your full sample. Remember that this may in fact be a finding in itself (see below).
- Can any open-ended questions be quantified? If you have used open-ended questions or those that allow the respondent to give fuller answers (e.g. *If Yes, please briefly explain why*), you can look for frequently occurring responses or patterns of responses that you may be able to put into SPSS. It may be better to wait until you have the full data set before doing this, but it's something that is worth thinking about at this stage.

Checking the findings

Another useful outcome of this process is that it will give you pilot data to play with. This may give you a hint of what to expect from the full sample and will also help you refine your questionnaire to get the most out of it. Although these results are clearly from a very limited sample, they may provide some food for thought about other questions that you may include in the final version. (See Chapter 10 to learn how to run the simple tests below.)

1. Run frequencies on everything. This will help you identify any redundant questions or those that may need to be re-phrased to give a wider range of responses (for example, if respondents from your pilot sample all answered *Strongly Agree* to a particular question).
2. Go back to your original hypotheses. Test these using simple crosstabs or correlations where appropriate.

Again, despite the limited sample, you may find things that don't work out as expected. This is not necessarily a problem; negative findings (i.e. ones that do not support your hypotheses) are still important (see Chapters 10 and 11) and may even turn out to be one of the most interesting things about your project. This may also prompt the 'But what if . . .' question. This is one of the key elements of research – trying to explain or account for findings, both 'positive' (i.e. in the direction you predicted) and 'negative' (i.e. completely baffling).

It turns out that X appears to have absolutely no effect on Y. This may be due to limited numbers of responses or it may be the beginnings of a more robust result.

But what if it's not X that has the effect, but Z. Why not include a question about Z in the final version? Just to check. For example, a student project on alcohol consumption and expenditure found that, while males and females claimed to drink roughly equal amounts, the women appeared to spend considerably less on a night out. Including a question on whom they bought drinks FOR shed some light on this (and possibly suggested that chivalry is not dead).

Making use of the pilot

Make a note of these discoveries and discussions as you go along. They can be useful in the final project report when discussing the rationale behind what you decided to do in the full version. They will also help clarify things to yourself and the group members when you come to describe the process weeks or months later. ('Why on earth did we do that?')

Think about ways in which you might use the (limited) results of your pilot questionnaire, perhaps even including these data in your report of the final project.

Piloting the process

Think about the practicalities of administering the pilot questionnaire as well. All of these lessons will prove useful when conducting the final project.

- Did the questionnaire take too long to complete?
- Did I run out of pencils?
- What problems did I have in recruiting respondents?

CHAPTER 9

Special Audiences – Work with Children

Both of us have experience of doing research with children and with families. Empirical research with children can be very rewarding and is popular with some students, so we have included this separate chapter on it. However, we should say at the outset: don't do research with children unless you feel confident about dealing with them and their caretakers directly. Children are a special group, requiring special techniques, and they are also potentially vulnerable to being upset emotionally or to being adversely affected educationally. Parents and teachers too can be inconvenienced and annoyed by researchers who haven't designed their project with children carefully, and who haven't consulted the relevant adults in advance about practicalities or explained their research goals.

Safeguards and consent

You will need a whole variety of safeguards in setting up a project with children, and unless you already have some inside experience of doing this – e.g. experience of working in a playgroup, or as a volunteer with a Cub or Brownie group, or in a former professional career (as some students do have) – don't attempt such research in a short-term project. Sometimes it's possible to do a project with children because you have a parent, or partner, who is a teacher, who can help you. A dissertation project, especially a three-year PhD, makes such a project more feasible because working with children, even more than with other human subjects, requires a great deal of prior planning and organisation before you carry it out. Before you embark on such a project make sure you do the following:

- Check with your tutor or supervisor about university regulations with regard to work with human subjects generally and children in particular.
- Check your proposed project with the university, faculty or department ethics committee.

- Make sure you have followed the advice given below about parental permission, school permission and children's own consent before you start.
- If there are likely to be problems with any of this, think about revising your project. For instance, if you can't gain access to children easily, think about asking *adult* subjects about their experiences and memories of childhood, or look at the ways in which children are represented in the media.[1]

Approaching children and families

The first step is to find some children – obviously! Standard approaches for student projects are via personal contacts. If you already know some teachers, or families, try them first. They may enable you to contact other teachers and parents. If you don't have personal contacts with access to children, it will be a lot harder to set up a study for a short-term student project. It is different with more formal, professional research.

Always contact children via their caretakers, never directly.

That said, make sure that the children themselves want to help you. If they don't, it's their right to withdraw and their parents shouldn't override them. Don't use children if they are unwilling, even if their elders are willing. The discrepancy between children's willingness to take part in TV programmes and their parents' willingness to let them do so was one of the strongest findings of our *Consenting Children?* study. On the whole, parents thought it was OK; children didn't. Children have the right to opt out. This should be made clear to teachers and parents, and to the children, when you introduce your research to them.

If you approach children via their schools (the easiest way of accessing a number of children), this must be done through the head

---

[1] See for instance M. M. Davies (2004) 'Innocent victims/active citizens: children and media war coverage' in A. Biressi and H. Nunn (eds), *Mediactive: Media War* (London: Lawrence and Wishart), pp. 55–66, and C. Carter and M. M. Davies (2005) ' "A fresh peach is easier to bruise": Children and traumatic news', in S. Allan (ed.), *Journalism: Critical Issues*, Maidenhead and New York: Open University Press, pp. 224–35.

teacher. If he/she is willing, be guided by their advice as to how best to proceed in setting up the study. The first stage is to write a letter to the parents, to be sent via the school, asking their permission. An example is given below. The simplest way to make sure that you don't involve the school in a lot of time-consuming chasing up of these letters is to say at the end:

> 'If we don't hear from you by the end of next week (*or whatever date the school suggests*), we will assume that you have granted your permission for your child to take part.'

The letter needs to come via the school, on their headed notepaper, so that parents are reassured that this is a proper educational activity. When you write to schools or parents yourselves, write on university headed notepaper and make sure with your head of school that this is OK. An example (of a parental letter) from a recent project carried out by Máire Messenger Davies is given on pp. 116–17.

Common issues of concern

Below is a checklist of issues that arise when working with children. Again, if these look too daunting, think about revising your project as suggested above.

Ethics: Check that you've explored the ethical procedures for setting up your project with your university or department's ethics committee.

Police vetting: With schools, you may find that you have to be checked by the police before you are allowed in to work with children. Don't be offended by this. It is a standard safeguard. An alternative is to ask your contact teachers to administer your questionnaire for you, but this is less satisfactory than doing it yourself. It is always good to have a discussion with children afterwards, to find out what they thought about the exercise.

Consent: Make sure you have parental consent by the use of a standard letter such as the example given above.

Will it work? Other issues are:

- Issues of comprehension – can they understand?
- Issues of 'affect' – will they be nervous, upset, irritated?

Format of permission letter to parents, sent via children's school

CHILDREN AND HUMOUR STUDY

Centre for Media Research, University of Ulster

Dear Parents/Guardians

We are a team of university researchers from the Centre for Media Research in the University of Ulster, who are taking part in an international study on children's humour organised by the International Institute for the Study of Young People and Media (IZI) in Munich. On 27 and 28 June we are visiting your school as part of this study. During our visit we want to show children aged between 8 and 11 (years 4 to 7) some children's television from different countries and to assess how the children respond to this. For this we need your permission for your child to take part. We hope you will agree as we think it will be an enjoyable experience.

The study will involve showing five clips of humorous TV material, all taken from children's programmes, and containing nothing unsuitable, to small groups of between 8 and 10 children and assessing their reactions. Children will be asked to operate a 'fun-o-meter' (like a computer game joystick) while they are watching (and laughing, we hope) and we will be talking to them about the programmes after they have seen them. We also want to film the children's reactions. The selected programme clips are: Pink Panther (USA); Angela Anaconda ('global'); Tabaluga TV (Germany); Open a Door (South Africa); Hidden Camera (Israel); Wallace and Gromit (UK/Ireland). We will also be talking about other humorous programmes the children might want to refer to in the post-viewing discussions.

Accordingly, we are writing to request your permission to involve your child in this study, which will take place in the school on 27 and 28 June 2005. Although we will require information about the children's names, all responses will be reported anonymously, and will be seen only by the school and the research team.

Please could you indicate your willingness, or otherwise, for your child to participate by filling in and returning the tear-off slip below to your child's teacher. If the school does not receive this slip back from you by 20 May, they will assume that you have granted your permission.

If you have any questions with regard to this study, please contact the school office directly.

Thank you very much in anticipation.

Yours sincerely,
Máire Messenger Davies (Professor),
Director, Centre for Media Research, University of Ulster at Coleraine.

Child's name: _____   Parent/
Guardian Name: _____

I DO/DO NOT WISH MY CHILD TO TAKE PART IN THE CHILDREN AND HUMOUR STUDY
(Please delete as appropriate)

- Issues of behaviour – what do you do if they misbehave? This is where the double safeguards of piloting first (even if only with some children you know from next door) and having a teacher or authority figure in the room with you when you carry out your survey or task are absolutely vital.
- Issues in qualitative research tasks: What kinds of materials do you use? Playful tasks such as the role-playing exercise used in the *Dear BBC* study, where several groups of five or six children had to be 'TV schedulers' and choose six out of thirty-two programme titles for a special children's schedule, are both educationally interesting (involving tasks such as negotiation, discussion, consensus-building, decision-making and critical judgements) and enjoyable. The children were given colour-coded badges and coloured cards with programme titles to organise, which made the task more playful.
- Issues of interpretation: what on earth are they talking about? This can be a problem in qualitative data – although it is still good to get some qualitative data (talk or written comments) if you can. Questionnaire formats, where children

simply have to choose an option (tick or circle a box), make subsequent interpretation a lot easier – another reason for using this valuable research tool.

- Issues of personal involvement: everybody has been a child – what's your own agenda here? Don't assume that your childhood experiences will be matched by other children's, and don't assume – if you have children – that this makes you an expert on other people's children. It doesn't! However, it is a very useful experience to have in terms of feeling more confident and comfortable around children.

Designing research with children

Some research questions are answerable with children, some are not. This may be to do with issues of 'suitability' (what you will be allowed to ask children); it is also to do with what children are capable of understanding and doing, which varies markedly, particularly with age, but also for other reasons. It's also important to find tasks that will be enjoyable and meaningful for them to do, otherwise they will be bored, unhappy and 'uncooperative; unlike adults (who tend to want to please researchers) children will *show* their dissatisfaction –this is another threat to **validity**. Even more than with adult subjects, the methodologies you choose for research with children need to be closely linked to your research question. And this question must be a feasible one.

Feasible media research questions for student projects with children

- Questions about taste: what children like.
- Questions about specific media products aimed at children, e.g. *Harry Potter*, Playstations (but beware being exclusionary – what about the kids in the class whose families can't afford these?)
- Questions aimed at children over the age of seven, who can (usually) read and write at least a little; who can understand instructions; and who will be accustomed to relating to adults other than their parents and relatives.

- Questions about differences between boys and girls.
- Questions about differences between younger (7–9) and older (10–12) children.
- Questions about media habits.
- Questions about advertising and products.
- Questions about children's opinions – including politics and cultural attitudes.
- Questions about their knowledge of the world and the media's contribution to this.
- Questions which enable them to demonstrate skills and knowledge that they are confident about and/or proud of. Research into popular culture often falls into this category, as even the most non-academic children can have specialised knowledge about TV or about video games. Popular culture also often transcends ethnic, religious and other cultural differences – hence it is easier to design questionnaires, or other research tasks, which you know will be broadly familiar to most children.

Non-feasible research questions with children: What not to ask

- Questions about sex and violence (parents and teachers are likely to object).
- Questions which require them to reveal socio-economic status (parental income) or other personal information about their families.
- Questions which require them to challenge their parents' value systems (e.g. about religion or ethnicity).
- Questions about pre-school, pre-literate or infant children. Research with this group is fascinating but requires highly specialised research techniques: possible if you are a psychology student in a good developmental psychology programme, less so if you are not. However it might be possible to address the questions you are interested in by surveying their parents.
- Questions which require children's extended effort and concentration over long periods of time.
- Questions which are disruptive of their routines and lives, whether in school or home.

- Questions which require them to behave badly. (Some classic experiments with children which attempted to measure the effects of media violence by requiring young children to show aggression towards other children, or toys, are highly suspect ethically – and less valid for this reason.)

Feasible research methods with children

- Short questionnaires (not more than 20–30 simple questions).
- Visual questionnaires (especially for under eight-year-olds) such as the 'smiley face' technique (see Figure 9.2).
- Three-point scales rather than five-point Likert scales (e.g. 'agree; disagree; not sure').
- Free expression sections: 'What do you think?'
- Drawings – but you need to be clear about what you want the drawings to express.
- Structured tasks – e.g. the scheduling task from *Dear BBC*.
- Group work which can be done in a classroom.
- Using simple technology with which children are familiar. Some computer programs can be used if both you and the children are familiar with them, and if they answer specific research questions. It is unwise to ask children to use technology that either they, or you, or both of you, haven't used before. However, useful work with children and technology has been done with more ethnographic approaches where the researcher has time to get to know children in their family setting, and where there is time to sort out technological difficulties if necessary (see e.g. S. Livingstone, *Young People and New Media*, 2002).

Questionnaires for children

Despite what you might think, questionnaires are a good tool for doing research with children, as long as they are appropriately designed. They have a number of advantages:

- They are anonymous.
- They include every child.
- They are carried out by each child individually and hence are less subject to peer pressure in answering.

- They are orderly: working with children in sociable and interactive groups is very enjoyable, but risky if you don't know the children and don't feel confident about keeping order. If every child is working busily on a questionnaire, it is easier for a young, unfamiliar inexperienced researcher to manage the situation (but always with a teacher or caretaker in the room with you, of course).
- Questionnaires are 'grown up'. Children are likely to be aware that adults are sometimes consulted in this way in public opinion polls and market research. The questionnaire is an adult research instrument, and children do like to be treated and consulted in an adult manner. This, too, is conducive to good order.
- They permit private responses – unlike group discussions, where again peer pressure may mean that some children say nothing, and others go along with the more dominant members of the group. In a questionnaire, answers are more likely to be the child's own views, not somebody else's. We found very strong evidence of the value of questionnaire privacy in some research we did for the Broadcasting Standards Commission (*Consenting Children?*, 2001). Parents and children were given the same questionnaire about children appearing in adult TV programmes. For every question, the responses of adults and children were different, with adults being more likely to approve of children appearing on TV than children were. This was a clear validation of the research hypothesis that parents can't necessarily speak for their children when it comes to 'consent' – at least to appearing on television. Of course, parents must be consulted when you are working with children, but it should not be assumed that parents and children are always going to agree (see Figure 9.1).

Designing a questionnaire for children

A questionnaire for children should not be long and it should be very simple. We give an example from Máire Messenger Davies' *Fake, Fact and Fantasy* in Figure 9.2. This was given to seventy-eight children between the ages of eight and fourteen years and none of them had problems reading or answering it. However, children younger than this might have had difficulty, and if we had included younger

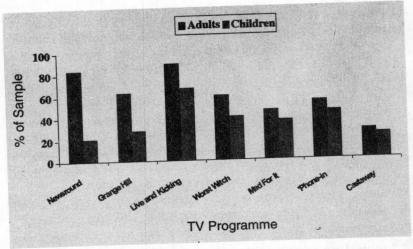

Figure 9.1. From Davies and Mosdell 2001: *Consenting Children?* Differences between parents' and children's responses to questions about children appearing on television. Respondents were asked 'I would like [child's version]/I would like my children [adults' version] to appear on (name of programme)': 'Agree; disagree; not sure'. The graph shows the 'agree' responses. (Base: 53 adults, 78 children.)

children in our sample, we would have made the questionnaire shorter and had a visual version. Some children in a whole-class group of older children may also have literacy problems. These should be identified in advance, and then a classroom assistant or extra researcher can be laid on to help them.

Visual techniques

With a group of younger children who can't read or write very easily, a usual technique is to read out the questionnaire to them, page by page, with each question on a different page and they all turn over the page together. Visual symbols for 'agree'; 'disagree' and 'not sure' (such as the 'smiley face') are a standard technique and can work very well. All the children have to do is to tick the relevant 'face'. Other visual techniques such as choosing between two or more pictures, or recognition of pictures of characters from programmes or films, can also be used. Work with children can produce some very enjoyable and imaginative solutions to research method problems, so don't be

If you wish hard when you blow out you birthday candles, your wish will come true.

True   **Not true**   **Not sure**

If people on TV adventure shows have a fight, they don't really hurt each other.

True   **Not true**   **Not sure**

There needs to be violence on TV to make the programmes exciting.

True   **Not true**   **Not sure**

Figure 9.2 Questionnaires for young children: the smiley face technique. 'Questions about "real and not real"' from Máire Messenger Davies (1997), *Fake, Fact and Fantasy: Children's Understanding of Television Reality*, Mahwah, NJ: Lawrence Erlbaum, pp. 168–73.

Programs like 'Full House' and 'The Cosby Show' happen in somebody's real house.

True   Not true   Not sure

TV ads make toys and candy look much nicer than they really are.

True   Not true   Not sure

Superman and Batman aren't really flying in the movies; it's a trick.

True   Not true   Not sure

Figure 9.2 (continued)

put off by all the needs for safeguards. You can have a lot of creative enjoyment with this kind of work.

Questions can also be administered via computer programs, but as we've said already, don't do anything with technology unless you are *super-confident* that it will work for both you and the children and their teachers/parents.

An alternative with non-literate children is to interview them individually and fill in their spoken answers, but this is very time-consuming and again, you may run into ethical difficulties if you are with a child unsupervised.

BSC STUDY: CHILDREN'S AND TEENAGERS' QUESTIONNAIRE

(Information about the project had already been given in a separate letter to the families, so there was no need to put an introductory paragraph at the top of this questionnaire. We also did not use the leading word 'Consenting', so did not put the title of our research on this questionnaire.)

My name is:

(this was a family project where names had to be identified, but the children and families were still kept anonymous in our report to the BSC)

_____

I am _____years old

Please look at the statements below and then circle one of the answers opposite;

1. I watch TV
    a) less than one hour a day
    b) 2–3 hours per day
    c) more than 3 hours a day
    d) never

2. I read books or magazines
    a) less than one hour a day
    b) 2–3 hours a day
    c) more than 3 hours a day
    d) never

3. I listen to the radio

a) less than one hour a day

b) 2–3 hours a day

c) more than 3 hours a day

d) never

4. I go to the theatre

a) at least once a month

b) six or more times a year

c) two or three times a year

d) once a year

e) less than once a year

f) never

5. I go to the cinema

a) at least once a month

b) six or more times a year

c) two or three times a year

d) once a year

e) less than once a year

f) never

6. I go to the library

a) at least once a month

b) six or more times a year

c) two or three times a year

d) once a year

e) less than once a year

f) never

My favourite TV programme is (name one):

_____

My favourite children's TV programme is (name one):

_____

My favourite TV personality is (name one):

_____

Now look at the statements below and then circle one of the answers opposite;

I watch TV with my parents	Regularly	Sometimes	Never
I watch TV with my brothers and sisters	Regularly	Sometimes	Never
I watch TV with my friends	Regularly	Sometimes	Never
I watch daytime TV	Regularly	Sometimes	Never
I am allowed to watch TV until	8 o'clock 10 o'clock	9 o'clock Later	
I talk about TV programmes with (circle more than one if you want)	My parents My brothers and sisters My friends No one Don't know		

What TV programmes do you watch with your parents? (list up to three, or leave blank if you don't watch any with them)

_____

What TV programmes do you watch with your brothers and sisters? (list up to three, or leave blank if you don't watch any with them)

_____

What TV programmes do you watch with your friends? (list up to three, or leave blank if you don't watch any with them)

_____

Name a TV programme that you are NOT allowed to watch:

_____

Look at the statements below and then circle one of the answers opposite

1. I would like to act   Agree   Not Sure   Disagree
   in a realistic drama
   programme like
   Grange Hill

2. I would like to be a   Agree   Not Sure   Disagree
   contestant in a game
   show like _Mad for It_

3. I would like to act   Agree   Not Sure   Disagree
   in a fantasy story
   like _The Worst Witch_

4. I would like to be   Agree   Not Sure   Disagree
   in the audience on a
   magazine show like
   Live and Kicking

5. I would like to be   Agree   Not Sure   Disagree
   in a real life
   documentary like
   Castaway

6. I would like to be   Agree   Not Sure   Disagree
   on a phone-in on
   Radio One

7. I would like to   Agree   Not Sure   Disagree
   be a reporter on a
   news programme like
   Newsround

Given only one choice, what kind of TV programme would you most like to be in? (Say why if you can)

What sort of TV programmes should young children NOT be allowed to watch? (List up to three if you can)

Is there anything else that you would like to say?

As you can see, we used the three-point scale rather than the five-point scale for our 'opinion questions' (and did the same with the parents' questionnaire, for ease of comparison). However, there are a number of other places in the questionnaire where there are up to six options (e.g. TV viewing). The questionnaire includes both closed (multiple-choice) and open-ended questions. The children who answered this took about half an hour to do it. Perhaps you can think of ways in which it could be adapted for other uses, or improved. Also, how you would code it.

Research with children: points to remember

1. Making contact and setting up the study: as we've said, use local schools, parents, teachers, etc. whom you already know. Convenience samples are the only ones that will work for a student project with children because of the trust issue, as well as the limits on time and resources which are inevitable with student work. However, you can still use your 'convenient' schools as a valid 'population' if your research question is sufficiently specific (see Chapter 4).
2. Parental permission.
3. School may require police vetting.
4. If you are showing film, television or online material, offer parents and teachers the chance to view it first. They may not want to do so and may trust you to choose suitable material for their children, especially if the material is uncontentious. However, if some of the material *is* contentious (because it has led to adult complaints,

as in the case of our 2001 BSC study *Consenting Children?*) it is wise
to cover yourself by asking adults to sign a permission form that
it's OK for their children to see it, if they don't want to preview it
themselves.[2]

5. If you are working in schools, visit the school and check out the
rooms and resources you will be using first. Make sure all equipment works; make sure all teachers involved know when it is you
want their children to take part. Make sure all teachers involved
have seen your research instruments, including questionnaires,
interview schedules, etc. Give them the opportunity to revise
wording, etc., e.g. if language needs to be simplified.

6. When conducting the research, whether with a class of children
or with children in their homes, have the relevant authority figure
(teacher or parent) with you in the room; this is a legalistic requirement, as well as a sensible practical one. In a classroom, it's better
for there to be at least two researchers too.

That said, do not let teachers or parents help or interfere with the
administration of the research procedures once you've started. It is
the children's views you want, not the adults'. It is always necessary to
impress on both the children and their caretakers/teachers that
research is *not a test*. There are no right or wrong answers to a research
questionnaire or a research task. Researchers are just as interested in
non-answers, or strange answers, as in what people might see as more
conventional, 'correct' answers. If adults interfere with children's performance (it's OK if all they want to do is help with spelling, or get
another piece of paper), this destroys the **internal validity** of the
research procedures and all your careful preparation will have gone
for nothing. Teachers and parents naturally can be very keen for the
children in their care to make a good impression; researchers don't

---

[2] In the case of *Consenting Children?* we used the requirement for parental vetting as a
positive element in the research design: we showed all the material to parents before
showing it to the whole family, including the children, and we were interested to see
whether the parental comments, approval or disapproval, were borne out by the children's reactions when they saw what their parents had already seen. In many cases,
there were very revealing differences between the two viewing sessions, and the
parents were surprised by their children's responses.

care about this. Indeed, we learn more from the mistakes and difficulties people have than we do from perfect responses. If all the answers to a questionnaire or research task are 'right', we run into the danger of producing a **'ceiling effect'**. Everybody gives the same answers, so there is no **variance** and nothing to measure, and no variety of scores to help evaluate differences between different people and different responses.

In summary

It may seem, after reading all this, that doing research with children is not worth the trouble because of all the safeguards and provisos you have to remember. However, as we've said, if you already have good contacts (with schools, or groups such as Cubs, Brownies or other youth groups) and with professional adults who will 'stand surety' for you, and help you with all the practicalities, doing work with children is one of the most enjoyable forms of research there can be. Be very clear about your research question and hypothesis, and, as we've said, steer clear of controversial or potentially upsetting topics: focus on what they *like* (or dislike), what they *think* and what they *do*, and you cannot go far wrong. Always pilot your research instrument, whether a questionnaire or a task such as the scheduling task, and consult your contact teacher or parent about its wording, length, practicality and so on. With children the practicalities ('The Six Ps' – see Chapter 5) are even more important than they are with other groups. Permission is a crucial one. Make sure you are safeguarded by following all the proper consent and ethical procedures; this is a factor in a very important seventh 'P' – Professionalism.

PART THREE

ANALYSIS: 'UNDERSTANDING IT'

CHAPTER 10

Data Analysis

Now that you have designed a questionnaire, selected a sample and collected some data, it's time to have a look at what you have found. Time for some excitement. But first, you have to enter the data into the computer so that you can perform all sorts of complicated counts and comparisons at the click of a button.

There are various software packages that will allow you to analyse your questionnaire data, but a user-friendly and very powerful option is SPSS. This chapter aims to introduce the SPSS environment. It assumes no previous knowledge of this software, and is by no means intended as a comprehensive guide.[1] This chapter is based on Version 12.0 of this software. If you are running a different version, then some of the windows may appear slightly different but the principles are basically the same.

It deals with entering data and running simple statistical tests, as well as covering some basic concepts of statistical probability.

Entering data

The first thing to notice when you have started SPSS is that there are two tabs at the bottom of the screen: *data view* and *variable view*.

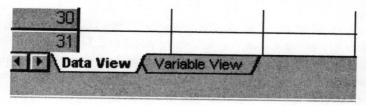

Variable view

This is the first step when entering your questionnaire data and basically allows you to set up the spreadsheet so that it reflects your questionnaire.

---

[1] A useful reference for statistics using SPSS is A. Field (2005) *Discovering Statistics Using SPSS*, London: Sage.

In *variable view*, each of the rows is a **variable** (something that varies) – usually a question – and the columns are attributes of that variable – what the variable is called, what the possible answers are, etc.

For example, your first question might be *'What is your gender?'* Hopefully, respondents will only have given one of two possible answers for this question – male or female. So, *Gender* is the variable, and *Male* and *Female* are *levels* of that variable.

You will notice that there are headings in the columns. Some of these columns require you to specify particular attributes, others are default values.

Name

Simply enough, what you decide to call the variable. There are certain limits to this – you can use alphanumeric characters (numbers and letters), but some symbols will not be accepted and there must be no spaces. Earlier versions of the software also had a character limit. As a rule of thumb, if you get an error message when you have entered a variable name, make sure there are no spaces or symbols and abbreviate the name if necessary.

To enter the name, click once inside the box under the *Name* column and type your choice of name (e.g. Gender).

When you click anywhere outside the box, a number of default values will be placed in the columns. Most of these will remain as they are.

Type

The format of the data that you are entering. The default value is numeric, meaning that you will enter numbers. This is useful since (referring back to Chapter 3) you have already coded your questionnaire in this format – where 1 stands for Female and 2 stands for Male, for example.

Width

A cosmetic point. The default is 8 – best leave it as it is.

Decimals

The number of decimal places that analyses will be calculated to. The default is 2. So, for example, if a calculation returns a result of 8.61235, SPSS will display 8.61.

Label

If you leave this box blank, any tables or graphs will display the variable name. This can be a useful place to extend the name so that it makes more sense or looks more aesthetically pleasing. You can use spaces and symbols for the variable label and the number of allowed characters is much higher.

Values

You must enter all of the values for each variable, i.e. all of the possible answers for each question, so that they are all available to you when you come to actually enter the data.

Click on the row of the variable you want to change under the column heading *Values*. Click the grey area with . . . in and a box will appear with *Value Labels*. Enter the *Value* (e.g. 1) in the first box and the *Label* (e.g. Female) in the second box. Click on *Add*. Click *OK* to finish once all values and labels are entered. If you need to change any values or value labels, select the value label from the list and change the value or the label by clicking and editing the *Value* or *Value Label* box and click *Change*.

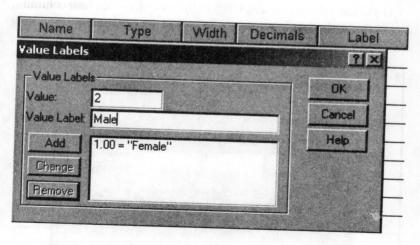

(This box appears when you click the grey . . . area of the first row under the column *Values*.)

A common mistake is to click *OK* before adding the final value. This will generate an error message and clicking on *OK* to that message will mean that the final value has not been added (you must click on *Add* before clicking *OK*).

Make sure that ALL possible answers appear in the box.

Missing

Another possible answer that people can give is not to answer at all. This is known as a *Missing Value* and can be very important. For example, if you find that a lot of people have not answered a particular question, it could indicate that the question was particularly sensitive (for example, many people are reluctant to give details of their income) or that the phrasing of the question meant that they felt unable or unqualified to answer it. This is another good reason for *piloting* the questionnaire (see Chapter 8) and testing the results of the pilot before collecting your 'real' data. Just as we have coded 1 for female and 2 for male, we need to assign a number for Missing. Usually we use a number that is unlikely to be reached in a list of possible answers. A common value for missing is 99. This is completely arbitrary, but you must make sure that the value will not be used as a code for any other answer.

Go to the column *Missing*. Click in the row of the variable you want to change and select using the grey . . . box. Click on the button next to *Discrete Values* and enter 99. Click *OK*.

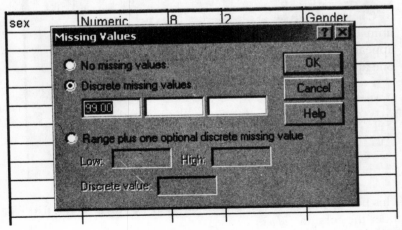

This box appears when you click the grey . . . area of the first row under the column *Missing*.

Columns

A cosmetic point. The default is 8 – best leave it as it is. This will change only if you stretch the column in *Data View*.

Align

A cosmetic point. The default is right – best leave it as it is.

Measure

The final thing to change. This refers to the type of data that the variable contains.

Remember that there are several levels of measurement (see Chapter 3). SPSS allows you to select *Nominal, Ordinal* and *Scale*. This may seem slightly confusing as much of your ordinal data will come from Likert scales.

As a tip, look at the icons next to each option.

- **Nominal** – not greater than, less than, higher in a list than, etc., just *different.*
- **Ordinal** – there is some order or progression in the way you have coded the data.
- **Scale** – refers to *Interval* or *Ratio* measurement, where the distance between points on the scale is always the same (as in distance, indicated by the ruler).

Click on the row of the variable you want to change under the column heading *Measure*. Click on the down arrow and a menu will appear containing three data types: *Scale; Ordinal; Nominal*. Select the one appropriate for your data.

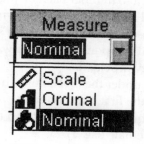

This box appears when you click the down arrow in the first row under the column *Measure*.

To recap, the headings you need to give some details for are:

1. name;
2. label (optional);
3. values;
4. missing;
5. measure.

The rest can safely be left as they are.

If you have made mistakes and want to remove variables, select the row by clicking inside the grey numbered area to the right of the screen and pressing delete.

You can also add new variables to the list by clicking in that area and going to the *Data* menu – select *Insert Variable*.

Once you have entered the specifications for every variable (basically, every question on your questionnaire), you are ready to begin entering data.

Put the kettle on and take a deep breath, this may take some time . . .

Data view

Click the tab at the bottom labelled *Data View*. This will bring you to a new blank screen, but you will notice that the columns now have variable names in them.

In *Data View*, each row is a person who filled out your questionnaire and each column is an attribute of that person – what their gender is, how old they are, etc.

Remember, it's a good idea to number each of your questionnaires before you input the data. This will stop you entering the same one twice and will also give a useful reference if there's something odd about a particular individual's responses or if you want to go back to any qualitative data that they provided.

Click in the top right box under the first column heading and enter the code for the answer on the first questionnaire.

For example, if the first question is Gender and the first person is female, enter the code for Female (e.g. 1).

If this is the first time that you have used SPSS, then you will see 1 on the screen. However, and this bit's magic, if you now click on the tiny button that looks like a luggage label (as in the above picture), that number will be transformed into the label that 1 stands for.

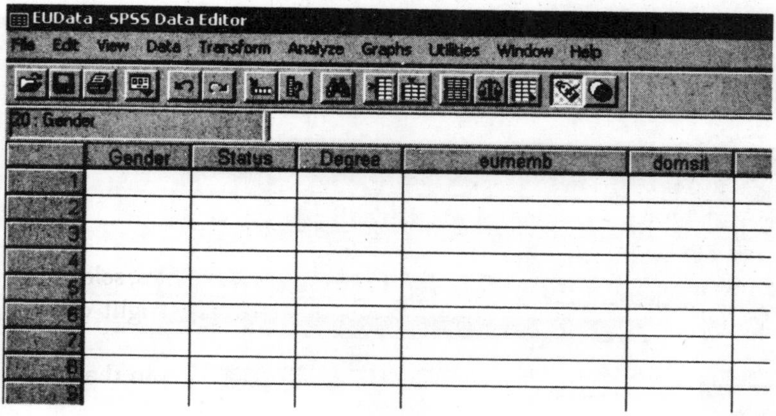

This also gives you the option of either entering the number directly or selecting from a drop-down menu for each variable.

Exploring the data

Once you have entered all your questionnaire data you can begin to look at what you have found.

The first step is always to run **frequencies** on every variable. This will give you some idea of what the data look like and will help you to spot any data entry mistakes (e.g. entering a 6 when you only have 5 values for that variable, or entering 55 instead of 5).

Frequencies

Frequencies are just simple counts of each level of a variable; for example, how many males and females you have in the sample.

1. From the *Analyse* menu –
        Descriptive Statistics –
                Frequencies . . .
    This will bring up a box like the one shown on p. 142.
2. Select the variable you want to look at from the list on the left (click on it once so that it is highlighted).

3. Click on the right arrow. This will remove that variable from the first list and place it in the *Variable(s):* list on the right.
4. Click *OK*.

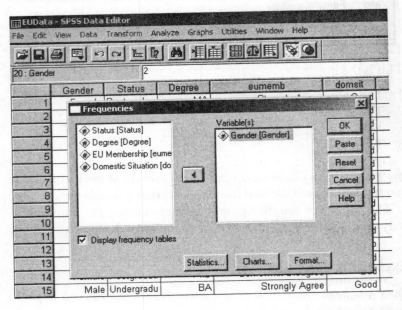

This will open up a new window in SPSS, titled *Output1 – SPSS Viewer*. Unless you close this window, each subsequent test will appear below the preceding one in this output window.

The frequency table from our EU example is shown below, for the variable 'gender'.

Statistics

Gender

N	Valid	20
	Missing	0

This first box simply shows what has gone into the test.

You can see that N = 20; that is, there are twenty cases in the table and that there are no missing values for this variable.

Gender

		Frequency	Per cent	Valid Per cent	Cumulative Per cent
Valid	Female	9	45.0	45.0	45.0
	Male	11	55.0	55.0	100.0
	Total	20	100.0	100.0	

This is the important part. You can see that there are five columns:

1. The values of the variable – *Female, Male* and the *Total.*
2. The *Frequency* (count) of these values – nine *Females* and eleven *Males* making a *Total* of twenty.
3. These counts expressed in *Per cent* – For example, nine *Females* out of a *Total* of twenty is 45.0 per cent.
4. These counts expressed as a *Valid Per cent* – this will differ from the *Per cent* only if you have any missing values. The *Per cent* expresses the numbers as a proportion of all of the people who returned your questionnaire. The *Valid Per cent* expresses these numbers as a proportion of all of the people who answered that particular question. The percentage that you choose to quote will depend on how many missing values you have. This is down to your judgement as a researcher.
5. A *Cumulative Per cent* – this adds up the valid percentages as you go down the columns. In this case, the first figure is 45.0. If you add the second figure (55.0) to this you get 100. This can be useful for combining levels of a particular variable – for example, if you want to know what proportion expressed some level of agreement to a particular statement you can combine the percentages for those who answered *Agree* with those who answered *Strongly Agree.*

Another useful tip is to click on the *Format . . .* button. The default is *Ascending values* that will display the frequencies in the order that the values were assigned. If you select *Descending counts*, this will display the values in descending order of frequency (i.e. the highest count first). This can save a great deal of time if you have a long list of values for a variable (for example, 'favourite TV programme').

Frequencies can be run on all variables, but there are other tests that depend on the data type that you have (nominal, ordinal, etc.). Two of the most useful are **Crosstabulation** and **Correlation**.

Crosstabulation

Crosstabulation (or Crosstabs) can be used with nominal data and any others. The table produced is basically the frequency of one variable within another variable – for example, how many female (Gender variable) undergraduates (Status variable) there were (as opposed to female postgraduates).

1. From the *Analyse* menu –
    Descriptive Statistics –
    Crosstabs . . .
    This will bring up a box like the one shown opposite.
2. Select one variable you want to look at from the list on the left (click on it once so that it is highlighted). Click on the upper right arrow. This will remove that variable from the first list and place it in the *Row(s):* list on the right.
3. Select the second variable you want to look at and click on the second right arrow you see. This will remove that variable from the first list and place it in the *Column(s):* list on the right.
4. To change the display to percentages, click on the *Cells* . . . button at the bottom of the *Crosstabs* box. Click next to each of the *Row, Column* and *Total* boxes until there is a tick by each. Click *Continue.*

Click *OK.*

The way in which you assign variables to rows and columns does not affect the table's contents but it's good practice to assign the *Independent variable* (see Chapter 6) to the columns, just to make the table easier to read.

This will bring up a table like the one shown opposite.

The first thing to notice is that there are only nineteen cases included in this table. This is because Crosstabs do not include any Missing Values (for either variable).

In the table opposite we have females running across the first row – four undergraduate and five postgraduate making a total of nine. Males run across the second row – six undergraduates and four postgraduates, making a total of ten.

Because you are unlikely to have equal numbers for every variable, you should express the findings of the table using percentages. If, for example, you had 200 undergraduates and fifty postgraduates, simply

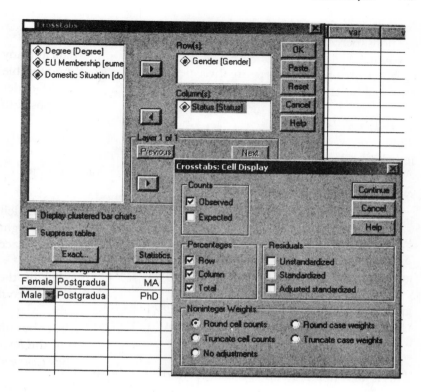

Gender * Status Cross-tabulation

			Status		
			Undergra-duate	Postgraduate	Total
Gender	Female	Count	4	5	9
		% within Gender	44.4%	55.6%	100.0%
		% within Status	40.0%	55.6%	47.4%
		% of Total	21.1%	26.3%	47.4%
	Male	Count	6	4	10
		% within Gender	60.0%	40.0%	100.0%
		% within Status	60.0%	44.4%	52.6%
		% of Total	31.6%	21.1%	52.6%
Total		Count	10	9	19
		% within Gender	52.6%	47.4%	100.0%
		% within Status	100.0%	100.0%	100.0%
		% of Total	52.6%	47.4%	100.0%

using the counts would obviously bias your results, but using the proportions (percentages) from each group will take the differences into account.

You will notice that there are three percentages below the count in each cell (square) of the table shown on p. 145.

1. *Within gender*

This expresses the count as a percentage of all of the males and females, and runs across the row to make 100 per cent.

If we take the first cell, four females out of a total of nine is expressed as 44.4 per cent.

Out of all the females, 44.4 per cent were undergraduates.

2. *Within status*

This expresses the count as a total of all the undergraduates and postgraduates and runs down the column to make 100 per cent.

The same four people expressed as a percentage of all the undergraduates – four out of ten – is shown as 40 per cent.

Out of all the undergraduates, 40 per cent were female.

3. *Within total*

This is less often used and basically runs diagonally to make 100 per cent. These four people expressed as a total of the whole sample – four out of nineteen – is shown as 21.1 per cent.

Out of all the people that we asked, 21.1 per cent were undergraduate and female.

To take the females and undergraduates example, think of it as having two groups of people. Some are undergraduates and some are female. Some are BOTH. The percentage that you use depends on the group of people that you are referring to, and this will depend on your hypothesis.

Layered crosstabs

It is possible to put more than two variables into a table, and this can be useful to investigate the data in more detail. For instance, using our EU example, if you wanted to look at the views about the domestic situation among all respondents who are both female and undergraduates, you could use a layer.

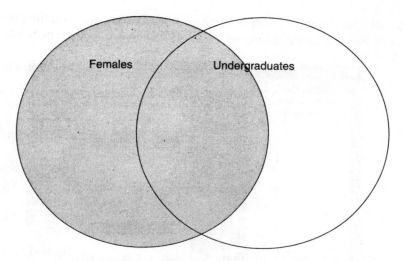

Out of all the females, 44.4 per cent were undergraduates.

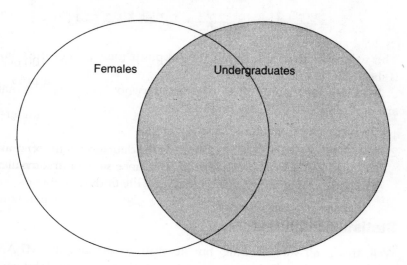

Out of all the undergraduates, 40 per cent were females.

Follow the steps above to create a Crosstab but add another variable into the Layer section of the table (as below).

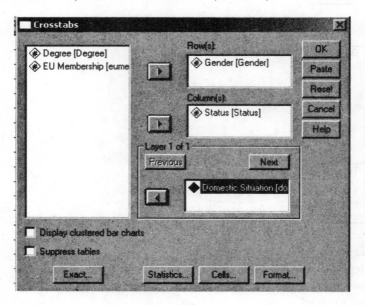

This will bring up a table like the one opposite (only part of the table is shown for the sake of clarity).

We should add a note of caution here – try not to create tables that are too complicated for two main reasons:

1. They are very difficult to read!
2. You should be careful not to subdivide the data too often – remember that we have cautioned against this since smaller and smaller groups of data will affect the validity of the findings.

Statistical significance

Well, this is all very exciting, but do your results actually MEAN anything?

Unfortunately, here we have to digress into the world of statistics. We will try to be brief.

You may have found some very interesting differences between groups of people and the answers they gave, but in order to make your

Gender * Status * Domestic Situation Crosstabulation

Domestic Situation: Very Good

			Status		Total
			Undergra-duate	Postgraduate	
Gender	Female	Count	2	1	3
		% within Gender	66.7%	33.3%	100.0%
		% within Status	66.7%	100.0%	75.0%
		% of Total	50.0%	25.0%	75.0%
	Male	Count	1	0	1
		% within Gender	100.0%	.0%	100.0%
		% within Status	33.3%	.0%	25.0%
		% of Total	25.0%	.0%	25.0%
Total		Count	3	1	4
		% within Gender	75.0%	25.0%	100.0%
		% within Status	100.0%	100.0%	100.0%
		% of Total	75.0%	25.0%	100.0%

arguments more powerful, you can also run certain tests to see whether these differences are likely to apply to a wider population (assuming you have been careful in selecting your sample) or whether they are simply due to chance.

The social sciences generally use a 95 per cent level of significance – that is, if the probability of getting the results you have is less than 5 in 100 then they can be said to be statistically significant.

Again this goes back to the idea of testing the *Null hypothesis* (see Chapter 2) – the seemingly perverse idea of trying to falsify your results. Think of it as the great detective Sherlock Holmes did: if you eliminate all the other possibilities then what you have is likely to be the truth.

Tests of statistical significance will give you a value that ranges from 0.00 to 1.00, where 1.00 expresses a probability that your results are entirely due to chance, and therefore not something that would apply to a wider population (see Chapter 4). So, what you are hoping for is a low probability – less than 0.05 (less than a 5 per cent likelihood of being due to chance). This is expressed in the following formula:

$$p < 0.05$$

In English, **p** (the probability of the result being due to chance) < (is less than) **0.05** (5%).

It is important to bear in mind that tests of statistical significance make certain assumptions:

1. The tests you can use depend on the type of data that you have. With nominal data, the only test you can legitimately use is *Chi-square* (explained below).
2. All tests assume that you have a representative, random sample (so that they can test whether your findings are likely to apply to the wider population that you have sampled from).
3. 'Significance' is a specific term in this context – it does not necessarily mean 'important'.
4. A test that is not statistically significant is NOT 'insignificant' – it may in fact be one of the most important findings of your research (see Chapter 11). Tests that give probability levels greater than 0.05 can be said to be 'approaching significance' if they are 0.06 or 0.07. Anything greater than 0.05 is expressed as p > 0.05.

Chi-square

This test is most often used with Crosstabs. In very simple terms, what the test does is build a table that has the same cells as yours and throws data into it on the basis that there is no relationship between the two things you are testing. It then compares these data (which you might expect to get by chance – there is no relationship) and the data that you have (which you are hoping is not due to chance). If the data you have are different from those which you would expect to get with no relationship between the two, then the test will return a probability less than 0.05.

To add a chi-square test to your Crosstab, follow the steps below:

1. Set the requirements for the Crosstab as outlined above.
2. Click on the *Statistics . . .* button.
3. Click next to the *chi-square* box so that it has a tick in it (see figure opposite).

A statistically significant chi-square will appear below your Crosstab and will look like the table shown opposite.

The figure you are mainly interested in is in the top right corner, under the *Asymp Sig (2-sided)* heading ('Asymptotic Significance' – please don't worry too much about what this term means!). Here, the probability of obtaining these results by chance is 0.000 (expressed to

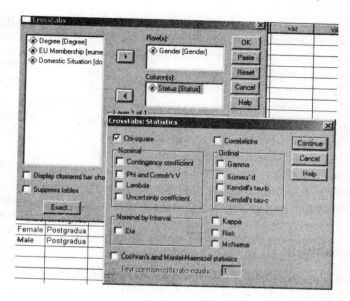

Chi-Square Tests

	Value	df	Asymp. Sig. (2-sided)
Pearson Chi-Square	123.000[a]	3	0.000
Likelihood Ratio	168.680	3	0.000
Linear-by-Linear Association	101.171	1	0.000
N of Valid Cases	123		

a. 0 cells (0.0%) have expected count less than 5. The minimum expected count is 8.34.

three decimal places – there are some numbers in there somewhere, but basically the probability of obtaining this result by chance is very low. It is certainly a lot less than 0.05, so we can say that there are significant differences in this Crosstab.

There are some important aspects to remember about chi-square in addition to those that apply to all statistical tests:

1. The test does not 'know' anything about your data. It simply looks at chance data.

2. Therefore, it does not explain any differences; nor does it tell you where these differences are. This is your job as a researcher and will be based on your hypotheses and your common-sense interpretation of the table itself.

3. Chi-square generally needs quite a lot of data to be robust (i.e. very reliable). You may find that there is a warning underneath the table that concerns the 'expected count' – this means that you have some cells that are empty or do not contain enough data. You can still use the findings, but they should be interpreted with some caution if the percentage of cells with less than the expected count is very high (note that the message below the chi-square illustrated requires each cell to contain a count of more than 5).

Correlation

Correlation is a slightly different type of statistical test which looks at the degree of association between two variables – whether scores on one variable are reflected in scores on another variable. This is most commonly used with data that come from Likert scales (see Chapter 3) and can give some indication of whether answers to questions that aim to measure attitudes, beliefs or consumption habits are related in some way. Using our EU example, we might hypothesise that people who think that the UK domestic situation is good will also approve of joining the EU (for whatever reason).

Again, there are important considerations to bear in mind when using correlations:

1. Data MUST be at least ordinal. This test cannot be used with nominal data. Data that meet this requirement can be tested using the *Spearman* correlation. Data that are of a higher level (interval or ratio) can be tested using the *Pearson* correlation.

2. The test only gives an indication of association – a significant correlation does not mean that scores on one variable CAUSE scores on another variable.

3. Again, a significant correlation does not explain WHY the data might be related. This is your job as a researcher, and you should always bear in mind that there might be a third variable involved – for example, people who think the domestic situation is

good and also approve of EU membership may do so because they are parents and the EU is proposing some specific policy concerning children.

To run a correlation:

1. From the *Analyse* menu –

   Correlate –

   Bivariate . . .

   This will bring up a box like the one shown below.
2. Select one of the variables you want to look at from the list on the left (click on it once so that it is highlighted).
3. Click on the right arrow. This will remove that variable from the first list and place it in the *Variables* list on the right.
4. Follow the same procedure to add the second variable.
5. For ordinal data, check the box next to Spearman, for interval or ratio data, check the box next to Pearson.
6. Click *OK.*

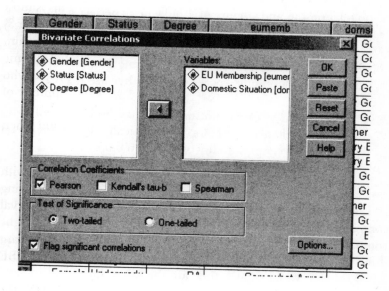

This will produce a correlation in the output window like the one shown overleaf.

Correlations

			EU Membership	Domestic Situation
Spearman's rho	EU Membership	Correlation Coefficient	1.000	0.620**
		Sig. (2-tailed)		0.004
		N	20	20
	Domestic Situation	Correlation Coefficient	0.620**	1.000
		Sig. (2-tailed)	0.004	
		N	20	20

**. Correlation is significant at the 0.01 level (2-tailed).

Correlations (both Pearson and Spearman) compare scores on one variable with scores on another and look for a relationship.

You can see from this table that there are four cells, some of which are redundant (see below), which contain three pieces of information:

1. The *correlation coefficient* – This is the product of complicated calculations that SPSS performs behind the scenes. Coefficients can range from 0 to 1 and basically express the strength of the relationship between the two variables. A figure of 0 indicates that there is no relationship and a figure of 1 indicates a perfect relationship.

   They can also be positive or negative – a positive correlation indicates that both variables are scoring in the same direction, while a negative correlation would indicate that as scores on one variable are increasing, scores on the other are decreasing (and vice versa).

2. The *Sig. (2-tailed)* – the significance level (the probability of getting this result by chance). As before, a statistically significant correlation would have a probability of less than 0.05.

3. The *N* – The number of paired scores (N) that went into the calculation.

Looking at the table you can see some cells are the same. Top left is comparing EU membership with EU membership, bottom right is comparing domestic situation with domestic situation. These both show perfect relationships, indicated by a correlation coefficient of 1.000 (as you would expect, they are the same thing) and so can be ignored.

Top right and bottom left are also the same – they are comparing EU membership with domestic situation – so you only need to look at one of these to see the results of the test.

First, the coefficient is 0.620. This may not seem particularly strong, but it is definitely closer to 1 than it is to 0. There is some debate about what constitutes a 'strong' relationship from correlations (see, for example, Wimmer and Dominick 2006), but very strong relationships are quite rare in the social sciences. Again, this is an area where the researcher must use common sense in interpretation.

Nonetheless, this indicates some sort of positive relationship between the two scores – the correlation coefficient would have a minus sign in front of it if it were negative.

Second, this relationship is statistically significant, as indicated by a significance level of 0.004 in the table. SPSS also usefully indicates this with the ** symbol next to the coefficient. If you look below the table you can see that SPSS tells us that the correlation is significant at the 0.01 level – even less likely to be due to chance than the 0.05 level.

As a final note of caution, correlations do not tell you WHERE the relationship lies, just that there is one. In this case, it could be that a lot of people are responding at the high end of both scales, but it could equally be that they are responding at the low end of both scales. To investigate the nature of the relationship you need to run a separate Crosstab to look at the data in more detail.

Chapter 11 deals with presentation of results in more details.

CHAPTER 11

Presenting Results

This chapter illustrates how to present the findings of your research, how students have used the tests outlined in the previous chapter in their research project, and how they have interpreted and presented their findings.

As examples, we have used various student projects conducted as part of MA programmes at the Cardiff School of Journalism, Media and Cultural Studies. Most of these were part of a ten-week course in quantitative research methods, but projects were conceived, conducted and reported in around five weeks. Details of the requirements and timetable are included in Chapter 12, but essentially the students were asked to design, conduct, analyse and report a project of their own choice. The reporting took the form of a class presentation and a 1,500-word journal article.

Presenting findings

Whether you are presenting your work as a report, journal article or as a visual presentation, there are several elements that are common to good practice.

Introduction

Our students are required to give a selection of academic sources as background to the project – a kind of mini-literature review that sets out the topic area, established thinking and gives an indication of how they came up with their ideas and hypotheses. This will put the research in perspective for the reader/audience and set the scene for outlining the hypotheses and presenting and interpreting the original findings.

Sample and demographics

It's always useful to begin by describing the sample from which your data come. This will put your findings in perspective for the reader/audience.

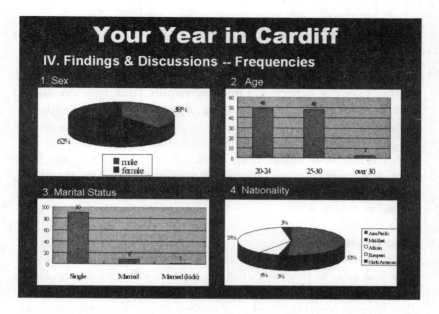

Whether you use tables or graphs is an aesthetic choice, but graphs are often preferred as they convey simple information quickly and easily. (See Appendix 1 for some simple instructions on creating graphs in SPSS.)

Above is a simple PowerPoint slide that uses a variety of graph types to demonstrate the sample from a project.

Key findings

Your key findings are those that directly relate to your hypotheses. Having run a number of statistical tests it's tempting to include all of them, since you went to the trouble of doing them, but it's important that you include only those that are relevant to the research and that relate to the hypotheses that were specified in advance of the analysis.

Not all of these will have worked out the way you hoped, but it is just as important to report these (see below) as it is to report the ones that came out as you predicted and were statistically significant.

'Negative' findings

Analyses that don't work out the way you had anticipated can often be baffling and disappointing. Try to keep an open mind if this happens as these can often be the most interesting and useful parts of your study.

First, assuming that your hypotheses were based on some reasonable thinking, try to work out why they might not have come out the way that you expected. This may require running some additional tests, but this is not 'cheating' if you can come up with an explanation.

Second, try to think about the meaning of this in the context of further research. If things didn't work out, try to work out why, but also how it could have been investigated differently. Perhaps the questions you asked didn't quite get to the heart of the topic or were unclear to respondents.

Clear presentation

However you decide to present your findings, it's important that you make it as clear as possible to the reader, who will not have the same in-depth knowledge of your project as you do. Opposite are two slides taken from a project that looked at student alcohol consumption. You can see that the first presents a fairly complicated **Crosstab** that is difficult to read on paper, let alone on screen. Fortunately, the students did a reasonable job of compressing these data and expressing them slightly differently on the slide that followed, which made things far easier for the audience to see their main finding on this point.

On p. 160 is a good example of how a graph can be used to express quite complicated findings. This is taken from a project that looked at how overseas students (non-UK in this case) and home students (UK in this case) were planning to spend their Christmas vacation. The group suggested that, based on the fact that international students had travelled some distance to come to study, they may be more likely to use vacation time to explore further. They had several breakdowns of these findings and explored them in greater depth, but the graph clearly demonstrates that international students appear more likely to travel during vacations than stick with a single destination.

Statistical significance

Ideally, you should always present the statistical tests that accompany your data, either with an example of the **chi-square** or **correlation**

Findings

Degree * How much? Crosstabulation

		Not applicable	1	2	3	4	5	Other	Total
Degree Undergradu	Count	0	1	5	10	5	15	10	46
	% within Degree	.0%	2.2%	10.9%	21.7%	10.9%	32.6%	21.7%	100.0%
	% within How m	.0%	16.7%	29.4%	50.0%	50.0%	60.0%	71.4%	48.9%
	% of Total	.0%	1.1%	5.3%	10.6%	5.3%	16.0%	10.6%	48.9%
Postgraduat	Count	2	5	12	10	5	10	4	48
	% within Degree	4.2%	10.4%	25.0%	20.8%	10.4%	20.8%	8.3%	100.0%
	% within How m	100.0%	83.3%	70.6%	50.0%	50.0%	40.0%	28.6%	51.1%
	% of Total	2.1%	5.3%	12.8%	10.6%	5.3%	10.6%	4.3%	51.1%
Total	Count	2	6	17	20	10	25	14	94
	% within Degree	2.1%	6.4%	18.1%	21.3%	10.6%	26.6%	14.9%	100.0%
	% within How m	100.0%	100.0%	100.0%	100.0%	100.0%	100.0%	100.0%	100.0%
	% of Total	2.1%	6.4%	18.1%	21.3%	10.6%	26.6%	14.9%	100.0%

Analysis

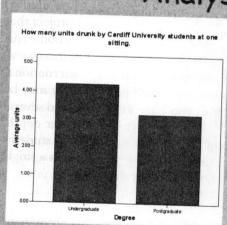

How many units drunk by Cardiff University students at one sitting.

- On average undergraduates drank 1 unit more than postgraduates.

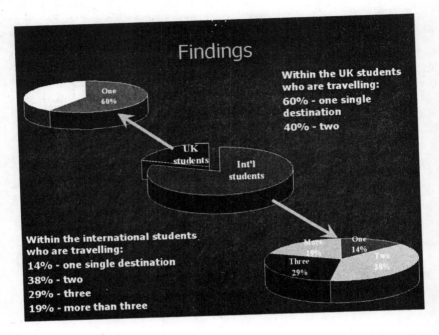

Findings

Within the UK students who are travelling:

60% - one single destination

40% - two

UK students

Int'l students

One 60%

Within the international students who are travelling:

14% - one single destination

38% - two

29% - three

19% - more than three

One 14%

Two 38%

Three 29%

More 19%

table or by using the notation $p < 0.05$ or $p > 0.05$. (See Chapter 10 for more information on running and interpreting these tests.)

Remember that tests that didn't turn out to be statistically significant should be mentioned; your 'negative' findings could be very important.

Replicability

An important requirement of any research report is that it details the methodology. This is so someone else could possibly **replicate** it – that is, run the same research as you have in order to test that the results stand up.

You should give full details of your sample and include an example questionnaire, as well as the details of how you administered and coded the questionnaire, and how you analysed the data from it.

Benefits

Finally, writing up a project like this can have benefits beyond getting a good grade for the research methods course.

A grounding in quantitative research, and practical experience of conducting, analysing, interpreting and presenting it, are important skills to have and it's worth pointing this out to potential employers. Some students have taken copies of work that they have done to job interviews and others have sent 'executive summaries' of research findings to companies that participated as a thank you for their help. This can result in a job offer!

Several former students have contacted us to say that the SPSS skills that they were so wary of at first have come in very useful in their careers at some stage.

CHAPTER 12

Information for Teachers

This chapter sets out some of the pedagogic aspects of teaching quantitative methods in the ways that we have over the last few years. Although we do not claim to teach quantitative methods in great depth, either theoretically or practically, we have found that a simple introduction can be extremely useful to students, especially those with a morbid fear of numbers. Since quantitative methods involve a certain rigour of thought and procedure, we have also found that a short, practical course in questionnaire design and analysis can introduce students to the skills involved in conducting any research project, regardless of the method they choose.

What do students learn?

We focus very much on the practical elements of this course – learning through 'doing. It is extremely difficult to teach quantitative methods to reluctant students through a series of lectures, especially if you are trying to illustrate the complexities of data analysis. The process of coming up with their own ideas, discovering and (hopefully) solving potential problems, analysing data that they are personally interested in and critiquing each others' work, means that the students learn a great deal (almost without realising it).

Whether the course takes the form of a few practical sessions or a longer core module, we have found the following elements and outcomes are common to introducing students to these sorts of methods. Believe it or not, much of this can be achieved in as little as eight hours of class time. We have included a sample timetable (below, pp. 166–9) to illustrate how this might be done.

Topic choice

Students are encouraged to come up with their own ideas for a short research project. The only restrictions are that they must be able to complete the project in the time allowed, with the resources available.

Generally, they form groups (around four or five in each group seems to work well) and begin by brainstorming for possible topic choices.

Students learn to function as a research team. This is an important skill as 'real-world' research, whether academic or commercial, is increasingly conducted by teams of researchers, often with cross-disciplinary backgrounds and skills. This is a useful experience for any individual student interested in conducting research. They learn that the world's problems cannot be solved by one investigation, and that some methods suit particular topics more than others.

Following on from this, the process of narrowing the research area into a workable project and further defining and redefining their questions to produce hypotheses helps to focus on the topic in hand, to shape their methodology, to define their sample (and population) and to begin to think about ways in which they might phrase their questions and design their questionnaire.

An additional bonus is that they begin to think more critically about published research, as they gain insight into the whole process through personal experience.

Introduction to statistics

Clearly, since this is a quantitative course, students should pick up a basic knowledge of statistics. This is more than the mechanics of SPSS and more than a grasp of the concept of statistical probability. We aim to encourage students to be sceptical about the everyday use and abuse of statistics that we all encounter on television, in newspapers and potentially in their professional careers.

We would hope that when a percentage is casually presented as a compelling fact during a news broadcast, students will automatically begin to ask:

- Exactly WHO was asked this question (the sample)?
- How MANY people were asked this question (the sample size)?
- What EXACTLY were they asked (the question wording and any leading phrases)?

Questionnaire design

A basic familiarity with SPSS (or other statistical programmes), however, will also lead to a better developed questionnaire. Once students have seen what the software can do, and what sort of analyses are common to questionnaire data, they begin to see how a questionnaire can be designed to produce data that will be more capable of answering their research questions and hypotheses.

Practical experience of designing a questionnaire will also reinforce the idea of keeping the hypotheses simple and focused, and also of maintaining strict **operational definitions** of the concepts they are investigating.

Collecting data

The process of collecting data is also a useful experience in the whole research process. It brings home the necessity to be organised, in terms of numbering questionnaires, keeping track of which group members have collected what amount of data, and so on. It can also be fun. It will certainly demonstrate how quantitative methods allow the researcher to gather large amounts of data in a relatively short time.

Analysing data and interpreting findings

This really is an intellectual skill and takes time to get to grips with. However, we believe that the fact that the students have generated their own topics and hypotheses adds motivation and meaning to the analysis side of things. What we are trying to foster here is not simply an understanding of basic statistics and quantitative methods generally, but also a rigorous, sceptical and disciplined approach to their work that is transferable to any form of research, regardless of methodology.

Presenting data

We often assess this sort of project in two ways – by a class presentation (usually using some sort of presentation software such as PowerPoint) and by a written account of the project in the form of a short journal article.

These have common elements in that they necessitate concise presentation and the ability to pick out the key findings of the project. They also require that the students target the presentation to a particular audience – they are encouraged to take the presentations seriously and to present their findings in an academic manner. It would be equally possible to construct an assessment where the target audience is different – for example, to present to a particular commercial audience, or a policy group (a test of their ability to explain quantitative findings to a 'lay' audience – i.e. those not too familiar with the terminology of scientific research).

Giving a class presentation brings further benefits. We tend to use PowerPoint to demonstrate the clarity of thought required to present the entire project in ten minutes – from background literature to future directions – and to present slides that are useful for the audience, without being crammed full of text or overwhelming with rainbow graphics and flashy effects. Of course, this has an additional benefit for the teacher in that students get some experience of being in a teacher's shoes – talking to a room full of people who are not necessarily fascinated by the subject matter. Also they should also begin to appreciate the hours we put into preparation!

A written report of the project can be useful as an example of concise portrayal of the project within a tight word limit, a skill that will often be useful later in their professional careers.

Project critique

A final requirement of the presentation of the project is that the students reflect on the whole experience and on particular elements of their research project.

It's useful to think about what worked and what didn't work; how the questionnaire or the sampling could have been improved; what would be done differently given a second chance, or more time and resources; how the study might be expanded further, or taken in a new direction, as a result of this initial attempt, and so on.

Again this is all part of the learning-through-doing approach, and we have found that often students gain the most from the mistakes that they made, and from the views and input of their classmates.

Assessing the work

In our sessions, we have found that a combination of class exercises and formal work is useful.

Class exercises

One or two simple exercises, completed during class time when the lecturer is present, that aim to ensure that students have grasped the basics of data input, analysis and interpretation.

As previously mentioned, we use our EU 'baby questionnaire' as an example – providing them with data to input that have been carefully constructed to give statistically significant results when analysed.

Project report and presentation

The requirements for these are outlined at the end of this chapter. The benefits have already been mentioned, but the point is to introduce students to public and written presentation skills for a specific audience, and this can be the beginnings of academic writing skills.

Sample timetable

This sets out a timetable for a four-session course with each session lasting two hours. Most of the work (apart from data-gathering) can be achieved within the class time. Although it seems daunting for students and teachers alike, we are constantly amazed at the quality of work produced by students during such a short exposure to quantitative methods.

As we always reiterate, this course is not meant to be a comprehensive explanation of the theory and practicalities of these techniques, but a simple, hands-on approach can give a meaningful and useful introduction to something that many students find difficult and off-putting.

Session 1
Taught content
- Why use quantitative methods?

Because they are compelling and 'scientific'.

Because they appear everywhere in the media, in reports and in published research.

Conducting a quantitative project will give students some understanding of the process of generating numbers and statistics, as well as the process of analysing and presenting them.

• Introduction to SPSS

We use our EU 'baby questionnaire' to illustrate questionnaire design – the demographic and research question components – and also to introduce the ideas of coding real-life data into numbers that can be analysed simply and quickly.

The SPSS environment is explained (as in Chapter 10) and students are talked through setting up one variable and entering some data.

Having completed the first part of the class exercise (see below), the procedures for generating Frequencies, Crosstabs and Correlations are explained and examples are given to illustrate how to read these tables.

Class work
• Introduction to SPSS

They are given a handout with twenty completed EU questionnaires and asked to complete the other four variables in variable view, and then to enter the data from the twenty completed questionnaires.

They are then given some fairly straightforward questions to answer using **Frequencies**, **Crosstabs** and **Correlation**.

This can often be a daunting first taste of quantitative methods, but most students find it satisfying that they can at least enter data into software that many have never used before.

Session 2
Taught content
• Introduction to statistics

Demonstrations of how to run **Frequencies, Crosstabs** (with **chi-square**) and **Correlation**.

This session also includes a section on statistical probability.
Most of this material is covered in Chapter 10.

Class work
- Running the tests

We give a handout with five simple questions about the EU data. Instructions are to type the questions in Word, run the appropriate tests in SPSS and then answer the questions in as much or as little detail as students feel necessary, with supporting tables copied from their SPSS outputs (see p. 189).

Experience of using SPSS on sample data can inform the ways in which students design their own projects and also give them ideas about the sorts of questions that SPSS can help to answer.

Session 3
Taught content
- Research design

Hypotheses and research questions – coming up with a workable idea for a small group project, given the time and resources available.

Sampling – an introduction to the ideas behind sampling so that students are at least aware of the considerations were they to embark on a full-scale research project.

- Questionnaire design

The importance of clear presentation and ethical considerations.

This includes examples of **demographic** and **research question** sections (see Chapter 6), as well as examples of **Likert scales**.

Class work
- Forming groups, topic choice and questionnaire design

Designing a draft questionnaire for piloting.
Thinking about the SPSS coding frame.
Finding relevant background literature.
This can be a useful class debate, and we usually end this part of the session by asking each group to give details of:

- the topic;
- the hypotheses;
- the sample.

• Designing a draft questionnaire

The groups are then required to begin to design their own questionnaire. Ideally, they will print out copies and ask classmates for feedback. This is all part of the **piloting** process and the class should finish with a more or less final version which they can take away to gather data before the final session.

Session 4

Taught content
• Statistics revisited

Much of the session on running the statistical tests is repeated so that students grasp not only the mechanics of SPSS, but also the concept of statistical significance and of how to interpret the more complicated Crosstabs and Correlations.

Class work
• Data analysis and report writing

In this four-session version we tend not to require a class presentation, but assessing the ways in which individual students have understood the process of using SPSS and the results of their own group project can be equally effective.

Group presentation guidelines

This will be a short presentation based on the group work that you have done during this semester.

Each presentation will last no more than TEN MINUTES, followed by time for any questions that the audience may have.

The presentation should ideally be made using PowerPoint, and should contain the following sections:

• Background and rationale – a brief introduction to the topic, explaining why your group decided to investigate it. This should include at least TWO sources of information (books, journal articles, websites, facts and figures, etc.) that are appropriately referenced.

- Hypotheses/research questions – what were you aiming to discover?
- Method – A description of your sample, how you designed your questionnaire, how you administered it, etc.
- Findings – THREE key findings from your analyses (with supporting tables and graphs). Remember, 'negative' findings (ones that you didn't expect) should be included.
- Discussion/conclusions – What these findings have told you about your topic.
- Critique – What worked and what didn't work; how the study could be improved; how you might plan to extend the study further.

CHAPTER 13

Conclusion and Summary

It might be more accurate to say that this brief chapter is a non-conclusion. This is partly because this book does not strictly need to be read in any particular order, although the first part should certainly be read before embarking on the later ones. We expect the book to be used as a work of reference, with student – and teacher – researchers dipping into it for answers to particular questions. We also expect it to be used in conjunction with more specific media research and other textbooks, which give more detailed answers to specific research questions – for example, for students who want to know more about qualitative methods, or for students who are particularly interested in ethnographic methods. We also expect students, once they have chosen their research topic, to do a lot of wider reading around this particular topic. For instance, if you are doing a content analysis on 'bias in the press', or a project on 'children's responses to toy advertising', we would expect you to read other studies on these topics, and these studies, too, may give you ideas for research designs and methods.

In our Bibliography and Reference section, we mention other books on research method and design which you might find useful. The four mentioned first, we consider 'core' texts, because we have used them extensively ourselves in teaching. However, other teachers may find different texts more accessible and useful, and so other standard research method books are listed here too. We have also listed some specific texts that we ourselves have found useful in specialist areas, such as content analysis, and audiences, including child audiences. But there are many other texts on these topics, and a major part of all research, whether in the humanities or in the sciences, is finding your own 'core' and 'specialist' texts that particularly suit you. So we do not propose these texts as a definitive list; they are simply those we have found useful ourselves, and we welcome suggestions for additions.

Our book is thus not the last word on research methods – far from it. It focuses quite tightly on basic research design principles and simple quantitative methodologies, because we believe that these principles and methods, drawn from social science, are a necessary underpinning to learning about, and doing, research generally. We also believe that basic numeracy – being able to understand and manipulate simple quantitative data (frequencies, crosstabs, ordinal, nominal, interval data, percentages, probabilities, and the like) – is an absolute necessity for anybody calling themselves a trained researcher.

'Do – and I understand'

No research method should be rejected without an understanding of it. We believe that it should not be possible for anybody in professional research fields to say that they 'can't do numbers', even if they don't want to use numbers in their own research. Everybody needs to be able to *understand* numbers in the research that they read, if nothing else. They also need to be able to guide students towards the most appropriate research methods for the students' own chosen topics; sometimes the most appropriate methods will be quantitative, using the basic and invaluable research tools, the questionnaire, or, in the case of content analysis, the coding frame. As we've said, we have proposed these practical approaches to research in the media because, thanks to our various enjoyable experiences of teaching research methods with many different kinds of students on many different kinds of course, we believe in the basic primary school pedagogic principle: 'Hear it – and you will forget. See it – and you will remember. *Do* it – and you will understand.'

Hence there is no real end of the story to give here: there will always be more to say and more to do, and further comments and amendments to be made when it comes to designing, and doing, research with human subjects, and research on human communication. Maybe some of it will come from you.

Good luck!

Bibliography and References

Core media research methods texts

Bauer, M. W. and Gaskell, G. (eds.) (2000) *Qualitative Researching with Text, Image and Sound: A Practical Handbook*, London: Sage.

Field, A. (2005) *Discovering Statistics Using SPSS*, London: Sage.

Machin, D. (2002) *Ethnographic Research for Media Studies*, London: Arnold.

Wimmer, R. D. and Dominick, J. R. (2006, 8th edn.) *Mass Media Research: An Introduction*, Belmont, CA: Wadsworth.

Useful media research methods texts

Alasuutari, P. (1998) *An Invitation to Social Research*, London: Sage.

Barwise, P. and Ehrenberg, A. (1996) *Television and its Audience*, London: Sage.

Deacon, D., Pickering, M., Golding, P. and Murdock, G. (1999) *Researching Communications: A Practical Guide to Methods in Media and Cultural Analysis*, London: Arnold.

Flick, U. (1998) *An Introduction to Qualitative Research*, London: Sage.

Fraser, S., Lewis, V., Ding, S., Kellett, M. and Robinson, C. (2003) *Doing Research with Children and Young People*, Milton Keynes: Open University Press.

Hansen, A., Cottle, S., Negrine, R. and Newbold, C. (1998) *Mass Communication Research Methods*, London: Macmillan.

Jensen, K. B. and Jankowski, N. W. (eds.) (1991) *A Handbook of Qualitative Methodologies for Mass Communication Research*, London: Routledge.

Lindlof, T. R. (1995) *Qualitative Communication Research Methods*, Thousand Oaks, CA: Sage.

Salkind, N. J. (2004) *Statistics for People Who (Think They) Hate Statistics*, London: Sage.

Sarantakos, S. (1998, 2nd edn.) *Social Research*, Basingstoke: Macmillan.

Seale, C. (ed.) (1998) *Researching Society and Culture*, London: Sage.

Silverman, D. (2001) *Interpreting Qualitative Data*, London: Sage.

Van Leeuwen, T. and Jewitt, C. (eds.) (2001) *Handbook of Visual Analysis*, London: Sage.

Williams, M. (2000) *Science and Social Science*, London: Routledge.

Content analysis: broadcasting

Davies, M. M. and Corbett, B. (1997) *Children's Television in Britain: An Enquiry for the Broadcasting Standards Commission*, London: Broadcasting Standards Commission.

Gerbner, G., Gross, L., Morgan, M. and Signorielli, N. (1986) 'Living with television: the dynamics of the cultivation process', in J. Bryant and D. Zillman (eds.), *Perspectives on Media Effects*, Hillsdale, NJ: Erlbaum.

Lewis, J., Brookes, R., Mosdell, N. and Threadgold, T. (2006) *Shoot First and Ask Questions Later: Media Coverage of the 2003 Iraq War*, New York: Peter Lang.

Wober, M. and Gunter, B. (1988) *Television and Social Control*, Aldershot: Gower Press.

Research on audiences: some useful readings

Abercrombie, N. and Longhurst, B. (1998) *Audiences: A Sociological Theory of Performance and Imagination*, London: Sage.

Ang, I. (1993) *Desperately Seeking the Audience*, London: Routledge.

Barwise, P. and Ehrenberg, A. (1996) *Television and its Audience*, London: Sage.

Tulloch, J. (2000) *Watching Television Audiences: Cultural Theories and Methods*, London: Arnold.

Media effects and special audiences

Barker, M. and Petley, J. (1997, reprinted 2001) *Ill Effects: The Media Violence Debate*, London: Routledge.

Davies, M. M. (2001) *Dear BBC: Children, Television Storytelling and the Public Sphere*, Cambridge: Cambridge University Press.

Gunter, B. (1992) *Violence and the Mass Media*, London: John Libbey.

Livingstone, S. and Lunt, P. (1994) *Talk on Television: Audience Participation and Public Debate*, London: Routledge.

General references

Aitchison, J. (1983) *The Articulate Mammal*, London: Hutchinson.

Bandura, A., Ross, D. and Ross, R. (1963) 'Imitation of film mediated aggressive models', *Journal of Abnormal and Social Psychology*, vol. 66, No.1, 3–11.

Carter, C. and Davies, M. M. (2004) '"A fresh peach is easier to bruise": children and traumatic news', in S. Allen (ed.), *Journalism: Critical Issues*, Maidenhead and New York: Open University Press, pp. 224–35.

Curran, J. and Seaton, J. (1997) *Power without Responsibility: The Press and Broadcasting in Britain*, London: Routledge.

Davies, M. M., and Mosdell, N. (2001) *Consenting Children?: The Use of Children in Non-fiction Television Programmes*, London: Broadcasting Standards Commission.

Davies, M. M. and Pearson, R. E. (2003) 'Stardom and Distinction: Patrick Stewart as an Agent of Cultural Mobility: A Study of Theatre and Film Audiences in New York City', in M. Barker and T. Austin (eds.), *Contemporary Hollywood Stardom*, London: Arnold, pp. 167–86.

Davies, M. M. and Pearson, R. E. (2004) 'To boldly bestride the narrow world like a colossus: Shakespeare, *Star Trek* and the European TV Market', in I. Bondebjerg and P. Golding (eds.), *European Culture and the Media: Changing Media, Changing Europe*, Vol. 1, Bristol: Intellect Books, pp. 65–90.

Davies, M. M., Lloyd, E. and Scheffler, A. (1987) *Baby Language*, London: Unwin Hyman.

Habermas, J. (1989) *The Transformation of the Public Sphere*, Cambridge: Polity (German original 1962, Luchterhand).

Kuhn, T. (1970) *The Structure of Scientific Revolutions*, Chicago: University of Chicago Press.

Livingstone, S. (2002) *Young People and New Media*, London: Sage.

Livingstone, S. and Bovill, M. (1999) *Children, Young People and the Changing Media Environment*, London: LSE.

Miller, T., Govil, N., McMurria, J., Maxwell, R. and Wang T. (2005) *Global Hollywood 2*, London: British Film Institute.

Pearson, R. E. and Davies, M. M. (2005) 'Class Acts? Public and Private Values and the Cultural Values of Theatre-goers', in S. Livingstone (ed.), *Audiences and Publics: When Cultural Engagement Matters for the Public Sphere*, Bristol: Intellect Books.

Popper, K. (1959) *The Logic of Scientific Discovery*, New York: Basic Books.

Rolston, B. and Miller, D. (1996) *War and Words: The Northern Ireland Media Reader*, Belfast: Beyond the Pale Press.

Wimmer, R. D. and Dominick, J. R. (1994, 4th edn.) *Mass Media Research: An Introduction*, Belmont, CA: Wadsworth.

APPENDICES

1. Graphs

One of the most simple and clear ways to present data is to put them in a graph. This can present your findings in a visually compelling way and spare the reader the task of wading through a series of complicated tables to get at your key findings.

The SPSS[1] program has a wide range of graph templates. It is worth experimenting with these, but beware of blinding your reader with style over content. The purpose of a graph is to display information in a clear and concise way, not to demonstrate that your printer can cope with 256 colours, or that what you really wanted to be was a graphic designer.

In journal articles and reports the two most common graph formats are the **bar graph** and the **pie chart**.

Simple bar graphs

Used to display frequencies. Go to:

1. *Graphs*
2. *Bar . . .*
3. Select *Simple* and click *Define*

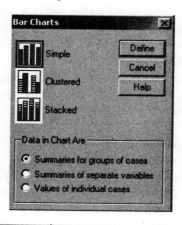

---

[1] This section is based on SPSS version 12.0. Other versions of the software may change some of the cosmetic aspects of graphs, but the basic procedures will be similar.

This will bring up a dialogue box like the one below.

1. Select the variable that you want to display from the list on the left and add it to *Category Axis:* using the arrow key.
2. Change *Bars Represent* to *% of cases* by clicking on the circle.

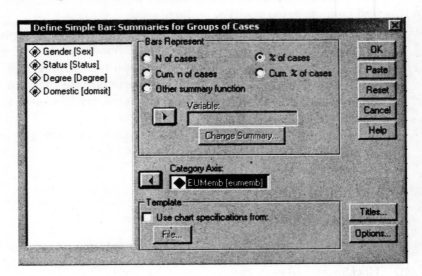

When you click *OK*, a new Output window will open containing your lovely bar graph. If you then double-click anywhere inside the graph, another window will open (SPSS Chart Editor) which allows you to change the appearance of the graph.

Play around with aspects of the graph's appearance. Each time you make a change you can see how it will look by closing the Chart Editor: click *Apply* and then click *Close*.

Changing the appearance of the bars

This will allow you to print in black and white.

Click once on the bars so that they are selected (they have a border around them, as in the Chart Editor box on p. 181).

Click on *Fill & Border*.

Change the colour by selecting a new colour from the palette.

Click *Apply*.

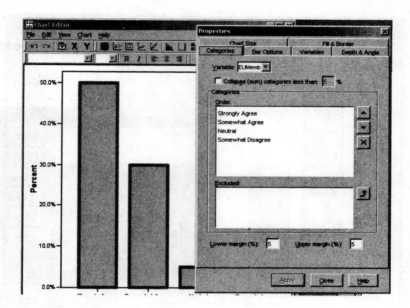

To change the pattern
Click on the bar.
> Click on *Pattern*, and select a pattern from the drop-down menu.
> Change the colour of the bar to white.
> Click *Apply*.

Changing the axis scales
Double click on the axis scale (the labels along the side of the graph (0, 10, 20, etc.).

From the *Chart* menu, select *Axis* . . . As above this will allow you to change the axis title and the placement of that title on the graph (*Left / Bottom; Right / Top, Centre*). You can also change the scale of the graph by typing in values for minimum and maximum and major and minor increments.

Displaying data labels
It can be very useful to display the values that are represented in graphs.

In the Chart Editor window, click once on the bars of the graph (or the slices in a pie chart) so that they are highlighted.

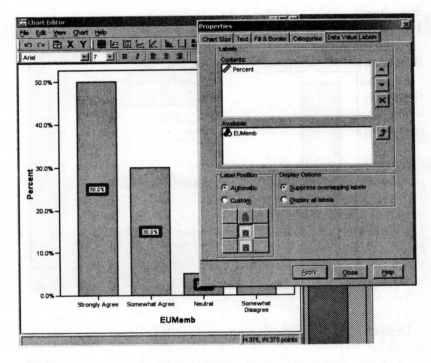

Go to the *Chart* menu and select Show Data Labels.

This will bring up a box like the one above, where the measure you have used (in this case percentage) is automatically inserted.

Play around
Double clicking anything on the graph while inside Chart Editor will bring up options to change that element's properties.

Clustered bar graphs

Bar graphs are very useful to display the results of crosstabs clearly and simply.

Follow the steps above but select *Clustered* from the first screen. This will allow you to plot one variable against another, for example, Gender against EU membership.

You will initially get a hideous rainbow of colours, but you can change the colour and fill style of each bar in the variable by following the steps above.

Pie charts

It's easiest to use these for simple frequencies.

Go to the *Graphs* menu and select *Pie* . . . then follow the steps outlined above for a simple bar graph.

This will give you a Pie Chart which you can edit as above, but with the added excitement of being able to emphasise the importance of slices by taking them out of the pie – click on a slice, go to the *Chart* menu and select *Explode Slice*.

Chart templates

If you are planning to use several graphs, you can save time by creating a chart template so that they all look similar – for example, so that they are all in black and white with patterned fills.

Once you have spent hours editing the appearance of your first graph, open the SPSS Chart Editor, go to the *File* menu and select *Save Chart Template*. This will prompt you for a filename (e.g. Graph-Style1) which you should save somewhere on your hard drive.

When you next go to create a graph, go to the *Graphs* menu and select the style of graph that you want to use.

Define the graph (the variable you want to use and the percentages or counts), but before clicking *OK*, check the box next to *Use chart specifications from*: and click the *File* . . . button.

This will bring up a dialogue box like the one below.

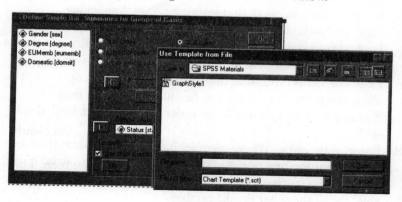

Select your graph template and click *Open*. This should make the graph appear in the style that you have so carefully edited. Or at least something vaguely like it . . .

2. Multiple Responses

Most of our students have had occasions where respondents ticked more than one answer on their questionnaire. There are a few ways of getting around this but a fairly simple one is to create new variables and then add them together in a *Multiple Response Set* to allow you to see how many times a particular response was chosen.

For example, a study investigating British culture may well feature the following question:

Which is your favourite choice of drink when you are in the pub?
Lager   Bitter   Stout   Wine   Absinthe   Gin   Vodka   Fruit-based
beverage

Although you have asked for the respondents' favourite, they may well choose more than one.

You cannot make any decisions about their favourite drink; you have to use the data that are given to you (and refine the question for later use). For the moment, you can make a multiple-response set to determine which drink was chosen most often.

1. Create a new variable in *Variable View* called drink1.
2. Enter the values from 1–8 that correspond to the drinks above (e.g. 1 = lager).
3. Enter another value, 0, that stands for 'Not Applicable'.
4. Copy the variable.
5. Look at your data and find the highest number of different drinks that any respondent chose.
6. Paste the drink1 variable until you have enough copies of it to allow this person's responses to be entered one at a time.
7. Rename the drink1 variables in order (e.g. drink1, drink2, drink3, etc.).
8. Enter your data: Where people have chosen more than one answer, put the first one into drink1, the second into drink2, and so on. When you have entered all their choices, enter 'Not Applicable' for all the other drink variables.

Once you have all the data, you can create the multiple-response set which will allow you to add everything together.

1. From the *Analyse* menu, select *Multiple Response* and *Define Sets . . .*
2. Highlight the variables that you want to include (in this case, all the *drink* variables) and add them to the *Variables in Set:* box using the arrow button.
3. Define the range of values in this variable – From 1 to 8 in this case (do not include 0).
4. Give the set a name and a label (the same as you would when creating a new variable).
5. Click on the *Add* button to place this new set under the *Mult Response Sets:* list on the right-hand side of the screen.
6. Click on *Close*.

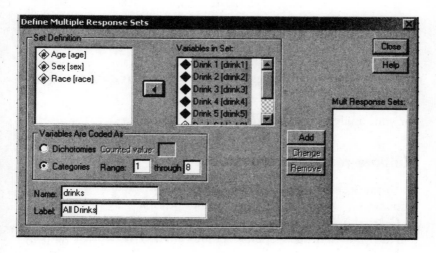

Multiple-response frequencies

You will now notice that there are other options available to you if you go to the *Analyse* menu and select *Multiple Response*.

When you select these new tests they do not appear in quite the same way as before. Overleaf is an example of the Frequency table for this data set:

Category Label – Fairly obvious.
Code – The value that was assigned to it within the drink variable.

Group $ Drink All Drinks

Category label	Code	Count	Pct of Responses	Pct of Cases
Lager	1	5	20.0	33.3
Bitter	2	1	4.0	6.7
Stout	3	4	16.0	26.7
Wine	4	3	12.0	20.0
Absinthe	5	4	16.0	26.7
Gin	6	1	4.0	6.7
Vodka	7	3	12.0	20.0
Fruit-based beverage	8	4	16.0	26.7
		-------	-------	--------
Total responses		25	100.0	166.7

0 missing cases; 15 valid cases

Count – How many times that value appeared regardless of which drink variable it was in.

For your analyses use the *Pct of Responses* figure.

Multiple-response crosstabs

You may want to look at some crosstabs that include this multiple response set. This is an ugly process but possible.

Go to the *Analyse* menu, select *Multiple Response* and *Crosstabs* . . .

Add your multiple response set and another variable to the rows and columns as you would do normally.

You will notice that when you add another variable you will have to define the range of that variable. Click on the *Define Ranges* . . . button and enter the minimum and maximum values of that variable.

1. Click on the *Options* button.
2. Check the boxes that will display percentages.
3. Click on the button to change the percentages so that they are based on *Responses*.

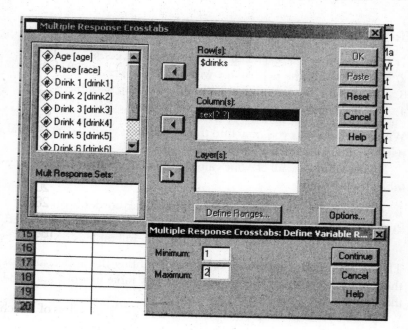

4. Click *Continue*.
5. Click *OK*.

This should present you with a very low-quality table that looks something like a crosstab.

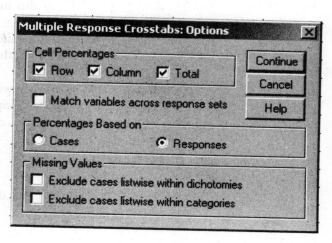

To read the table:

1. The first figure in each cell of the table is the count.
2. The second is the percentage within the row variable.
3. The third is the percentage within the column variable.
4. The final figure is the percentage of the total.

With large data sets you may find that the table is spread over several pages or that some of it is not visible at all.

If you cannot see all of your values displayed in either a frequency table or a crosstab:

1. Click once on the table so that it has a black border around it.
2. Click and hold down on the square in the bottom right-hand corner and drag this downwards until the full table is revealed.

There's not much you can do in terms of editing the appearance of these tables, so probably best to create a new table in word and type this data into it.

3. Example SPSS Exercise

Using the data you have (see data in spreadsheets, pp. 55–6), use the appropriate statistical procedures and tests to find answers to the following questions:

1. Were there equal numbers of subjects (people) from each of the four degrees in the school?

   FREQUENCIES

2. What percentage of all subjects (people) think the overall domestic situation in the UK is very bad?
   What percentage think it is neither bad nor good?

   FREQUENCIES

3. How many women and how many men strongly support Britain's membership of the EU? Express these as a proportion (percentage).

   CROSSTABS

4. What was the distribution of men and women across the four degree programmes? Is this distribution significantly unequal?

   CROSSTABS/statistics = chi-square.

5. Is there any evidence that people who think the situation in the UK is good are also more likely to approve of membership of the EU?

   CORRELATION + CROSSTAB

6. Think of one more question of your own to 'interrogate' these data, and run the appropriate statistical procedure on it.

4. Questionnaire Design Guide

Presentation

If the questionnaire looks professional, so do you. Make sure you spell check! Spend some time on the layout so that the questionnaire looks clear.

Don't make it too long.

Think carefully about the questions that will give you the most useful data. It needs to be completed in a few minutes (especially important if you are stopping people in the street) – 20–30 questions at the most.

The majority of questions should be multiple-choice so that respondents can answer them quickly.

Make sure that your instructions are clear – state whether you want respondents to circle or tick answers and whether they can choose more than one option in particular questions.

Be polite. It's useful to have some sort of introduction at the beginning which explains who you are and what you are doing. Try not to give too much away though. You should usually guarantee that all responses are anonymous and will be used only for academic research.

Always remember to thank respondents for their time at the end. You may also want to include a space at the end for 'any other comments'.

Sections

1. Demographics

This usually comes first as it is a non-threatening way of introducing people to your questionnaire. Think about personal characteristics that will influence the way in which people answer the questions related to your research. For example, will a person's nationality (or country of origin) affect their responses?

Other things to consider might include: age; gender; nationality/ethnicity; religion; education; income; number of children (and their ages), etc.

Potentially sensitive questions are often phrased so that they are not too specific, for example, using a range of ages or incomes (e.g. 18–21; 22–25, etc).

Think carefully about how you will ask for people's nationality – you are not likely to get equal numbers of respondents from Wales and from Mongolia.

2. 'Lifestyle'

Cultural consumption, taste and attitudes may be relevant to you. You can use multiple-choice or Likert scale questions to investigate this – for example, where people get their news, which newspaper they read, how much television they watch, etc. Do people who read broadsheets think differently about the issue in which you are interested from people who read tabloids?

You may also be interested in how often they purchase a particular product or type of product, where they purchase it and how much they spend.

You may be interested in how often they visit a particular facility (cinema, shopping centre, the Graduate Centre), etc.

3. Research questions

This is the most important part of your questionnaire. It is standard to use Likert scale questions here, where the respondent is asked to give their level of agreement to certain statements, for example:

SPSS is pointless
Strongly Agree   Agree   Neutral   Disagree   Strongly Disagree

Make your statements clear and try to elicit answers that will cover the full range of the scale (be careful not to offend people though). Make sure your respondents will have enough knowledge to answer the question and that the answers are not too obvious. You may also want to consider grouping questions that have the same answer format, but be wary of setting it out in a way that generates automatic responses.

It may be possible to put in some 'decoy' questions to avoid giving away your research hypothesis.

4. Open-ended questions

You may want to include one or two (not more) questions where respondents can answer in more detail. The answers can be post-coded later. This allows you to collect some qualitative data or to gather answers to questions that are difficult to predict. If you use these, put them near the end of the questionnaire – people may be pushed for time and not want to have to think too much.

Other points

Think carefully about how you will code the questionnaire as you construct it. You may want to put your variables into SPSS as you go along.

Too many 'Neutral/Don't Know/Undecided' answers are not desirable. Make the questions bold and thought-provoking. You may also want to include a response of 'Do not wish to answer' for potentially sensitive questions.

If you are concerned about respondents answering randomly, you may want to have a couple of questions that are aimed at the same topic but are worded differently, perhaps even with the scales reversed. This will also avoid 'response set' – automatically answering 'agree' to every question.

Make sure your questions are clear and are addressing exactly what you want them to. Avoid double-questions, for example:

How much do you want to be rich and famous?

Personally, I wouldn't mind being rich but I'm not sure I really want to have to dodge paparazzi every morning.

Avoid hypothetical questions, for example:

When you become rich, what will you spend your money on?

Make sure your respondents have the knowledge to answer the questions, and try to avoid technical jargon. For example:

When you buy your speedboat, will it be the RS105 or the T47 Raptor?

ALWAYS pilot your questionnaire – test it out on other people in the class or on your housemates. This will ensure that your instructions and wording are clear.

Good luck!

Index

Note: page numbers for **chapters** are in **bold**. Page numbers with n (e.g. 144n) refer to a footnote.